DEATH AT MY PLEASURE

The Story of SONNY: SERIAL RAPIST, SERIAL KILLER

"They silently hunt in the shadows to seize, torment, and murder the innocent unsuspecting"

DETWRITER

Copyright © 2018 by Detwriter

All rights reserved. No part of this publication may be reproduced, distributed, or transmitted in any form or by any means, including photocopying, recording, or other electronic or mechanical methods, without the prior written permission of the publisher, except in the case of brief quotations embodied in critical reviews and certain other noncommercial uses permitted by copyright law.

ISBN: 13: 978-1727883336

ISBN 10: 1727883330

Table of Contents

	AUTHORS' PROLOGUE	iv
CHAPTER ONE	THE SECRET	1
CHAPTER TWO	THE BEAST WITHIN	26
CHAPTER THREE	WHO I AM	44
CHAPTER FOUR	IDLE TIME / A PLAN FORMS	55
CHAPTER FIVE	AUNTIE MAME	61
CHAPTER SIX	TUDORSHIP	79
CHAPTER SEVEN	SONNY	103
CHAPTER EIGHT	THE PLAN	133
CHAPTER NINE	EXECUTING THE PLAN	167
CHAPTER TEN	HORROR CHAMBER	212
CHAPTER ELEVEN	FLYS IN THE WEB	249
CHAPTER TWELVE	SUSAN	278
CHAPTER THIRTEEN	ACCOMPLICE	310

Prologue

With years of experience in law enforcement and exposure to some of the most demented of heinous and unnatural criminal minds, I was encouraged by my teammates to write several short stories combining the horror of both factual and fictional serial rapists/killers. Relying on a scrapbook of long ago memories interfacing with many accounts of serial death dealers, I created the composite characters in this novel that will leave you forever remembering the potential consequence when you or a loved one abandons survival awareness for just that one brief moment. The horrendous tortures described are not illusionary pornographic fairy tales but gleaned from crime archives, police reports or media accounts. Reading through these accounts of the cruelty of madmen, the chosen descriptive form and passages of acts and record may suggest to some a pornographic and faux theme, however and to the contrary, the intent is not prurient but to graphically convey images strong enough to forever burn into the readers' mind the actual consequence and plight of that one second of misfortune or inattentiveness resulting in a victims' captivity and ultimate demise. These descriptive passages and scenes you are to shortly read about are not figments, fantasies or imaginations of a fiction from a cheap paperback but the poisonous interpretation of norms by psychopathic monsters from within the vilest souls of such deviants as the infamous Marquis de Sade or the vampire king, Vlad the Impaler or maybe that neighbor that just this morning, smiled and waved "hi" to you. . The inhuman creatures that reign these tortures and deaths on their fellow man are breathing physical manifestations from deep within the burning furnaces of Hell.

The purpose of this novel is just not to just shock the reader into a cataclysmic abyss of terrors haunting in the dark, but to provide to the reader a vivid dissection of the minds that stalk everyday life. Many of these killers defy forensic profiling and exist incognito beneath the radar of neighbors, co-workers, sociologists, mental health workers, sanity trackers,

and professional law enforcement agencies. Serial rapists and killers are often the most difficult of criminals to apprehend. Many possess high intelligence, cunning, and a superior ability to plan crimes in great detail. Others evade law enforcement by random geographical wanderings, committing cross country, a murder in one state, then crossing a state or county line to murder the next victim, eluding apprehension by the absence of the confines of locality, predictability and pattern.

The main criminal subject featured in this novel is "Sonny", a handsome, young, muscular white man with an anti-social and psychopathic dark side. These written words will allow you to safely enter into a world of cruelty, barbarism, atrocity, torment, pain and horror. This is Sonny's world. You will be witness to a number of abductions, rapes, tortures and deaths. You will be in his mind as he rapidly transitions from a sexually aggressive student of his matron Auntie to a fiendish and monsterish abomination of mankind. The manifestations of Sonny's desires and acts chill the blood; the cunning underpinning the execution of his abductions are a warning to all of how vulnerable we all are in this world of distractions and unconcern. Most frightening is that Sonny is not a singular bad seed, there are many with similar intent, and many right now who have taken a shovel and begun to dig a shallow grave to hide their current victim's remains.

If this journey into horror awakens just one person to the dangers of the monsters about and the fiendish and cunning traps, or has alerted one to make a single observation of a suspicious environment, then this novel has accomplished its mission and achieved its reward.

CHAPTER ONE

Opening the morning newspaper the front page headline reveals in bold glaring, attention getting type, "Serial Killer Strikes Again, Police Baffled and With No Leads." You, with intense interest for details, read every word twice. The reporter informs you that the body of another young woman has just this morning been discovered by joggers along a wooded section of a very popular jogging trail. The body was placed there sometime during the pitch of last night. The body of the young woman was nude, hands bound, legs spread into an exaggerated "Y" and sitting forever silently with her back propped against a tree. The article goes on to state that according to the joggers who discovered the body, breast mutilations were obvious and a feather protruding from her body (the reporters' editor clipped "vagina" and replaced it with "body"). Police refused to discuss or confirm any details of the crime scene. The reporter, before the police closed off the area, was limited to what she was able to photograph and a brief interview with the two joggers who

discovered the body. The jogging trail is only one mile from your house and your wife and daughter use this same trail on the weekends. You know, according to what you have read in the news print, this is the sixth body discovered, all nude, all in some type of fixed position (back against a tree or post), so far always a young or middle aged woman, hands bound with packaging cord, breast mutilations, a small white feather protruding from the body, and the victim's legs forced open and spread in the killer's characteristic exaggerated wide "Y."

You smile. You know that the police are no closer to apprehending or even identifying a suspect then they were when the first body was found. You know that your wife and daughter are safe from the killer. You understand the message of the body position, the spread legs and mutilations. You know the panic or thoughts going through the minds of your neighbors as they recoil in terror from the terrifying fact that a serial killer is stalking this part of the city, their part of the city. You smile again. You know every young woman will be temporarily safe from being the next victim for now. You know that the killer will not, as is his habit, be hunting another victim for another two to six months. You know it takes two to six months before the killer will be satisfied that he made no mistakes to draw the attention of the police investigators to his person. Equally while waiting for police trails to go cold, you know the killer will begin to patiently hunt out and focus on the next victim. After a very careful search and assessment of personal habits, he will repeatedly track her in her daily wanderings to determine where the strike zone will be; a parking lot, an activity site, her home maybe. The strike zone will be repeatedly cased to be certain to assure those three minutes it takes to overpower and duct tape the victim will be without interruption. He will also be aware of her personal articles and look for any signs to suggest that she has a handgun, mace, or a sharp weapon in her purse or on her person. You know and remember only too well, that young redhead, victim number three, whose body to date, still

remains undiscovered, was almost able to get her gun free from her purse and shoot her assailant. Luckily for her assailant during the struggle as she fought to free her pink toned revolver, he was able to deliver a forceful enough strike with that ten inch piece of taped re-bar held ready in his right hand that immediately stopped her aggression and dropped her harmlessly into those powerful arms. A major lesson in any contact crime, guns are really dangerous, always be aware if the victim is carrying or has the potential to have a concealed weapon on their person or in their belongings. You smile when you think that the next victim will not be number six, as the newspapers herald, but will actually and factually be number eleven. The first four murder victim corpses that were buried before it was decided that you needed a distinctive brand as a message to the community that you are still out there and remain very much undiscovered and deadly. How do you know of all these things; you are the serial killer of course.

No one would ever begin suspecting a friendly, agreeable, church going, local business man and family man as yourself of these hideous crimes; assault, abduction, rape, torture, mutilation, and finally the cold blooded murder of a bound helpless victim. With no circumstantial binds to link you to the murder victims, and no physical evidence left at the crime scene, the frustrated police investigators will hope for that one lucky lead; that tiny overlooked calling card that will provide the clue to your identity. You know there will be no lucky lead, you won't be telling on yourself and the only other way would be if a victim escaped or you got careless and left that police hoped for calling card piece of evidence or some other unusual circumstance like a curious police car or heroic pedestrian coming to the victim's rescue.

With much patience and observation, you have chosen the next victim. As your custom, you carefully choose areas unrelated to past targets, to prevent police from patterning a probability model. You have chosen a light

industrial type office area, very low vehicle and pedestrian traffic. This area has great potential. It is many miles away from the last scene. There are no parks close by and the street area is well lighted. There is no close by apartments or residences. The alleys are dark with weak lighting only over delivery doors. None of these buildings in this stretch have night watchmen or guards, and police patrols are almost non-existent. The area is made up of service providers, which means that there is little attraction for thieves and that translates into very little crime and little police interest. Stamp and petty cash burglars would be the only criminals attracted to these offices.

You first noticed her while you were scouting past her building late one afternoon after quitting hours; she was locking the doors to her office. The large overhead sign advertises the services of an insurance company. By chance you noticed her locking the main office door, signifying that she is likely the last to leave. You circled the block and discovered that she was walking, unaccompanied and seemingly unafraid, to the bus stop. Definitely, worth a second look.

It is time to execute the first phase of the Plan; victim contact and selection. Later that week as a follow-up with the pretext of looking for a business referral contact, you walked in the lobby and with a friendly smile, inquired at her desk if a Mr. Jeb Lester worked there. Already knowing the answer as she thumbs through the directory you candidly observe that she large heavy breasts, a thin waist, light body frame, no wedding ring, dresses well in a yellow sleeveless blouse and blue pleated skirt, a pretty face, a cute smile and dimples. You also watch the movement of her arms as she flips the pages of the directory, to see if she has the disproportionate muscle tone of someone that works out and would have above normal strength for someone weighing ninety five pounds. The caveat being, of course that those muscular girls could be very dangerous in the event of a struggle. Seeing that she did not appear to be gym toned,

you continue your candidate profile. She is obviously in her twenties, blonde and works in that office as a cheerful receptionist and probably was hired by a man obsessed with a fantasy of jiggling breasts. "I'm sorry sir we don't have anyone by that name here in this branch office or at any of the other local offices. Could Mr. Lester be an independent broker that sells our products? Sorry, is there anything else I can do for you?" she smiled. "Yes there is as a matter of fact, but not now. You will be perfect, made to order for what I need", you think as you smile and say "thank you, I might have gotten that name wrong, I'll go back and check that name again and get back to you; thanks ever so much" and you walk away. "Hmm, wonder what he beaver is going to look like and taste like. I sure hope it's' not a hairy Neanderthal or Troglodyte one. Some of these good lookers can really fool you and when you peel those cute lacey panties down expecting a rosy pink and bouquet smelling yummy and instead you discover something that should refrained by a leash and will take a chair and a whip to tame .Yep, you knew know."

Driving past her office and then parking on a side street with a view of her office door, you begin to pattern her route. You know it will be dark by 5 pm and by 5:30 pm after the quitting time stampede; all the area offices are usually vacant so the chances of anyone observing you are very slim. As part of the plan, you had to observe the victim's routine, so you sat in that alley with several packages you marked for delivery to one of the businesses occupying an office with a delivery door in the alley. If a police cruiser would stop and the officer would ask, you can always present the package, explain that you got there too late to deliver it, thank the officer and pick up your clip board scribble something on it, start the van, pull away, abort the abduction and begin the victim cruising in another part of town. As there were no curious police interventions with this one, the plan light is still green. So, on several nights, you clocked that at 6:10 pm sharp she locks up the building and never hesitating, leaves the building and

DEATH AT MY PLEASURE

walks to the bus stop, two blocks away. With no other lights on in the building except for the lobby light, you know that she is the last one to leave, every night. Walking to the bus stop, she must pass two unlighted alleys. She does seem confident walking alone but you notice that she obviously exhibits common sense caution when she gets to the alley veering away from its darkness and walking to the center of the street. You know this slight deviation well because you first had to check the alleys out for cameras and finding no cameras, spent four nights within the darkness of its depths watching her walk past at 6:13pm.

On Wednesday, (always choose a mid-week day, for some reason people are less suspicious of others in the middle of the week) you explain to the wife that you will leaving to take some night time and dawn first light pictures of river barge traffic, to try to get that just right photo to put in a magazine special (you are an amateur photographer / publisher who occasionally snaps a good enough photo to put interest to a magazine or to add to your company's portfolio of art choices for client projects). The wife knows and tolerates that this hobby and these photos are your passion and by often refusing to allow you to pursuit them uses this as a means to punish you for your most current transgressions, however slight they may be, against her. As she allows you to pay yourself, via a special company account, a generous professional photographer's fee, and inasmuch as that money is immediately confiscated and funneled into the kid's college fund, she allows you this occasional freedom. Damn do you hate this woman, and can never believe for a moment, that you ever held a spark of love for this insensitive, selfish, rude, and cruel person. If only she knew what a Master game player you really were. You dream of having her bound by handcuffs and forcing a cattle prod deeply up into her bowels and then triggering the electric current across the two metal contact points causing her to go screaming into convulsions. You always smile at the thought of

that image; the bitch screaming in pain and begging for forgiveness and mercy. Someday, just maybe.

Once in the van, you pull over to the riverside public park and park in a secluded point sheltered by large bushes. Exiting the van and by striking up conversations with the two or three regulars you are familiar with, make it obvious that tonight's mission is for you to snap several special photos of the river barge traffic. As you chat with the regulars you gradually walk into the night shadows and your image becomes lost in the increasing darkness. You check your watch it is 5pm; time to put the plan in action. Yesterday, as a major part of the plan, you even changed tires, substituting an old balding, little tread left, garage sale set for the everyday non-felonious ones (as a strong piece of scene and forensic evidence, cops always when possible, make tire tread molds. More than one criminal has been convicted and got life or the lonely one way walk based solely on a prosecutor overcoming the reasonable doubt question with the circumstantial evidence that the matching tire tread print produced and satisfied the jurors).

You walk back from the dimness into view of the regulars; you briefly explain that you are going downstream to the river bend. In the darkness you sneak back to the van. Once back inside the van you completely change your clothing. You are donning clothing that was rummaged from the Good Will box or bought with cash and cheaply at one of the box stores. You know how important it is that any evidence they find at the crime scene will be kept fruitless towards profiling or linking you to the crime scene. For each time, you have made a habit of buying a pair of cheap tennis shoes at the big box store, and then purposefully cut a groove in the sole, a different spot on the sole for each crime scene. After the crime you will cast the shoes off the bridge and into the river, where the shoes along with the victim's clothing and any evidence that will not burn will be carried away by the current downstream to rest in some deep,

debris filled, backwater eddy and rot. You even change socks before slipping on the notched tennis shoes.

Several years ago, as part of the execution of your Master abduction plan, you bolted anchor clips to the van floor and walls. You also drilled and mounted four shiny metal plated two inch eye bolts, carefully and strategically spaced and soundly anchored to the floor; two spaced thirty six inches apart towards the drivers' front and two spaced forty inches apart towards the rear doors. Each eye bolt has a thirty four inch piece of packaging cord tied to it (this is a cord that when tightly knotted, the knots never slip). These are tie downs for the victim's hands and feet to keep the victim in a spread eagle position. If a nosey cop were to ask, "why officer those are cargo tie-down spots for my camera equipment delivery, as you know camera equipment is so sensitive to bumps and vibrations, a slight jar and the photo shoot is wasted." For less than ten dollars, you have bought five thin plastic, disposable painter tarps. Carefully you spread them out and secure them to the clips. No one would ever suspect that these tarps were intended for something other than the splatter of paint. Once after the splatter plastic has performed its use and the plastic sheets become evidence, you will bundle them up and burn them in the back yard fire pit telling your wife, if the bitch even demonstrates the intelligence of curiosity to ask, that they were used as backgrounds in a photo shoot.

Clothing already donned, you strip off six two feet lengths of duct tape and gently spot stick them to the van ceiling. The next check off is the cotton ski mask, another item for the river. The last items are the box cutter, a heavy bladed EMS set of scissors, the surgical gloves (another purchase from the dollar store), the piece of rebar that has been carefully and meticulously cleaned of fingerprints and then carefully taped with duct tape likewise cleaned (while this item, as well as the pliers, will be cast from the bridge, it is an item that could be recovered by a forensic dive team and acetone smoked for fingerprints on the tape or metal, so finger

print removal is crucial), a six pack of good reservoir end condoms (never the cheap ones, they do break when one gets carried away in the heat of passion, and one is almost always guaranteed to be in the heat of passion), a small bottle of bleach, a small plastic water pistol, a pair of cheap box store pliers, and just for the dramatics, a homemade garrote (a short piece of wooden doweling on each end of a triple strand of white cord, and a small spool of exceptionally strong package cord (which will be incinerated with the other burnable evidence). All the personal evidence from the victim's purse will also be burned in the fire pit; credit cards, driver's license, anything that will burn to ash or melt into a plastic glob. The only thing you leave on the victim's body is her jewelry. Clothing is cut into strips, purses sides cut open, beepers, belts, etc. thrown from the bridge. A different spot and different bridge is chosen for each victim and with three different bridges crossing this river, there is never an after rush hour moment when any one of the bridges is not absolutely void of traffic, both pedestrian and vehicle. To prevent late night travelers from stopping to ask if you need help, you always lean several fishing poles against the bridge hand rail and turn on a portable battery powered lamp. "Just got here, nothing biting yet" or "Just trying to catch a fish dinner to feed my family, officer."

A major part of the plan requires the abduction scene setting to have certain things either present or not present. There, obviously can be no cameras. There can be no bright illumination or light poles beyond the common little 60 watt alley delivery door way lights. The alley must be wide enough for the van. The alley must be vacant of after hour activity. There must be several large dumpsters. A passerby must not be able to see very deeply into the darkness of the alley. Intersecting streets must also be vacant of activity. It is very important that there be no apartments or homes close by that might feel obligated to investigate any possible screams from the darkness.

After parking the van between two dumpsters and the alley wall, driver's side out, you don your rubber surgical gloves and take up your many times proven homemade rebar blackjack. You set out the eye catching props, position yourself beside the dumpster and building wall, and tense up in excitement ready for that predatory strike that will lead to the capture, abduction and absolute control of this new victim. You briefly think about her breasts; will they be solid or soft? Will she scream when you squeeze them or just grunt in pain? Will she have a pleasantly sweet vagina or will it reek of bathroom odors? You snap your attention back to the business at hand, your mind must be focused or the plan will fail. You check your watch, it is 6:12 pm; time for her to be walking past the alley. You can hear her heels clicking on the pavement approaching the alley. You hear no other sounds.

Crouched in the darkness you moan loud enough to be heard from the street. You moan again slightly louder and mumble the words "please help me". You hear her clicking heels suddenly go silent. She heard. You know what is racing through her mind struggling to weigh out what she should do; ignore the pleas and go to the bus or help someone in distress. Will her intuitive instincts to flee overcome her kinder side wanting to help an injured person in distress? You moan again and this time just a little louder and as pathetic as you can make the words, you mutter louder "help please, for my children's sake, help me, please." This is a crucial point to the plan; will she approach the alley with some caution, scream for help, or flee to the bus stop and look for a phone to call the police.

Her mind processing the sound commands her feet to become immobile as she rapidly sorts options. She is a very self-confident woman who has never considered herself in any danger walking in the dark to the bus stop. After two years of being a very ardent as time available student, she has achieved green belt status in Tae Kwon Do. As another precaution, every night, immediately after removing the key from the office door lock, she

returns the key to her purse and then from her purse she removes a six inch needle point sharpened nail spike (a gift from her brother) that she carries in her right hand and stays at the ready until she boards the bus for that 20 minute ride to her home stop. She looks so forward to the day when she won't anymore be standing in all kinds of weather waiting for public transportation. The two block walk to the bus stop after a long day at the office is a bummer. But the bus ride is a necessity of her budget; she is saving her money for a down payment on a little red sports car and will be able to make that down payment in just two more months.

It is a long, twice a day, morning then evening, lonely walk, but no one could feel safer. Being a person that is always there to help others, it is with little hesitancy that she weighs out to assist a seriously injured crime victim or to be as a majority, close her ears to his pleas and continue on with her life. The combination of the martial arts and the spike provides her the margin that she believes makes her invincible.

Only on a few occasions have potential victims resisted the lure of providing help for a stricken fellow human being causing you to immediately abort those abduction attempts and move on to another restart and another victim. You hear her heels clicking, but clicking slowly now, she has made a decision to help; she has taken the bait. "Help me please, I can't get up. They robbed and beat me. Please help me." "Where are you at" she shouts, the fear and indecision in her voice very evident. "Over here between these dumpsters and the van. They beat me then dragged me between the dumpster and left me for dead." "I'll go get help." "No, I can't wait, I need your help now, please, for my little daughters sake, please." "I still can't see you." "Please lady I need your help. I am lying on the ground next to this van by the wall. Bless you. I can see your feet, I'm on the other side, between the van and the wall; please hurry before I bleed out." As a prop that you know will successfully grab her attention for those important first several seconds, you have long ago

prepared a pair of old blue jeans and wired a pair of bright tennis shoes to the pant legs. You pushed that waist part of the jeans beneath the front of the van so that just the legs and shoes are visible making the victim believe that you had crawled beneath the van to escape your assailants. You know she will focus on those blue jean legs and move forward just enough to present her unsuspecting back to you.

As the beautiful, blonde, Good Samaritan lady very slowly and cautiously walked to the wall side of the van, your patience and cunning has paid off. The spider awaits the fly and the web is ready. Quickly she glances inside the van's windows to make certain that no assailants are hidden and waiting, seeing nothing suspicious she is now focused on the blue jean prop. She takes the bait, and does not suspect that you are not lying beneath the van's undercarriage, now oblivious to the fact that you are the hidden danger she should be looking for and who is now patiently waiting and hiding in the shadows of the dumpster. With her focus concentrated on the blue jeans prop and as she passes between the van and dumpster and turns to face the front of the van, she has her back now completely to you. "You poor man, I'm here and there is no one here to hurt you. I'll help you to the bus stop and"……..she never finishes that sentence. With a downward hammer stroke, you use the rebar blackjack to knock the young woman unconscious. One grunt and she collapses to the alley pavement.

As she falls you hear something metal drop from her hand that makes a ringing sound on the pavement. It distracts you for but a split second. You see the spike, very quickly pick it up and in almost one motion slide open the van door and toss the spike towards the back of the van door. The nervy bitch had a spike and was going to kabob you if she had a chance. Gotta remember during the games what this violence prone bitch is about later. Back to business at hand, you carefully avoid the blood oozing from her head wound and quickly grab her, lift her dead weight body up, and push her through the van side doors and onto the plastic sheeting. You

guess a dead body weight of around 105 to 110 pounds. Still a back strain, those 80-90 pound girls are a dream to toss around, but the tradeoff is they usually have tiny, tiny tits and that's not where all the fun is; soft, beautiful, squeezable, pliant breasts are where the fun is at, most defintely. You quickly pick up the blue jean prop, toss it through the van door, then hop in and close and padlock the door (you thought it was a great idea to put a padlock on that sliding door to prevent escapes or surprise intrusions).

Knowing how important timing is to the plan, you strip off a piece of the pre-cut duct tape and bind her hands. A second strip is used as a blindfold. A third binds her ankles. The fourth is used as a gag; duct tape when applied correctly seals the oral cavity so well that to avoid suffocation it forces the victim to breathe through their nose. The fifth is used as a second insurance binding for her hands. Your weakness begins, you must touch her. You push your hand up inside her blouse, under her bra and onto her breast. You curse the insensitivity of the rubber gloves. You gently touch the nipple. Squeezing her globes tightly and not feeling any foreign masses or resistance within the soft masses, you think "These are real tits, no silicone bags here" then smile. You quickly withdraw your hand and slide it up beneath her skirt, pushing aside her panties and gently force and wiggle your finger inside her, the rubber of the gloves a liability making fingering her dry and resistant womanhood a little bit more difficult. Your finger tells you that she is a fallen woman, the virginal gatekeeper probably long gone when she was a teenager and flopping in the back seat with some passionate hard dick boyfriend of the moment in daddy's car at a drive in movie or remote part of a lovers' lane or City Park. Withdrawing your finger, you present its bouquet to your nose then drag it across your tongue. This girl is perfect. Your penis begins to harden in earnest. Not now, there are things that must be done first. You smile; it is such a good feeling, a successful capture. "Time for that later", you think, the main need now is to concentrate on getting safely to the "spot."

You climb over the motor compartment, start the van and with a smile of satisfaction, put the transmission into "drive". Your worse nightmare is over, a successful capture and then stranded at the scene with a motor that won't turn over. You pull from the alley and head to the "spot." It is a forty minute drive, but you could drive it blindfolded; you drive it every morning and every evening. To be sure that you are not being followed, you do not drive directly but make several off route turns and U-turns. Satisfied no one is tailing you, you return to the route to the "spot". You are the default owner / manager of a large print shop. Hired by your father-in-law you started as a simple multi-color press machine operator and gradually out of the nagging of your wife were promoted to a print salesman. Your unimpressive personality traits doomed you to being a very less than successful salesman, and your father in law purposely delighted in sending you out to a potential client and after your failure at selling a print contract, would send out one of the A-team wonder boys or girls to successfully bring that business in the fold. You always suspected that those two cute Hollywood starlet girls, Heather and Kim, with absolutely no communicative skills had to include a blowjob or two as part of their sales promotion to close a sale. The boss didn't care, as long as he was seeing signed contracts they could have blown monkeys at the zoo to get the ink on the paper.

It was no secret that your father-in-law intensely disliked you. It was no secret that your wife had no respect for you and bullied you. Everyone in the company knew. Everyone smirked behind your back. Your weak personality, absence of self-confidence, extreme and boring dedication to details, overall failure to connect with living matter, and strangely, all those negatives shadowing a high IQ, while filling the FBI model for a person likely to commit terrible heinous crimes against humanity, none-the-less was easily and mistakenly recognized at a glance by most common souls as a very dull person that could very easily get lost in a crowd of two. You

dreaded the annual holiday family get together, where your father in law and daughter would tell shop stories of your grandiose failures and everyone would laugh as if the story was a very funny joke. Your only defense was a smile as you melted into another room. Of course, when your father in law passed on, you inherited the CEO spot and became the on-paper owner/manager of his very successful small business. From day one, every employee understood that your wife, the lovely drone and bully, was calling all the shots, your authority for decisions was limited to minor supply purchases. If they only knew, the piss would drain from their bladders in fright.

As a habit you cruise around the outside of the compound fencing checking for parked cars. You have made a company policy about security and the alarm system, no one is allowed in the building after hours for any reason. Still you always check. You have the remote keys for the compound main gate and the remote keys for the truck bays. You have keys for everything; this is your secret kingdom where you reign. Using the remote, you unlock the perimeter security chain link gate; pull the van through then carefully relock the gate and then pull up to the garage door. Taking the remote door opener in hand you press the green remote up key unlocking and opening the automatic garage door, and also with the remote, you press the light button and trigger the inside light switch illuminating the entire expanse of the truck bays. You pull inside. You quickly exit the van and double check the lock on the garage side door and place the manual lock override on the garage door. You also lock the doors from the building to the garage, just as insurance in case someone should wonder in. Satisfied that the area is locked down, you re-enter the van. It's play time; your prick is singing for its reward! As part of the early development of this evil master plan, you had made certain to meet the local police precinct captain, Captain Finch, to explain that there will be many times when you work late and the lights will be on in the garage. Occasional lunches and a

nice and expensive personal Christmas gift to Captain Finch guarantees that the desk officer will at precinct roll call remind all area cars that unless a crime is on view to patrolling officers they are not to be concerned with any after hour activities in the building.

Climbing in the back of the van and towering over this latest victim, you check to see if she is conscious; no this one is still out. That last one had recovered enough to struggle and it was a physical challenge over powering her to get her hands and legs tied to the eye bolts. Flipping this one over on her stomach, you take your heavy duty EMS surgical shearers and begin cutting up the back of her skirt, her panties, her blouse and then her bra. You carefully cut out the sleeves which then releases all her clothing from her body. You now roll her over on her back and lift her eye lids to see if there is any retina response. Eyes still dilated, she is still out. "Good", you mutter, as you replace the blindfold and take notice that there is no more blood flow from the superficial head wound. You can't help but notice how her extra-large soft breasts sag and gently roll to and rest on the side of her ribs. You also cannot help but notice the size of her nipples and the bullseye encirclement of those nipples by large dark pinkish areolas. You feel that tinge again beginning in your loins. Now the dangerous part begins; there is always the possibility of a lucky punch or chop incapacitating you if she suddenly awakens and begins to struggle and break free, and if she was able to force open the van door allowing her to escape within the building and with so many phones and offices to hide in, it could be a disaster for you. Stretching her bound hands over to the right eye bolt, you double check to see if there are any signs of consciousness. With no signs of her coming to, so carefully, using the cord, you tie her left hand securely to the anchor. You then cut through the duct tape freeing her hands and quickly pull her right hand over to the left eye bolt and securely tie it to the anchor. Now for the feet. Once that last ankle is tightly bound, she is naked, secured, spread eagle and ready for the party.

It is seven thirty and you have at least two hours to enjoy the bountiful promising success of your hunt.

Within minutes she begins to come to, you wish you could watch her eyes as they gradually clear and she begins to swing from bewilderment to panic as she realizes her plight; abducted, naked, and bound to the cold plastic covered floor. You see her muscles contracting as they begin to test and struggle against the cord bindings. You enjoy the panic that you sense tensing and growing in her body. She probably thinks that she is alone somewhere in a grungy basement or a vacant house. It is time for you to explain the rules. You grab one soft breast with the pliers and crush its tissue with the increasing pressure on the pliers handles. You smile as she arches her back to escape the pain and mumbles a scream. Releasing the pliers from her breast; "Hello there, I hope I have your attention, my name is Jerry. I have chosen you to be my sexual partner tonight. In a minute or two I will remove the blind fold and the gag. I have removed all your clothing and have tied you down to floor anchors. There is no escape. If you co-operate, I will free you. If not, then the consequences are of your own decision and making. I am a man of strong bodily desires. I intend to make love to you in many ways, in your vagina, your mouth and your anus. I will also treat you to oral; I love the smell, taste and feel of my tongue on and in a warm, moist vagina. I know that almost every woman loves the sensation that oral produces as it sends those welcome fiery signals to every nerve ending in your body. Your vagina will betray you, it will moisten with anticipation and it will want so much more. I promise you that. What, you're shaking your head no, I am surprised, a good looking woman like you should have had plenty of wonderful experiences and orgasms with handsome boyfriends with, no doubt, the most athletic and exploring of young eager tongues. No matter. I suggest that you pretend that you are enjoying it, do so and I won't have to get ugly. If you fight, the consequences of that too is your decision. Although I don't encourage it,

you are welcome to scream as loud as you like, there is no one within miles to hear you. Each time you scream, I will be forced to punish you. If you get cute and try to bite my penis or hurt me in any manner, I will slowly cut and skin your nipples off. I don't think you would want that, would you? You cannot begin to imagine the pain and just think a beautiful girl like you with those gorgeous breasts scarred so hideously that she will have to hide those beauties for the rest of her life. (Always give them a thread of hope that there will be eventual freedom). I am going to remove your blindfold and gag now." With that you tear the duct tape binding the blindfold from her eyes and hair. You always do the hair first, they always scream when the duct tape pulls the beautiful tresses of their hair out by the roots, so to keep the noise down it's the hair first then the gag. You rip the duct tape from across her lips; the shock of the adhesive caused pain on her lips always causes them to gasp. After preforming this drill on previous victims, you know the game and the predictable responses. You expect them, and you are never disappointed.

"OK, now I am going to ask you a few questions and you are going to answer truthfully. First at all times, you are to call me Sir, understand?" "Yeah". "Are you stupid or are you a slow learner, what did I just tell you to call me?" "Sir, I am sorry." "That's better, don't forget it's always Sir, always." "Yes Sir."

"Before we begin, I am going to take several photos of you. I have a regular portrait lens and a macro lens for close-ups. I intend to take a few full body lengths, a facial, some close-up shots of your breasts and nipples, and some close-ups of your pussy, with the lips both closed and separated. Now sweetheart, when I take the facial, you will smile for the first one and on the second you will stick your tongue out as far as possible, understand? Later after I have made sweet love to you, I will cum on your tongue and you hold it there until I can get a photo. That's always such a neat shot, a

beautiful girl with her mouth wide open and a pool of cum floating on her tongue. Can you do that as well?" "Yes Sir".

You momentarily think about the camera work, this is the part you really like, posing each victim to snap close up photos to remember them by and focusing that macro lens within millimeters of their nipples and so close to the drapery of those labias that later when you pull them from the files, you will almost be able to smell that smoky sexual scent. You love this little camera that you bought with company money. Your father-in-law really bitched at paying six hundred, eighty five dollars and sixty five cents for a camera and another four hundred and thirty six dollars and eighteen cents for two special focus lenses. You just wish the cocksucker was alive to see what you were using that camera and special lens for. Unless you get careless and leave some film lying around, there is very little chance of anyone discovering the film as you use the safety and the comforting confidentiality of the company dark room to develop it. Once the photos are developed and hidden in a safe deposit box, should they ever be discovered or you are caught with them, and they not linked to an investigation pointing towards you, you can always claim you found them in the maintenance shed and you think one of your employee's has a bondage fetish and likely bought the films at an adult bookstore fair and you intended to show them to the good Captain at the police precinct and ask if that someone was breaking any laws. "Yes, I understand that, but why didn't you immediately report it to Captain Finch?" "Very simple, I was waiting for more evidence. I watch TV police shows and I know you need lots of evidence to make a case, so I was just being patient."

"What do people call you?" "Connie, Sir." "Are you a virgin, Connie?" "No, Sir." "How many men have you made love to, Connie?" "Since high school, I don't really know anymore, maybe about thirty, maybe fifty, Sir." "Did you commit oral sex on these men, Connie?" "Not for every guy, Sir." "How many, Connie?" "On most of them, men always want that. My

girlfriend says men like to cum in a girl's mouth because it makes them feel like it's a master and slave thing, Sir. Even right now if I want to keep my job, I have to suck my Ethiopian boss's cock once a week. He is definitely not a boyfriend, Sir. He is a fat disgusting pig, he has body odor, his dick stinks, and his cum tastes funny." "Connie, do you catch your boyfriends' ejaculate and swallow, or when you feel that first hot squirt of cum on your tongue, do you jerk his cock out of your mouth and let the guy do a space shot?" "I can deep throat, catch their cum and swallow without gagging, I don't mind, Sir. Sir, what do I have to do to get free? If you let me go, I promise I would never tell anyone, never, please, Sir. If you let me go, I will give you the best blowjob ever, Sir. I can get all of your cock down my throat and I can wiggle my tongue like a wagging puppy's tail while it's all the way down there. It makes my boyfriend cum right away and they all say it's the best blowjob ever. Of course I don't do that for my boss, the fat smelly asshole. Please Sir, I won't tell anyone, I swear, please, Sir."

"Connie right now I'm going to do oral on you to get me in the mood and get you ready for my penis, I suggest you be still until I tell you it's ok to talk, understand? "Yes, Sir, I'll be quiet." You pull down and remove your pants and flash a straining five inch cock. Dropping to your knees, you begin to lap Connie's pussy. "Do you like this Connie?" "Yes Sir it's wonderful." Connie played the game all women play; every guy that eats pussy thinks he is the best. So few men do much more than unimaginative and barely stimulating tongue strokes across and up and down the labia canvas, and the ladies, in an effort to please, pretend it's taking them to a level of pure ecstasy never achieved by a mortal woman before. Connie knew this sick guy was falling short, but was wise enough not to insult him. She knew most men are not in the passion heights league with lady lovers; that being when a female eats pussy it is with understanding, knowledge, and it's with real intense passion. The giggle joke in ladies rooms and during bridge parties is "no one eats pussy better than a pussy." Probably

no truer statement ever made. Those few times with that butch roommate sure set forever high goal posts for the men in Connie's future life who attempted and failed miserably at the pleasure potential of their wiggling tongue in her honey well.

After the unimpressive lap time, you move up her body and sheath your dick with a condom and plunge your dick in her spit lubricated vagina. Eight or nine jabs and you groan as you fill up the jizz bag. As you climb off of her corpse like body you are thinking "that pussy wasn't very tight. Bet her boyfriend has a horse cock." You command her "Open your mouth slave; do not swallow or spit it out" as she complies you upend the dick rubber by the nipple end and let all the collected semen drain into her gapping mouth. "Now it's time to take a camera shot. Listen carefully, I want you to open your mouth and cup your tongue and hold my cum in a puddle on your tongue so I can get a good close up. Fuck it up and I will have to really punish you and I know you don't want that to happen, do you? So, let's get it right the first time. OK?" Ballooning the semen in a pocket between her cheek and gum line, Connie replied in a very garglely voice "Yes Sir, I can do that." "Open your mouth" you command as you twist the focus ring on the macro lens. "Now curl your tongue like a spoon and let it float in the valley." Once you have taken several degrading open mouth floating cum puddle photos, you bark another command, "Now swallow every last drop and then open your mouth and stick your tongue out for another shot." Connie complies and you set aside the camera, its work done. "Time for a little break. Rest sweet Connie, and we will play again in ten minutes or so; I think my cock will be ready by then."

"When will you be releasing me Sir?" "You bring it up one more time and I am going to make you really sorry. Now shut the fuck up about it, when I decide it's time to release you, I will let you know. We still have a lot of fun ahead of us. Now, just do as I say." Frightened by the prospects of more pain, Connie just in an exhausted and defeated response, blurted out

another "Yes, Sir". "Now Connie it's time to show me your little cocksucker tongue tickler trick. Just looking at your beautiful tits and that hungry pussy gives me a boner again."

Will that semen ever become the evidence that when she swallows it becomes a forensic archive that could send you to death row? Doing the research, you feel pretty safe doing this, you read in a forensic magazine that semen is destroyed by stomach acid and any semen trapped in her esophagus can be destroyed by a household 5% bleach douche. As you start to squirt, she starts to gag; you pinch her nose and force her to swallow. "Like that whore, I promise there will be more. I was blessed with DNA that usually lets me get hard and ejaculate three to five times during one of these sessions. I think it has something to do with the eroticism of you being my slave and I am in total control." A pleasure thought occurs to you; you jab your fingers into her cunt and begin punching it in and out. Within five minutes of finger fucking her, your dick is case hard again. Forcing her lips apart, you push all five inches into her delicious mouth and the feel of her tongue squirming on your cock feels like a magic carpet and triggers the next ejaculation. You have always been glad that you were not born with a huge horse cock, five inches fits just perfectly and comfortably down almost every throat. Again you had to pinch her nose to get her to swallow. "Will you release me after I suck your dick Sir?" "Did I tell you it was OK to talk and didn't I tell you not to bring up releasing you again? Are you that stupid Connie?" "No Sir, I'm sorry, Sir." The very nerve of this ungrateful bitch. "You have a consequence now, Connie. I specifically told you to talk only on my command. I don't like to punish girls, but you did break a rule."

Reaching over you strike a hammer blow with your fist into her stomach. The impact of the strike naturally drives the air from her lungs and causes her body to try to fold up. Impossible with the bindings so she just beats her head against the plastic sheet covered floor. When she gains control of

her breathing again, she blurts out "OOOh, Sir please don't hurt me again, please." "Again you talk without permission Connie, now I have to punish you more. I was hoping that you would be someone special and be someone I wouldn't have to punish. I am sorry but now you have forced me to teach you to be polite." Placing a new set of surgical gloves on, using your left thumb and fore finger, you spread her now lubricated vulva open and then force two fingers, then a third, then the pinkie, and finally with one hard shove, you push your fist past the labia gateway sentinels and as deep up and inside as it can go, which is to the forearm slightly above the wrist. That last boyfriend must have a beer bottle cock. Poor Connie is really screaming now. You twist your hand back and forth. She screams louder, you smile. You relax your fist and allow your hand to slide from her slippery vagina. "Feel better now, Connie? Connie, I would like to say I'm sorry but that pain was caused by you, behave and we won't have to punish you anymore, understand" "Yes, sir" she whimpers out. "Connie there is so much fun to be had for the both of us and this show is just beginning." "Please sir I will do anything you want, you can fuck my ass, I'll swallow every drop of your cum, but please don't hurt me again and please let me go." "There you go again, speaking without permission. You know Connie; your chattering is starting to get on my nerves." Suddenly she is becoming aware that you are more than a demented, psycho rapist.

Realizing the seriousness and hopelessness of her plight, Connie is now on a verbal offensive, thinking maybe a different tactic will change the order of things. "Bet you tortured puppies and kittens when you were a little boy. Bet all the other boys bullied you and probably had a special name for you; didn't they? Maybe they called Jerry the fairy before they jabbed their dicks down your tonsils? You probably had callouses on your knees working line ups of big stinky cocks. You are one sad motherfucker, you know that and now I know that. Fuck you, you midget dick coward cocksucker. I bet your wife pisses in your face. You are a fucking coward. Bet she makes you

call her ma'am. Untie me and give me a chance, I'll tear your balls off and make you eat them, you loathsome dead dick, asshole. Bet the boys have been ass fucking you so long you couldn't shit in a wash tub. You can't get a woman to look at you so you do this, you no good, tiny dick cocksucker. Bet your wife laughs because you're a one pump hump, you evil, sick motherfucker. You eat pussy like you're licking an asshole, bet you got plenty of experience doing that too." "Connie, I'm shocked at your profanity; we can't have you being so profane, such talk for a pretty young lady. A little duct tape and we'll have peace and quiet again."

You grab the tape roll and replace the gag. You make certain it is air tight. "Now, that's so much better, I can concentrate on my toys." "Do you know who I am Connie?" She shook her head no. You enjoy seeing the terror, horror and shock flame into their eyes as they suddenly realize the totality of their predicament. Your cock is getting hard again. "I'm the guy that killed all those girls and I am so sorry but it looks like you are going to be my next victim. Think for a minute, I am the last voice you will ever hear and the last face you will ever see." When told that, she put every effort into struggling and pulling against her cord bindings, and all to no avail. "Sorry, dear Connie, there is no escape, be a good girl and it will be easy, be a bad girl and you will really, really regret it. Understand?" Connie nodded her head "yes" hoping that something or someone would intervene and rescue her from this fiend.

"Oh, by the way Connie, I found that spike that you had in your hand. You were going to stab me with it weren't you, you bitch? Move your eyes up for yes or sideways for no." Fearing the consequences, she frantically shakes her head in a side to side "no" gesture. You push the spike up to her face then take the spike and slowly drag it across each of her eyes. "Well, I once read about a serial killer who used something like this to poke out the eyes of his victims, would you like that Connie?" Again, Connie shakes her head vigorously from side to side. Once her head stops moving

you take the spike and push it ever so slightly up first one nostril then another. You see the immediate register of pain in her eyes. "If I were to push really hard the spike would follow your sinus cavity upwards and penetrate your brain, killing you instantly. But we won't be doing that, it would rob me of all the fun we are going to have. If I were to poke out your eyes, well you know, I can't really do that either because it will interfere with my brand but what I can do you cruel bitch is to push it up your ass and give you a little taste of the pain you meant for me, you slutty cocksucker." With that said you release her right ankle from its binding and force her leg up towards the van roof exposing the valley that shields her pink little button. Holding her leg in this elevated position by pushing your shoulder against it and cramping it stationery, she is powerless to move. Not wishing to make a bloody mess, you center the spike point on the pink artifice and slowly push it in on an angle intending to only slightly puncture the sphincter muscle; deep enough to cause pain but not deep enough to cause huge hemorrhaging. The pain is immediate as she arches her torso in response. Liking the results, you jab her several more times. Removing the spike and releasing her hips and then securing her ankle again to the floor anchor bolt, you look into her agony filled eyes. "Just a little taste Connie, maybe later I will give you more of what you intended to give me, maybe later, but I think you got enough of the feel of that steel to realize how bad a person you are to want to hurt someone else with this terrible weapon. Jerry smiled, "that's funny poetry, the "feel of the steel", isn't it Connie?"

CHAPTER TWO

As a preliminary step of your practiced horror routine, you smile in anticipation as you remove the device from its hideaway inside a camera bag; a readily and inexpensively available electric TENS shock muscle therapy impulse transmitter. Small and very light weight, it carries at the high volume settings an extreme electrical charge. You examine the probes and flip the power switch. The green light is on and the charge meter indicates 100 percent. It's time for pain therapy now. You reach beneath her buttocks, and slightly lift and turn them to be able to slide an electrode up into her rectum. Once the electrode is centered on her tight pink doorway, you then force it as deeply into her rectum as the length of your finger allows. Allowing her ass to settle back on the van floor, you take the other electrode and insert it too as far up into her vagina as you can force your finger. Electrodes in place it is time to turn the music on. You begin with a low volume and gradually increase the power until you can see a reaction in her stomach muscles. At full power it is so exciting to see her body arch each time you twirl the power knob and

it reaches the max, ten. This girl is not reacting to the intensity of the higher shock volumes; the shocks are not triggering the muscle contractions in her as they have done to the others. Thinking that it may be a breakdown of a circuit, you make a mental check to have these electrodes later scoped out with a meter. Not satisfied with the exercise, you pull the electrodes from her insides and set them aside for that later amp meter diagnostic check. Now is time for the nipple fun. Replacing the pad electrodes with clip types, you attach an electrode clip on each nipple and twisting the dial to the highest number to send the maximum current impulse through her gorgeous huge jello-ish tits you almost cheer as her tits quake from the current that is now racing through her conductive mammary cell tissues.

After thirty minutes of electro torture, you allow her to take a small break. You wish you could know what is racing through her mind. You like to see the tiny beads of fear and pain sweat break out on her face, tits and flat stomach. Glancing at the vee of her legs, you notice there is a pool of urine beneath her ass and you can still see yellow drops dripping from her pussy. Grabbing the paper towels, you soak up her piss. Ripping the duct tape from her mouth you calmly comment just as you would to an employee "Connie we really can't have this. You made a mess, what do you think we should do about this, tell me, before I get angry and decide to do your nipples again." Crying and sobbing Connie responds "Sir, please, I want to be a good girl, but the electric caused me to piss myself. I will try to not do it again Sir." "Open your mouth wide you disgusting cunt." With her mouth wide open you squeeze the piss from the paper towels directly down into her throat. Holding her nose she has no choice but to swallow or drown. She swallows, they all swallow.

"Connie, did you like the taste of that; yes or no?" "Yes, sir." "Good, since you like piss so much, now, I think it's time for me to relieve my bladder, and I will be pissing slowly so there is no reason that any of it should spill from your mouth. I strongly suggest that you gulp it down. If any of my piss

spills, I'm gonna stick that spike up your asshole again, got it?" "Yes, sir." "That's' the right answer." Straddling her chest, you unzip your fly and wiggle out your cock. Pushing her lips open, you begin to dribble your bladder down her throat. She fights gagging and manages by gulping, to stay ahead of the steady stream. "Good job, Connie, you didn't lose a drop and because you were such a good girl, I'm going to reward you by extending the break a few more minutes, what do you say?" Weakly she responded with a "Thank you Sir." "Now, I am going to replace the tape gag and you better hold your head still." She watched with crazed and panicky eyes as you pulled more duct tape free of the roll and smashed it across her mouth. At least she could still breathe through her nose she thought.

Once you have decided she has rested enough to have regained a full reserve of energy, it is time to move on to the finale. The steps in the branding method phase of abusing poor Connie's body doesn't all quite require a heartbeat, so it is almost time to release her soul and make her body the ultimate unprotestingly pleasure center.

"Now Connie, break time is over, do you believe in brand advertising?" Connie shook her head "yes." "Sweet little Connie, to be certain that I get complete credit by the police and media, I have to leave them a brand. My brand consists of removing your nipples and areolas, incising a X on your left breast, a Y on your right breast, burning all the hair from your vagina and ass, and forcing a decorative feather into your medium rare pink meat vagina. As a final branding I will be douching your vagina with good ole household, brighten the laundry, bleach." As you describe these inhuman things, Connie's struggling reaches a pitch where she is actually shaking the van fighting those biting bindings. You smile. You reach in the mercantile plastic carry out bag, and remove the garrote. Connie stops struggling and with panic and fear demonstrated in her eyes, she stares at what you now have looped in your hands. Not having ever seen a garrote before, she has no idea that this the thin rope with wooden handles in your hands could very well be a vehicle of death, her death. "Connie, this is a garrote used

by the special soldiers to silence a sentry. They sneak up and loop the garrote around the sentry's neck, place their knee in the center of the sentry's back and pull with all their strength. It takes but several minutes for the brain and body to totally die. It is very efficient, quick and silent. You smile at her and switch positions between her head and the driver's seat. You drape the garrote from a clip on the van's overhead. Her eyes never leave the garrote. Almost believing that she could stare the garrote away and now realizing what that simple deadly device is for, it is like a magnet and her eyes cannot ever leave it. You again focus on her breasts. They are magnificent. You gently take each in a hand and begin squeezing. You squeeze as tightly as you can, until you are exerting maximum crushing pressure on each one. You see the degrees of pain register in her eyes and hear her muffled screams beneath the duct tape gag. Releasing her breasts you kiss them and carefully nip the nipples and softly bite within the pinkish circle of her areolas. It is important not to leave punctures. If one were to leave bite impressions outside that soon to be removed trophy sphere of love, a good forensic examiner would be able to cast a dental impression and suddenly the crime investigators would have hard evidence. Not going to happen. This torturous foreplay once again awakens your manhood.

"Now first I am going to make love to you again." With that you slip on a condom and lying on top of her you slide your penis deep into her. You enjoy very much the warmness of her body radiating into your cock. Her eyes are still staring intently at the garrote thinking that there lies the only article of danger. You know she will be focusing on that device, all of them do. To extenuate the pleasure of being inside her, with a rapid and sudden movement, you thumb and finger pinch the areola slightly behind the nipple to produce the maximum amount of breast pain. Connie bucks and twists against her bindings each time the crushing pain floods her pain receptors. The body contortions are causing an additional sensation and movement within her vagina and those muscle movements transferring

directly to your penis. You pinch her areolas again holding that crushing pressure for thirty seconds, releasing it when her reaction begins to diminish. You let her rest for fifteen seconds and then again you crush the end of her breasts with that very painful pressure. Each time she reacts and struggles against the pain you can feel that delightful, vaginal muscle clasping pressure on your cock. The pleasure is overwhelming and you feel the jet of cum race through your cock, explode and flood the inside of the condom. You slowly ease your condom encased dick out of her pussy. "Oh that was so sweet dear Connie. I hope you were able to enjoy it as well. There is more pleasure to come, dear Connie." There is only one better sexual sensation; and that is about to begin. This is a special reward for your cock.

You slide down her body and examine her vagina. It is very wet and slippery. You begin your secret rituals, first the tip of the tongue outlining and tracing both labias; the tongue spearing the clitoris; and finally complete tongue penetration into the depths of her womanhood. You can feel your cock getting hard again. The record for erections was that tight pussy redhead who couldn't have weighed more than seventy pounds. You hated killing that one, but you were cursed with the universal curse of serial killers and victims, you had no means to keep her captive and alive. Regretfully, all you have is her nipples floating in a preservative and two dozen photos. That girl was so good you kept her alive for almost seven hours and you fucked and cummed six times that night, which is quite an accomplishment for a forty one year old man. She was so entertaining, with that one, you barely got home before sunup.

With your dick again hard, "Thank you dear Connie I do so enjoy eating pussy. Eating your pussy made my cock hard again and eager to fuck, but poor Connie, this will be the last fuck you ever have. Please make it special for the both of us. If you weren't such a pottie mouth girl, the gag wouldn't be necessary and you could scream how much you love it. But, alas I find it hard to be romantic with a woman calling me obscene,

belittling names." Very, very slowing you slide your cock, centimeter by centimeter, a little in and a little back out, and finally plunging it fully into the warmness of her treasure and then with full penetration, you can feel the excitement of your balls passively resting on the warmth of her ass.

Fucking her hard now, actually slamming your body against hers, you grab both of her breasts and again begin twisting and crushing them. The response to the pain is instantaneous, she begins bucking and thrashing her body up against yours. You release your grip and use the thumb and forefinger to clamp just behind the nipple in that most excruciating of painful breast grips. Her body accelerates it's struggling. Your cock is hammer head hard now. Just a little longer, just a little longer.

Releasing the nipples you suddenly and forcefully pinch her nose closed. Just two digits, a thumb and forefinger have become instruments of her death. The garrote was a tease focus decoy, Connie's death will come from another method of suffocation, the duct tape has sealed off her oral airway, and by tightly pinching her nose, the compression closes completely her sinus cavity and you know from experience that this method of execution will immediately and absolutely prevent the flow of oxygen to her lungs. She will be conscious for five minutes or so, and you will witness through the panic and desperation in her eyes that she is absolutely aware that she is slowly being murdered.

This is the exciting part, the sensation reward for your wife neglected cock. You must hold tight to prevent her head twisting or lifting upwards and breaking loose from your thumb and forefinger. She bucks, twists and tries to roll her head sideways. With her nose compressed and sealed in that death pinch and a hand full of hair in your other hand she is powerless to struggle free. The struggling produces the effect you love most; very strong muscle contractions within her vagina. Fucking that seventy pound redhead, you had a dozen times released your nose grip to allow her enough air to begin the suffocation cycle over and over, allowing you to

feel those vaginal muscles strangle and massage your cock. That was a night to remember. If only there would have been some way you could have kept that bitch alive as a slave; just too damn bad for you and for her. She did seem like she enjoyed it.

Those desperate muscular struggling panic reactions of a woman who knows she is being murdered create such extreme internal body movements and protestations that normal routine sex pales in comparison to and no longer satisfies you. You love this feeling, it is unlike any sexual feeling you have ever experienced before; orally, anally or with best and most exotic methods of masturbation. You know of course that this extreme vaginal response can only be triggered with extreme pain to the body and panic to the mind; it is an unintended consequence of muscle contraction response to pain and panic. Connie struggles arching her back and screaming silent screams. You must hold tightly to her nose and hug her body tightly to prevent her contortions from expelling your dick from her pussy. On the few occasions that your wife allows anal sex, the "rabbit hole" you called it (usually only after a rare night of her having too many cocktails partying), even at that point when you are fucking your wife's tightest orifice, you have never experienced such a muscular grip on your cock, never.

As Connie's struggles weaken, you focus on her rising breasts, straining for life. Such beautiful mounds, those light brown nipples that taste so wonderful. In seven minutes her body has one last huge contortion; she has passed to the other side. You release your grip on her nose and with a plunge you force your dick deeper into her, spilling your evil seed into the condom. As her vaginal grip relaxes in death, so does your whole body. With now only passive pressure holding onto your cock, you sigh and completely relax draping across the now cooling corpse of poor Connie. After several moments of rest you extract your now shrinking penis and begin to regain a little composure. To be double sure, you feel for a pulse. No pulse, poor Connie is now on the other side. You wait; another minute

or so, and triple check to be sure there is no spark of life. You have to be absolutely sure there is no life left in these bodies. One fuck up and it could mean the long lonely walk on death row.

It is now absolutely safe to free her hands and feet. You cut all the nylon binding cords free and stuff them into your burn bag. The excitement of her fight for survival has renewed your sexual energy and your naked cock is again standing at the ready. You roll her corpse over and placing a condom on, enthusiastically force your penis into her still warm ass. You fuck her ass with as much power in the long stabs as you are able to mustard. Amazing, within thirty seconds, you feel that hot jet traveling from your balls, through your cock and exploding in her tightness of her ass, filling the nipple of the condom. You are sweating and almost exhausted as you pull your softening cock from the corpse's ass. You would like to take a rest break, but there is much more work to be done. Turning her back over, breasts up, you linger for a moment and unable to resist, you push her legs open and again perform cunnilingus on and in her vagina. The vagina bouquet is spicier now, almost every victim has a bladder release in that final death throe, and that is a vaginal flavor you enjoy so much more than the bouquet from a fresh one.

You quickly dress. It is time to dress the corpse with your police taunting distinctive brand. You click the lock on the blade of the box cutter to expose two inches of the razor sharp edge. Grabbing her left breast and with practiced surgical precision, you carefully cut around the circumference of her areola and gently and very carefully slice and peel it to sever it from its mound, the soft elastic fatty tissue of her breast. You would love to sever each nipple by gnawing it from its breast but you know that it would ruin its later erotic souvenir value. Then with equal precision, you slash a large "X" beginning with the first diagonal line three inches from the vacated nipple/areola and crossing through the exposed whitish fatty tissue. If she were still alive there would be blood spurting and squirting from both the excised skin and the deep incisions from the letter,

not so with a stilled heart, only a pink seepage identifies with the gaping wound. You do the same with the right breast, forming the letter "Y". You carefully place each severed nipple and areola flap into a brown plastic jar marked "photo developer, part A" which contains a taxidermy solution you prepared of common borax soda, salt, and alcohol. If kept immersed in the solution, the tissue specimens will stay preserved for decades. These are the only souvenirs you allow yourself as a reward for the execution of another perfect crime.

Taking the hand held butane torch, you ignite the flame and carefully burn all her pubic hair until there remains only tiny ashes and her vagina has the color of a medium rare steak. Immediately the van's interior is flooded with odor of scorched hair. Turning her over, you do the same with any hair on the backside of her vagina and anus. You carefully wipe the ashes from the vagina and anus. Pushing her legs apart, using two fingers of your left hand you slowly separate the drapery of her labias, then pushing the nozzle of the plastic squirt pistol filled with bleach inward and past the labias, you squeeze half its contents in her vaginal cavity. You open her mouth fill it with bleach and using your finger force open her throat to allow that caustic fluid to drain deep down in her esophagus to destroy any semen evidence. With another squirt, you rinse the inside of her mouth out with the bleach as well. You then roll the corpse over and again with the left hand force open her asshole and push the nozzle of the pistol as deep up into her anus as possible then squeeze the balance of the household disinfectant into the orifice.

With practiced precision, you clean up all the bindings, any fluids, and all burnable evidence from the altar of horror. You dress with the throw away clothing and head out to a dump spot along the jogging path that you have with much attention to detail, carefully chosen for tis body. You glance to your dash clock; it is now 10:46pm; too late for jogglers and bicyclers and too early for patrolling police cars. During one of those friendly public relation lunches with the police captain, you discovered after asking a

crafty question, that all the city and county cops do roll call and change shifts at 11pm. So between 10:30 pm and 11:15 pm the only area patrol cars out and about are those that are stuck on a radio call complaint. You drive past the spot three times, spacing the time between, at 2 minute to 5 minute intervals. The first trip is torturously slow and the second and third at a normal cruise speed of 25 mph. You see nothing suspicious. On the fourth you quickly pull off the asphalt and drive over to a grove of small oak trees. Pulling the van aside one, you park, hop over the motor cover, unlock the inside door padlock, slide the door open and quickly drag poor Connie's remains to the base of a small oak tree.

Before leaving the truck bays you had lightly rebound the hands and now just have to drag her over and pose her sitting with her back propped against a tree and then force her stiffening legs in an exaggerated "Y." The breast mutilations will be obvious and as an added signature, you partially push a feather into her vagina. The feather insertion is something you read in a tabloid that a long ago murderer did to his rape victims, and after being apprehended told the police it was a symbol of the sins of Eve in the Garden. You know it will drive the police crime profilers crazy trying to make a connection between the bloody mutilation alphabet letters, the suggestive alphabetic position of the legs, and the peeking feather. The searing of the pubic hair and bleach will be obvious to the forensic technician. You purposefully leave a shoe impression in the soil by her body. Double checking you are convinced that you have left nothing unintended at the scene. You pull away from the scene and very intently look as far as possible in all directions for anyone or anything that could cause problems and connect you to the scene. You want to be certain to identify any potential for a chance connection or intervention by a patrolling police car, or a late dog walker.

Driving to the bridge, leaving the van idling and the headlights on pointing westward, you hop out of the van switch on the electric lamp and point its reflector light towards the east shore preventing anyone from either side

from observing anything yet leaving the southern rail side in deep shadows. You quickly remove your rod prop and cast the fishing line into the dark swirling waters and then lean the rod against the bridge railing. No one about, so you bundle all her clothing up (just her clothing nothing else) into a tight ball and using a concrete block, weigh down all of the physical evidence you wish to cast into the silent currents of the river's cold depths. No traffic tonight. Once you are satisfied that everything not for the burn pit and related to poor Connie's existence has been removed from the van and trusted to the rot and degradation of the deep waters, you pitch the last bundle out to the welcoming wet bosom of the river and watch it splash and immediately sink into the depths. Looking about again, you see no one. You gather up the light and fishing pole and head in the direction of home. Ever careful and somewhat satisfied that no one is following; you still take a very exaggerated route home with several loops and U-turns. With no dogging or reappearing vehicles in your rear mirror, you are safe from interdiction.

Finally arriving home, you bundle up all that is burnable and go straight to the fire pit. Once you have all the real evidence balled up, you ignite the hand torch and put the flame to the plastic. In less than five minutes all the evidence to link poor Connie's existence and demise to you is melted into a smoldering plastic glob. Satisfied that you have successfully incinerated tonight's sins, you return to the van and do a very thorough check for anything you might have overlooked. The van is clean. Now into the garage, with the speed jack, it takes you a practiced thirty minutes to replace the worn tires with the road worthy set. The throw away clothes are the last to go. Into a plastic bag and tomorrow on the way to the office, you will drop them at the local charity collection dumpster, where you are sure, a homeless person will sort through them and grab anything suitable for personal use or resale. The last thing to do is to take care of the trophies. In the jar marked "photo solution" are two wrinkly, pale circular orbs of skin and tissue. Naturally, both have a raisin shaped nipple

dead center. You quickly place the jar and camera into the overnight safe that you keep in the garage. Everyone in the family and even some of the neighbors know that the purpose of the safe is not for personal valuables but for protecting bring home client projects. You were very careful when you made everyone aware of the purpose of the safe. The curiosity and/or suspicions of neighbors have sent many a felon on that one way walk. Discovery of a single set of nipple trophies would be enough evidence for a death penalty verdict from any jury. You are obvious to that fact and have planned accordingly.

The overnight storage safe is a grand old bank antique. It cost you over five hundred dollars to have a false back installed in it. This would only likely be discovered by someone with experience with old safes or someone that measured the inside width and compared it with the outside width. A good investment, you always thought. These souvenirs will be taken to the office and added to the collection you have in the rented commercial storage locker. Years ago, you wisely rented that commercial storage locker using a long ago terminated employee's picture less ID card and explained to the vendor that you were a scientist and collected rare preserved fish samples and expedition photography artifacts and needed a climate controlled safe space for these valuable specimens. As a further prevention of any intrusion into the privacy of your storage locker, you pay the monthly rental installments biennially and with all cash. The rental policy of the storage place is to notify owners when the rent is due and give them a 30 day grace period before cutting the locks and selling the contents. The renewal date is extremely important and a date you can never, never overlook. What a shock it would be for someone to buy the contents with the coded twenty three brown jars and at first be confused by the jar contents and then horrified when the realization of what the preserved tissues were. Again, you make absolutely sure you also pay the bank deposit box rental fees far in advance, as there would only be a righteous indignation with no confusion as to who should be notified if a bank clerk

were to open the box and suddenly see all those incriminating photos. There was enough condemning evidence in those heinous photos to not only get you on death row, but to get you denied a last meal. Society can be a very cruel administrator and caretaker of the law of man.

Trusting not to memory, you have a small code book that you keep hidden in the tire well of your car that corresponds with the photos of each victim hidden in a personal safe deposit box again using the name of that long ago employee. The code book tracks the victims' name and victims' number on the photo envelop and specimen jar. It is not much fun or sexually arousing if you can't remember each victim. You have developed a sequence you follow each time you decide to visit your trophy room; first review the entries in your code book and select a memory, and then you drive to the bank, key into the safe deposit box, select a numbered envelope containing a full set of victim photographs and then drive to the storage locker. Once you have opened the storage locker (you, long ago thinking ahead, rented one with climate control and proper illumination) you enter and lock yourself in. Then matching the number on the envelope with a numbered jar you sit at the small café table and chair and carefully lay the photos out on the table top. Opening the jar, you remove the preserved skins. Drying the trophies with a paper towel, you begin to feel the excitement growing in your loins. Dragging your tongue across each areola and nipple, and pausing to mouth and lightly suck on each nipple, your cock demands attention. Standing, you unbuckle and drop your trousers and underwear, allowing your cock to wave in anticipation. Holding both breast skins in your left hand your rapidly masturbate your penis with your right hand. Within thirty seconds your cock jets, spews and oozes its creamy warm cum onto the breast skins. The breast skins now resemble gravy over biscuit breakfast fare. Your left hand lifts the semen drenched skins upwards to your face. You examine the texture closely; first smelling of it then, like a viper use your tongue to slurp and cleanse the semen from their uncomplaining surfaces. After a final inspection to ensure that no

drop escaped that hungry tongue, you gently return the silent skins to their embalming solution. Exhausted, you collapse onto the chair. You lift the facial photo and gently place it against your lips. After five minutes of rest you wipe any residues from you up with the toweling and dress. Returning everything, it is now time to make that trip back to the safe deposit box. Using these playtime episodes allow you to space the frequency between victims and reduce the potential for a lucky break for police investigators. But, still it would have been so great to have a video of each victim's torture and murder, but such evidence is extremely dangerous to have and would slam dunk you into death row.

Having a victim photo archives in the safe deposit box and a safe space in the rental locker with victim body artifacts serves a great purpose in the prevention of law enforcement suspicion or apprehension, it reduces the frequency of your need to stalk and hunt. With the occasional cruise by on a free afternoon and by locking yourself in the space, opening one or two of the jars, retrieving the pliable skin patch, and the fire of kissing the nipples, vividly relives each capture and murder allowing you to violently masturbate and ejaculate away the dark urge and desire for a fresh body. The sexual relief satisfies you enough that you can space captures anywhere from three to six months apart. This is an investigative killer for the police as it greatly reduces the potential for a witness or incidental vehicle stop by police and also allows the panic in the community and pressure on the police and local government to temporarily subside.

Into the house you go for a quick shower and then into the bed and a quick kiss for your semi-awake wife. "I'm really sleepy so make it quick, how'd it go, any good money shots tonight?" "Yes, I got a couple of really good sunsets and a few of the barge traffic." "Will you be bringing any photo money home tomorrow?" "Yeah, probably, but I am really horny." "How much?" "I don't know yet, maybe five hundred dollars or so." "That isn't very much money, I can't keep paying you for something that is crap, if you don't start getting better saleable shots, I'm thinking about cutting off your

photography commission; you probably shouldn't have it anyway. Then you won't have any place to escape the family. Do you want that to happen?" "Honey, feel my dick, it is really ready. Could you roll on your tummy, can we play rabbit hole tonight. My little rabbit is frightened and would like to scamper into your wonderful hidey hole, please, sweetie? It won't take me long to cum, I promise." "Not tonight, I told you a hundred times, you get to rabbit hole fuck me only when I see the cash. No cash, no fucking me in the ass. Besides it hurts and is disgusting. I like it the other way around. It's more fun with me working the dildo in your ass; you do seem to like it and you do moan so. But nothing for you tonight, I'm tired and need to go back to sleep, so turn the light out. If you're that horny go jackoff in the bathroom; won't be the first time will it?" "OK, OK, honey how about tomorrow, maybe tomorrow?" "Yeah, if you got the cash, maybe tomorrow." Boy do you hate that bitch. The bitch is just like some ugly, cold, mechanical vending machine, nothing goes in any of her holes, absolutely nothing without upfront coin. It's a good thing that you got your rocks off so many times tonight, "good sweet Connie, thanks honey for saving me from my cunt denying, money hungry, selfish Neanderthal wife."

You wake up and cook your wife's breakfast; you know how she hates to wait for it so it better be ready and the coffee just right, not too much sugar and not too much milk. Not only is she a bully, but she treats you like a servant. Heaven help you if you fuck something up. Shit, remember the time you shrunk her good alpaca wool, deep plunging vee, tit displaying sweater? There was hell to pay for that and still is every time she remembers it. She claimed it was irreplaceable. Lying bitch! The one thing she loved so much about it was that showcased her big tits and grape sized nipples so well that when she wore it the men at the office would crowd around to peek down that wide open and inviting ample cleavage and as an extra bonus, the fact that it was the boss's wife's tits they got to stare at and fantasize about. More than once you caught them staring down her open sweater at her jiggling tits and when you caught their eyes, they knew

you knew what they were lusting about but all you could do was to give them a nasty paper tiger boss look. Your wife did so enjoy embarrassing you in front of the employees. All the employees would politely turn their heads or walk out of the room when she started on you. You knew what they all were thinking; the wife has bigger balls than the pussy whipped boss man. Some of the girls even felt sorry for you. How could you live with and take that from such a bitch. That was a big mistake agreeing to continue as her employee, as operational CEO. Should have listened to that attorney and cut a deal where she either was a stay at home or started another printing shop location. That way you could have hired a fuck bimbo, who for a secure and slightly over rate salary would be only too happy to gargle your cum in the stock room. But, what choice did you have; the printing company belonged to her family and she was first in line for inheritance rights. Another nasty thought, now with all the profits flowing directly into her bank account, what was to prevent her to someday say "Damn, he's boring, maybe time to move on and get something with a spark, maybe I should call my lawyer tomorrow and have him file divorce proceedings?" What a wonderful dream; escaping this trap and forever free of that dominant bitch's nagging; the negative part, the money stays with her.

You yell upstairs, "time to get up sweeties, breakfast is waiting." Your two sweet little daughters fly down the stairs and in unison shout; "what did you get for us daddy, what?" "Got you both a nice surprise, you can open them after breakfast, OK?' "OK, daddy."

In a stuffy, poorly air conditioned downtown police precinct a familiar conversation is being carried on. Precinct Captain Lewis asks "You guys crack the case yet?" "No luck Skipper, our guy always waits anywhere from two to six months before he strikes again and it is never within a geographical pattern. The FBI profilers are as baffled as we are."

"Captain, we are still coming up with no leads on this sick bastard. The tire prints and shoe impressions could be from anyone, even several copycats. But there is a common denominator with a twist, a very strange thing at every scene, when we are able to collect tire prints, they always match each scene, but the shoe prints don't. Its' almost as if he's wearing new tennis shoes each time, Chief. According to the FBI forensic people, the tread pattern of the damn shoes are cheap box store shoes and can be bought from at least ten stores in the metro area, and that gets us thinking that maybe he lives here in the city. The pathology reports from the FBI indicate that the adhesive residues, the duct tape binding and ligature burns on all their wrists and ankles all come from a similar binding material, like the nylon cord twining pattern from a heavy duty packaging cord. The impact contusions on the victims are all very similar, so apparently he using the same type of blunt object to club them unconscious. There is never any tissue beneath the victim's nails from a struggle. There is never any semen in or on the victim; either he is using a condom or the bleach destroys it. Not a single pubic hair. The slashes on the breasts are from some type of razor blade and the feds are betting it's from a cheap dollar box cutter. We haven't gotten a single phone call that even remotely gives us a subject lead. We have no idea the significance of the two letters carved into the vic's breasts; they could be mathematical or alphabetical, no idea. We are sure the bleach is to destroy any of his bodily fluid evidence he might leave in the body. He burns the pubic and anal hair to be sure none of his body hairs have shed onto the victim, and no one has ever heard of any rapist sticking a feather in a vagina. We have checked the central and national crime data base twice to see if we could get at least a partial match of a MO, but have come back clueless each search. We did come up with one partial match. In New Mexico there was a rapist/killer who killed four old matrons. He would scout them out on his delivery route. Make the delivery and come back late at night with another box feinting a delivery. He would push his way in, beat the old lady, rape her and force her to perform oral sex, strangle her with a phone cord, and

then cut her nipples off. We know it's not him, because one old lady, number five, was suspicious when he came back after delivery hours and had her .38 (her son had given her a home protection gun for a Christmas present) ready and when he tried to force his way in, she shot him twice in the face and he died in the doorway."

"Well Sgt. Samuels you guys in homicide are paid the big bucks to crack tough cases, something will turn up, and something almost always turns up. One stupid mistake and it will lead you right to his door. The odds are always in our favor, the more perfect they think they are, the more likely they are someday going to leave a major calling card at the scene or on the victim or during the abduction. With the mayor and every Tom, Dick and Harry screaming at me, I don't want to see this one in the cold case file. I'm sure you boys understand; no one likes to get sent back in uniform or put on the cemetery patrol. Meanwhile we can all be positive and hope that he's gonna grab some pretty little girl one night and she will pull her dainty pink lady revolver out and shoot his cock off." Every cop in hearing distance laughed; but all the homicide detectives knew exactly what he meant, and weren't laughing; that uniform and cemetery crack wasn't intended to be a joke, the Skipper intended it to an incentive.

CHAPTER THREE

The above person and criminal scenario could easily be someone you know and it could very well happen in your own community; a neighbor, a church goer, a service man, a teacher, anyone. It does happen and happens often enough that people must always stay alert to their surroundings. One of the worse personal crime threats and terrors to ever rain down on a community is the discovery that there is a serial killer committing unabated and random murder in the community. Serial killers are often very intelligent and are usually cursed with egos that compel them to taunt and challenge the best of the police department investigators and profilers. In addition to control and some degree of depraved sexual pleasure; murder and torture to a serial killer is a way of stroking their egotistical lives while terrorizing the good citizens within an otherwise normal community. The pressure and demand from community leaders and the media for a quick arrest and closure that an active serial killer investigation brings on the police department, often one understaffed and with little margin in the budget, leads to the panic not only of the

citizens of the community but in job fretting police officials and politicians as well.

Serial killers often, but not always fit in neat little FBI profile boxes that can give investigators everything but a name and an address. Formerly, police departments relied on pure luck, a mistake at the crime scene, a snitch, a rare escaped victim, or an angry woman to identify the killer and close the case. In years past, if the serial killer was a transient and killed in many different states, the absence of police to police communication usually meant the only way the killings would stop was if the killer was unlucky in his victim selection, was incarcerated on another charge, or had naturally or untimely reached his or her "dust to dust" end. Development of cutting edge data base technical advancements in law enforcement electronic communications has improved the success of LE investigations. Serial killer crimes can now be profiled and eventually identified if there are any common pattern elements in the physical evidence, such as marks on the victims, sexual deviance, sexual assaults on the victims, particular types of torture, age of the victims, bindings, unusual type of death, type of weapons used, as commonality in profiling. However, and still to this day, if no common denominator is identified and the perpetrator is a transient killer, a killer that has no preference for method, or an extremely detail oriented disciple of the devil, many, many cases wind up in the unsolved, forever open, cold case files.

Once routine but unspectacular crimes with similar modus operandi are connected, and generally if no child abduction and multiple deaths are not associated, local law enforcement will first expend huge amounts of exhaustive man hours while tracking countless leads before the FBI and their unlimited budget, forensic resources and manpower assistance is requested. Should a child be involved or a linked series of heinous murders, the FBI are often invited from the get go. The FBI can often, but not always, immensely reduce goose chases. Local FBI bureaus monitor

local crime and often run parallel investigations before officially being committed to a hunt.

Generally, when more than three cases are tied together with similar evidence (all raped and throats slit; all raped with cigarette burns; panties stuffed in the victims mouths; similar mutilations, a certain piece of clothing missing; similar body placements or disposals; etc.) anonymous sources within local police departments usually begin to leak to favorite reporters that there is a serial rapist or killer about. No police department welcomes within its jurisdiction the threat of a serial killer or rapist. Realizing that these cases often become very complicated and difficult to solve, they usually make that phone call to the FBI to tap into the endless resources and personnel assets of the FBI to cross check files for similar crimes nationwide; to check crime sheets for similarities, to do case histories, to do the forensics on crime scene evidence and to do a thousand other things that local departments do not have the budget, talent, experience or resources to tackle.

Serial killers generally fall into two basic major categories further branching into a number of sub less distinctive or definitive categories. The two major categories of police interests are categories of opportunity or the category of a defined hunter. An opportunity killer will seek chance encounters to obtain a victim, no one is safe. A defined hunter will carefully stalk victims either through a victim selection process using a common denominator, such as a type of dwelling, a campus, a mall parking lot, etc.; or selection of a victim through association with a particular activity, abduction from laundromats, sport events, a particular type of afterhours bar, etc. A sub category of a defined hunter is a specific physical or life style choice (as in straight /gay/ bi-sexual); a particular color of hair (as in blonde/ brunette / black/red); an age group (child/teenage/middle or old age); a physical trait (busty/ obese/ thin); a race ethnicity (white / black / brown / yellow); an economic level (trailer community / suburban /city/ghetto); a profession (prostitute / secretary/ housewife/ retiree); this list is endless. However,

once investigators can isolate the category, especially if it is a hunter type category, and a sub category is identified, the trail begins to warm.

Investigators begin to investigate these latent repeat crimes and murders by determining first a geo-location and pattern. With no definition of brand or pattern or location boundary, investigators must hope for a shred of crime scene evidence or a lead, be it a tip from a crime hotline or an accomplice or spurned lover. The fact that often these serial killings are mostly random and scattered is especially challenging to police investigators. When a singular crime is committed within a community, investigators are apt to spend huge amounts of hours conducting interviews, searching crime profiles and databases for area suspects with similar MOs. This type of investigation effort for a typical common crime more often than not ends in the identification, apprehension, and conviction of the perpetrator. Serial crimes require a much more intensive specialized type of investigative procedure and evidence luck.

A common thread of a particular serial killer or serial rapist is branding; many leave a signature, often a very revolting and heinous indignity upon the victims' body to proudly broadcast to authorities, "I did this, me. I am smarter than you, now come and find me". There are a number of pattern categories and traits that professional law enforcement employ to composite a rough idea of the actual every day bubble of a killers world. Communication across jurisdictional or geo boundaries allows migration of suspects in and out of jurisdictions and greatly thwarts case and suspect development. It helps not if the killer is a migrant as that singular frightening fact of mobility often aids to the continuance of a crime spree. Mobility often shelters and overlooks that fact that the serial killer has likely been murdering targets for decades. Serial killers often have many and definitive pattern habits which allow the brighter of police profilers to narrow investigative leads and eliminate many false positives in the rush to apprehend the perpetrator.

Serial killer creatures can usually be defined as a male. Most have very serious but demonically concealed mental disorders which trace back to early childhood and were either ignored or categorized as a "phase" that the child or young adult would grow out of. By the time that these mental trackers are easily identified, the deranged person is appearing in a Court of law for a criminal act. The Courts are not interested in diagnosing psychopathic behaviors, they are more interested in clearing dockets and therefore have little inspiration beyond disposing of cases involving these aggressive and anti-social personalities by either incarceration or counseling, neither of which effectively diminishes the future danger to society. Victims are generally females, though there are many cases of record of men that sought out other men for various reasons, mainly directly linked to a "hate" fixation; be it racial, sexual, or ethnical.

The word torture derives from the Latin verb "torquere" to twist and is defined in major dictionaries as "the act of inflicting of severe excruciating physical pain as punishment or revenge or as a means to obtain sadistic pleasure".

The word rape originates from the Latin rapere (supine stem raptum), "to snatch, to grab, to carry off" and is defined in modern times as the "unlawful sexual intercourse or any other sexual penetration of the vagina, anus, or mouth of another person, with or without force, by a sex organ, other body part, or foreign object, without the consent of the victim".

A majority of rapes do not usually include, beyond the mental duress, mental torture, and the pain and fright of being a temporarily powerless victim of a sexual assault, major physical torture. Most rape victims physically survive the crime while physiologically suffering forever the horror and haunting of a captivity, forced body invasion and penetration sans the infliction of a method of torture.

Conversely, rarely does abduction and pleasure killing not include both initial victim rape as means of control, sexual pleasure, torture and

subjugation for the perpetrator, rapidly accelerating into severe horrific measures of extreme physical pain and culminating in death.

Rape and torture are usually the prerequisite hallmark of a serial killer. The very psyche of a serial killer prevents or precludes any form of mercy or compassion. Additionally, serial killers are often secretly ashamed of their cowardly acts and by extinguishing the life of the victim, self-justify their acts by their superiority in the erasure of the acts by the total and fatal subordination of the victim. In categorizing serial killers; one serial killer profile seeks to erase the acts from both the perpetrator's conscience and the judgement of their fellow man through the fastidious disposal and concealment of the victim's remains from detection; while another more common profile seeks the self-glorification of a notoriety of establishing a well-publicized, criminal brand.

It is important that everyday humanity understand the boundaries of the differences in the type of criminal abduction; one has hope, one is absent of hope. A ransom kidnapping always gives the hostage the hope and likelihood of release while a serial killer's captive will ultimately know no hope and face unimaginative torture pain and an eventual and untimely gruesome end.

Prevention by awareness and avoidance is a major key in staying out of the clutches of an abductor. Law enforcement and personal safety instructors time and again present the same message in bulletins and seminars; full time awareness of your environment. Citizens must personally accept responsibility for their own safety and must adhere to a state of unrelenting consciousness with an absolute awareness of their surroundings. A first step in personal safety is the application of the "what's wrong with this picture?" theory. Police academies, from the FBI's Quantico to tiny village law enforcement training centers teach police recruit officers to always scan the environment for the out of place or for suspicious behavior. More crimes are prevented, and the key word here is

"prevented", by someone noticing something suspicious and then either phoning 911 or alerting others. Once a criminal or someone about to become a criminal is exposed, rarely will that person linger at the scene. Citizens are drilled to make a practice of scanning and really "seeing". Notice the car parked with a person sitting doing nothing but focusing too long on passersby pedestrian traffic; a stranger following you to your car all the while scanning the area possibly for cameras or witnesses; a suspicious stranger standing within a radius of twenty five feet of your car; the stranger strolling through a residential neighborhood; a vagrant watching people enter and leave a convenience store; a pattern or routine of anyone not known to you or out of place in the environment; you must alert to anything that makes you uncomfortable or suggests a flag of abnormality.

There will be many times when this instinct proves to be an embarrassing false alarm, but a people trapper or people hunter only has to be successful and glide under your radar once. A majority of these people trappers or hunters will always have one thing in common; their eyes will be constantly scanning, both for a victim and for the presence of cameras, rescuers or law enforcement. Always look to the eyes, if they appear scanning, that person either likely has criminal intent or is a cop searching for the about to be law breakers. Keep forever acid etched in the back of your mind, that trapped people rarely survive their captivity.

Good Samaritans must be absolutely certain that they are not being baited into an ambush. Many who have responded to what appeared to be a situation of distress or disaster have discovered too late that had they had taken one more second of assessment or taken one more precaution they would not have found themselves bound and headed to the destiny of an untimely and monstrous death in a remote or hidden human slaughterhouse. Few have lived to tell the tale. There are tens of thousands of these fake scene incidents in the crime books; a majority being robberies, but there is enough abduction to warrant special attention. By police definition a hostage situation is normally the taking of

a person against their will as a means of escaping the consequences of a criminal act or a kidnapping for ransom. A hostage situation is not the same as abduction; the fate of the victim in the abduction is usually sealed and ends in victim fatality.

Awareness of surrounding is the key element to defeat the most ingenious of people trappers or hunters. Any single or tiny flag that conflicts with the staged bait should be that one flag that precipitates caution and the need for rethinking another response. Evil will always lurk in man. Evil will always be present in society. A majority of mankind will elude the consequences of a major encounter with evil. For the right of the decimal point minority, one tiny mistake in judging a situation can be disastrous and allow that evil to triumph converting that baited and trapped vibrantly alive and breathing collection of protozoa into an unidentifiable and unpleasantly decomposing mass, often times to forever remain undiscovered and lost to loved ones and to history.

Unfortunately it is often too late when the death candidate discovers the plight. Hope is opportunity and opportunity translates to life. The victim must be prepared to recognize and advantage every opportunity, however slight. Opportunity can take many forms, alarming others in the vicinity of your plight, the rebinding of ligatures; the transfer and movement from one place or position to another; a distraction of the captor; a loose binding; the availability of a sharp instrument; a quick and violent punch or kick to the captors' throat; anything or any means that could convey serious and incapacitating injury or be fatal to the captor that will provide an avenue for escape. There is no fairness nor Marquis of Queensbury rules to escaping an agonizing death; all options must be recognized and kept open for instant and extremely aggressive action.

Once you have been trapped, the abductor is not interested in any deal you may try to make for your freedom. You must remember he is a student of the Marquis de Sade. He will be merciless. He is only interested in

domination and delivering pain. He is not interested in any money beyond what you may have in your purse. A trip to an ATM while offering him cash, is filmed by bank cameras and increases the likelihood of his identification and his risk of apprehension. He knows that. Even the slowest of criminals know that police check ATM and drive through teller banking video records and banking activities of post abducted victims. Bargaining with every imaginable method and technique of sex will not be a very persuasive bargaining chip; after all you are completely in his control and refusing to submit to any desire will likely result in the employment of a violent and painful incentive. Trying to appeal to his sympathies regarding babies, small children, sick relatives will not penetrate his psychopathic barrier wall. Pleading will not deliver any change in the course he has chosen for your demise either. The serial killer has baited and trapped you or the hunter has abducted you for two motives; control and his pleasure. With you bound and helpless, he can subject every single artifice to sexual assault; he can subject your body to the most horrific of tortures; by pain or the promise of pain he can drive you to commit the most disgusting of perverted acts and make you describe how much you love it and him. Once you are trapped or captured and in his control, your only avenue to freedom is escape and an escape engineered and carried out solely by your cunning and with the resources at hand.

The victim must realize that passivity or subordination to his domination will very likely be fatal. The victim must use cunning and always be prepared to rally and exert the strength of every muscle to overpower or in any way possible debilitate a madman. There will be no second chance. The only sacred rule in dealing with abduction, rape, torture and murder is to not make the initial mistake of being taken in by the bait or circumstances. Taking that extra time to return to a store and ask for an escort or noting the emphatic heart touching situation and driving or walking on while immediately making it obvious that you are using your cell phone to notify police; it can professionally help the injured or distressed

and it definitely without questions, can save your life. In any situation, before you commit to any Good Samaritan act, call 911, report your location and describe what you see. Criminals will often abandon the attempt if it appears the victim is speaking with a police dispatcher. The core purpose of criminals is to not get caught; by notifying police of a situation or suspicious person you have flipped the tables and greatly increased the odds of apprehension should the felon persist with the intent of his felonious endeavor.

Serial rapist/killers can sometimes neatly fill a model profile and other times be a challenge to the best crime profiler the FBI has to offer. These psychopathic misfits can take any form, from the meek neighbor next door to the manager of the super market. Many are family men; many are drifters. Most exhibit contemporary and text book commonality. All will add that little personal touch or "brand" in their preferences for the infliction of pain and suffering, or that special mutilation, body positioning, or in the method of executing the victim. A majority are of Jekle and Hyde constitution; the true deviant personality and behavior surfacing in the planning, disposition, capture, sexual torture, physical torture, and execution of a victim. Control is the number one factor, allowing the deviant to master the inadequacies of his psyche. Each arrest and conviction of a serial rapist/killer adds a new page to the professional profiler's handbook and sometimes a new chapter to the psychology manual.

A serial rapist/killer is often discovered to be of split personalities; one that is a perfect fit in a community; the other a calculating and challenging sinister mind seeking to frustrate the best minds of a homicide department. There is another type that often forever evades the best efforts of police investigation; the transient or pass through opportunist that travels the interstates and never remains for long in the crime vicinity. All have a single purpose, to bait, trap, control, capture and subject their victims to unimaginable and heinous torture and ultimately murder their

victims, often in the most gruesome of manner. Many eventually face the judge. More often than realized by the public, the sudden cessation of a series of killings is not due to the applied efforts of the FBI and police homicide departments, but to either the killer's demise to a natural or unnatural death or the killer's incarceration for another crime. In the case of the a natural or unnatural death, the victims' families never receive closure; in the case of the second circumstance, the killings generally continue once the killer either serves his sentence or is paroled for his/her lessor crime. Another theory regards the length of the sentence and the age of the killer once he/she serves out the term of sentencing or is paroled. A middle age killer who receives a thirty year sentence for a lessor crime and enters the penitentiary when he/she is forty five years old and then returns to society after serving a thirty year sentence is far less likely to resume murdering his/her co-habitors of the planet at the age of seventy five.

Upon the successful apprehension of a serial killer another issue becomes immediate, how many victims did he/she really kill? Serial killers rarely confess to anything beyond the initial evidence, hoping that a smart lawyer seeking to make a name will one day free the defendant on a law or trial technicality. Only after the hope of freedom evaporates, does the serial killer then begin to use the legal system to his/her advantage. Fully knowing the value of closure both to the police in closing cold case unsolved files and closure for the victim's family the serial killer often uses the yet unnamed victims and the location of their remains as a bargaining chip. The more common attitude of convicted killers is to prefer to forever declare their innocence hoping that some future Clarence Darrow will discover a tiny flaw in their conviction and force an overturn and free them from death row. There are thousands of lonely and undiscovered graves across this country, testimony of those forgotten victims.

CHAPTER FOUR

Sitting in the mall parking lot across the street from the small convenience store lost in the gentle peaceful quiet and loneliness of the snowfall, Sonny was enjoying the luxury of a bad cup of coffee and a cigarette, in the warmth and comfort of his specially outfitted van. While reflecting on the little stressful things of everyday life that can weigh so heavily on anyone's mind in a time of solitude, Sonny was also on the watch for that special opportunity. Every set of tail lights that parked in front of the store brought Sonny's attention and focus to the purpose of why he was sitting in a parked van in a snowfall on a very cold, very windy and wintery day. Sonny was hunting and on a search for a proper victim. Sonny was keenly observing every person that the need for another cigarette, or a loaf of sandwich bread, or maybe an ice cream or chocolate treat, forced them out onto the wet and slippery low income streets of Chicago's lost wards.

Sonny was the alpha hunter, his prey any woman that Sonny felt he could trick for just those few short moments it took to get control; or if worse came to worse, those few extra moments it took to over power and force her into the van and in either event, a new victim for fun city. In his hunt it was four major considerations: a by-themselves victim, the victim age, looks, and size. The plan dictated that once a victim was selected that the opportunity in the form of a lonely stretch of road be present; with minimum risk factors; vehicle traffic, cameras, police patrols. Equally important was the confrontation hazard, is the victim likely to be easily overpowered should she become suspicious and the police ruse fail. Once the plan was initiated, Sonny knew that there would be only one option should the victim break free and escape; it would be necessary to use his weapon to shoot her to death and flee.

He knew he had to have a plan, a very refined plan if he wanted it to be two things; a) successful and b) and keep himself a free man. Every successful criminal had a plan. Daily setting aside one hour in the early part of the day and one hour before lights out, in those lonely periods in his prison cell, Sonny polished and re-polished his plan. He called it the "Hello Officer" or the HO Plan for short. He went over his list of items countless times, weeding out or changing the items he wanted for both the capture van and the slavery parlor. Money was not a big concern, while in the penitentiary, Sonny, unlike those hundreds of jailbird scammers, really did have a rich Auntie that died and left him an inheritance of her $550,000.00 life insurance policy in a familial attempt to rehab him. The plan was simple but required a lot of visuals and props, including a van that would pass as a police paddy wagon type prisoner transport vehicle. It would all begin by him casing an area convenience store first for a dead spot that was not being recorded by security cameras, either the stores' or a neighboring retail. He would cruise the roads to determine which had lower late night vehicle counts. Once he located a store that fit the profile, Sonny would then patiently sit in a dead spot carefully watching each and

every vehicle that pulled onto the convenience store parking lot. With a pair of small binoculars, he would focus on the driver to see if it was female, she was alone, and her rough age and body size. If she matched his victim profile he would then wait until she exited the store and pulled off the lot. If she chose the road he selected as being the safest for his charade, he would follow her and as soon as she reached the stretch of road he selected, he would flash his phony police lights and make the felony stop. Impersonating a police detective he would pull the victim over to the roadside explaining to the victim that there had been a crime committed by someone driving a similar vehicle. Handcuffing the woman, he would then seat her in the van and shackle her to the prisoner bench. The plan was simple and had produced enough imaginary victims that Sonny could recite the routine in his sleep.

In his last three years in prison, Sonny, who was a minor part of a homo rape gang, felt his sexual urges spiral up to become an almost overwhelming haunting curse. He thought about women and dominating them from the moment his eyes opened until the moment his eyes closed at night. He imagined them bound and helpless struggling against their tethers while begging for their freedom. He imagined absolute control allowing him to do as he wished to their bodies. At night as he closed his eyes, he could hear their screams. He conjured up method after method to induce pain and prolong their suffering. He fantasized the tortures invented and graphically described in a book of the life of Marquis de Sade, a several paper novels of bondage, rape, and torture; books he had stolen from a book vendor, read and re-read and memorized when he was a teenager. In these fantasies, Sonny was the Master. In reality of everyday penitentiary life, whether he was fucking a punk in the ass; holding a punk in a straggle hold while one of his buddies drilled for oil in that loose fitting, fatigued asshole; was getting his cock swallowed by someone he bullied; or was sucking the dick of someone who bullied him, his mind wrapped around violently raping a begging, screaming beautiful full breasted

woman. His dreams were porno fantasies that would blush the most degenerate of his prison mates. The images of these women's struggles enticed and produced rivers of semen that flowed nightly from his loins. Any Inquisition torturer would have been proud of this eager student of pain.

As he was counting his days to freedom from the walls, halls, and hairy balls of the prison and its inmates, Sonny clearly and distinctly knew what was calling to him from the other side. Over countless mental rewrites and interviews with a number of very seasoned and accomplished rapists, some incarcerated for rape, some incarcerated for other things, while skating on the consequence of their rapine crimes, he benefited from their tutelage. Rarely is anyone doing time for all their crimes. During his interview of fellow inmates, he always, always asked "what led to you being caught, evidence or bad luck?" This was a conversation constantly being had throughout the American penal system; prison is a finishing school for career criminals. It offers the future chance to escape the tentacles of law enforcement by learning from the mistakes of others.

Sonny cataloged each answer and after a very careful examination of the tiniest detail of each, he was able to decipher a pattern for law enforcement success, responsible for solving and closing in about 40 percent of their cases. Of the other 60 percent were another 40 percent by snitches and at least 20 percent as unsolved and forever open casework destined for a cardboard box and filed away in a musty police file room. Law enforcement success and crime busting wasn't generally a clue requiring super sleuthing; it was something unintentionally left behind on the scene or on the victim by the perpetrator. It was not Sherlock Homes' intuition, but hard, obvious evidence overlooked, dropped, or otherwise present that would lead anyone in police work, from a probationary patrolman to a seasoned homicide investigator, on a conclusive trail of whodunit.

Joining this revelation of crime scene evidence plus a little tip here and a little tip there, Sonny homogenized each to make a composite of a plan to produce victims, minimizing the risk of identity and capture. The first rule was to never have an accomplice. Half of the yard population would complain that the reason they were serving time was that a buddy had ratted them out to cut a deal. The second rule was to never tell a woman about even the smallest detail of a felony. Sooner or later it would become a bargaining chip that a bitch would use to hold your love as a boyfriend, shake you down for drugs or money, or to get even with you if you dumped her or fucked her friend or her sister or her mother.

A major class in the exercise yard was evidence. A shred of fabric that matched a shirt, a shoe print, drops of blood on your clothes, anything overlooked or one careless moment was enough for the coppers to slam you back in a cell. Manage your crime scene like a military inspection, look at everything and look everywhere. Fire and common household bleach are your best friends.

Witness suspect identification, even if it is a very general and partial make of your face, can be a very bad thing for a law breaker. As part of a successful crime enterprise, a criminal must reduce the potential for the witness to recall any specific or dominant characteristics of their facial features or if the felony is heavy enough, the options are few; leave them alive and hope you won't be tagged by the cops, or kill the victim on the scene, or kill the victim and dump the body, or disappear the victim in as quiet and innocuous method as possible. On July 30, 1975 someone or some bodies chose to murder and then disappear the body of Jimmy Hoffa and after thousands of leads and 40 years later, the LE folks are no closer in finding it and still are searching for Hoffa's body.

Sonny also had a strategy on ending his prison sentence. After serving out his full term Sonny would have no obligations to report to a parole officer. Sonny considered this a wonderful thing and worth the extra year he spent

inside. Parole meant reporting to a parole officer, having a job, or at least providing evidence that he searched for a job, and subjected Sonny, the dwelling where he was living in and anything and everything else in his possession to a legal warrantless search, anytime the parole officer thought it fun harassing an ex-con or suspecting a backward slip. Having served his time in full, his freedom would not be subject to the parole board looking at his record of suspected rapes and violence against other inmates and giving those good parole deciding community people the opportunity to keep Sonny incarcerated. They would if released early, never for a second believe that Sonny posed no risk to the community. Penitentiaries are like hotels, limited bookings available, and as such there is always pressure on the patrol board to release the less threatening of low life; however sexual and violent assaults against fellow inmates were a poison pill with parole boards. Not the case here; with all time served, Sonny walked through the gates a free man. With no restrictions on his release, Sonny immediately faded off the law enforcement radar. First stop would be his Auntie's Mame's estate attorney.

CHAPTER FIVE

Sonny and Auntie Mame had the most interesting and unusual of relationships. Sonny's rich Auntie Mame was a widower of ten years when Sonny reached his sixteenth birthday. Auntie Mame had heard from his parents that Sonny was having academic and social problems in high school. Being a former school administrator, Mame had agreed to help tutor and possibly refine or reform his social skills. Twice a month Sonny's parents would practically force him in the family car and drive him across town to Mame's small townhouse where he was commanded to mind Auntie Mame and pay attention to her tutoring. The first month was torture, Sonny did improve in his classroom attention with his grades beginning to climb, and pretty much was able to pretty much steer clear of trouble, but he just did not seem to respond to any of Mame's standard bad boy reform protocol. Mame tried the academic carrot; do well in her practice tests and she would treat him to a movie of his choice or maybe a nice restaurant.

Mame's tutorage plan took a different course and the consequences began to change both their lives one Saturday morning, Sonny woke up and as usual being the routine, stripped down and wrapped a towel around his waist and headed for the shower. The bathroom door was open and Sonny walked in before realizing that Auntie Mame was in the shower. He could see her shadow through the opaque shower doors. For being 67, Mame still had a hard, man eye catching and gonad teasing body. She had large hard breasts that did not in the least sag, there was little fat on her hips and her waist line was still much narrower than her hips.

Sonny just stood there and looked. There was no modest desire to retreat from the bathroom. The shadow of Mame's body moving on the other side of that frosted glass was a young boy's eye magnet. Sonny had never been with a woman, and here was a real, live naked woman. He wanted to see, he had to see. He stood there quietly and stared through the shower door glass. He watched his Auntie slowly soap her body. He could see the shadow of her hand soaping between her legs and across and around her breasts. He thought he could hear or imagined slight moans. He was aware that his cock was beginning to harden. It was a good feeling. The hell with modesty and the hell with her being his Auntie, he was not leaving; gun fire could not have had him flee from witnessing the motion of her sensuous form. This was a performance he had to see and he had a stage side, front row ticket to savor every second of it.

When the shower door opened and Auntie Mame pushed her head through, she was shocked to see Sonny standing there speechless but obviously enjoying the voyeuristic sights she unwittingly was the singular attraction in. Immediately she fired two questions at him; "How did you get in here and how long were you watching me young man?" "You left the bathroom door open and I was going to take my shower so I came right in, I didn't know you were in the shower, honest Auntie Mame. Maybe 10 minutes. Are you mad at me Auntie?" "Why didn't you just leave?" "My feet froze; I'm so sorry Auntie Mame." "Sonny, now you tell exactly what

you saw." "Well, when I came in you were soaping your belly and legs and boobs." "Did you like what you saw?" "Yes, you are really gorgeous and I really did, are you mad at me for watching you?" "No, you're not in any trouble." "Should I leave now, Auntie?" "Yes, I think you should leave." "Can I please see the rest of you, please Auntie. I have never seen a real woman's naked body before, and after all I am here to learn and you are here to teach me, please."

Mame thought for a moment, "what would it hurt, after all he was gawking and what he hadn't seen I'm sure he imagined, so why not. Plus it is kinda voyeuristic and sensuous to know you have a drooling admirer, almost like a burlesque matinee. For optics, I might even throw in a breast wiggle." Mame smiled, and it was impossible for Mame to not notice that Sonny's little soldier was standing at attention and trying to poke through that towel hoping for a summons. "OK, Sonny, I guess we can do this just once, but as soon as I get to the towel rack you're gone, understand?" With that Mame slipped the rest of her body though the shower door. Her mat of snowy white curly pubic hair matched her premature snow white tresses. The lips of her vagina were pink and glowing from the stimulation of the hot water and the friction against it by that natural sponge. Her tits stood out and the nipples were at attention. She heard a slight moan from him as she purposefully shook her shoulders and that motion quaked and rippled through her breasts. Her huge brown areoles magnified the effect of her harden and standing proud nipples. "Good gracious, Auntie Mame has a better body than most of the school's cheerleaders" he thought. As she glided to the towel rack, he said "you sure are beautiful Auntie Mame. Can I hug you?" "No, Sonny it's time to leave, now beat it and don't you dare ever say anything about this to your mom or dad or any friends, or you will be in big trouble, understand." "Promise Auntie Mame, I am a boy that can keep a secret." Mame smiled to herself, she knew he would be jacking off tonight and he wouldn't be using or needing the stimulus of any

of the fuck magazines or fuck novels she knew he kept secret and hidden under his bed.

The next Friday night when they were laboring over a math problem, Mame asked him, "Sonny what is wrong, you know this material and don't seem to be able to concentrate, what's the matter. You have problems with mom and dad or at school again?" "No, every time I get near you I keep thinking about the shower and how beautiful you are." "Sonny its best you forget all about what you saw in that shower. You know what a woman's body looks like now and I am sure that before too long you will dating cute girls and exploring their secrets. Now just forget it and let's get back to our lessons." "I can't forget what I saw and I don't want any other girls, I want to kiss and touch your special places Auntie Mame, I really, really do." When he said special places, Mame knew that Sonny was doing his research in those cheap paperback fuck books that all boys sooner or later end up believing.

"Sonny, you are talking stupid now. It can't be and you know it can't be, so get it out of your mind before it causes a big problem, understand? Besides I am way too old for you." That last sentence triggered an avalanche of hope in Sonny. "I don't think you are old at all Auntie and I have an idea, you know you always talk about if I do a good job I get a reward, right. So how about each time I do something good, you let me watch you undress and shower. That would be so swell. How about it, can we do that. I promise I will just sit and watch and I won't tell you how beautiful you are. I won't say anything about how wonderful your boobs look and how I would love to gently feel them. I won't say how anything about your nipples and how I really want to kiss and nibble them. I won't say anything about those lovely tiny white curls down under covering those sweet pink wrinkles that look so delicious that I would love to stab my tongue in. I promise, please a special reward, please." "Sonny, now you are really talking stupid. Now forget this nonsense before I tell your parents

that I can't help you anymore. Would you like that to happen?" "No, Auntie, No."

After listening to Sonny's litany of promises and advance suggestions, Mame knew that Sonny was taking pointers from steamy paragraphs in his paperbacks and between memories of her naked body and his own fantasy was having a sexual awakening and was ever so desperate to move up from masturbation to the next level. He was likely learning far more from his cheap paperback fuck novels then he was from Mame's tutorage. But his pleadings and fantasy did open a door long sealed in Mame's libido. Mame was very much aware that suddenly she too had a few thoughts of that shower and his pleading, desirous eyes and as pleasurable as those thoughts were, they were wrong, really wrong. Mame was certainly no prude or lifeless matron, never would she be content as other dead husband matrons, with a monthly book club, a weekly game of cards, a monthly social dinner, and an otherwise sexless life.

Several times now after Sonny had returned home to his parents and she was alone in the townhouse, Mame allowed herself some minutes of pleasure as her fingers teased her vagina into a revival of the electric storms of passion long ago pushed behind the curtains, but never totally abandoned from her life. Mame knew the benefits of the solo double digit sex club too well; she smiled as she thought of all the pleasures and ecstatic heights those slippery stabbing fingers had provided her since the passing of dear Bob. With a further thought to the rekindling of the ashes of those wonderful feelings, Mame even went into the storage cage and retrieved several almost forgotten dildo toys that she and Bob had used to heighten their weekly experimentations; Bob really enjoyed dual penetration, inserting a dildo into her anus and the rubbing contact sensation it produced as his cock plunged in and out of her vagina. Occasionally, Mame would use the dildo on Bob sliding it in as deeply as it would go; she was sure it always did two things, made his cock harder and made him ejaculate a larger volume, and Bob did seem to enjoy that

penetration. Many an evening she and Bob would just lie in bed sipping wine and watching and discussing the most disgusting and degrading porno movies Bob could buy downtown at the Adult XXX shop. Afterwards, sometimes it was sweaty sex and other times it was just a good night kiss and lights out. Now, it was solo passion, tame by Mame's past standards, but welcomed. With no foreplay, Mame had to rely on a tube of shaving cream for lubricant. The creamy white lather was surprisingly slippery and with just a little around the dildo and a little dab pushed onto and past her the drapery of her labia lips, it did a far better job than those very expensive tubes of sexual lubes. Her vagina ached and forcefully thrust upwards to swallow and conquer that plastic intruder. What a familiar sensation as she gently and slowly fed that plastic impostor into the jaws of the beast. Mane could feel a long forgotten and neglected energy begin to awaken. At first her motions in teasing that beast were gentle and she allowed the penetration to be a slow gradual push and pull, increasing in depth and force to complete consumption and herculean thrusts. Her body became on fire. Oh, how she missed Bob and the feel of a real flesh javelin deep inside her. Within seconds of the accelerated and forceful penetrations she could feel the wonderful creep of an orgasm. Mame's body exploded with the ecstasy those ten inches of pliant plastic phallus awakened. With no shame or embarrassment Mame found herself panting and bucking and jamming and with passion tremors quaking the very essence of her soul. The beast was still there and it was just as wanting, hungry, savage, and as hopelessly selfish as it had ever been.

More than a few times in past years she thought about how wonderful it would be again to have a physical relationship and light fires that had been out for over a decade. Sure, with her body she could still attract men, she had no trouble doing that; she had been out on a few dates since Bob died. Each time, because she was a widow, the men automatically thought that she was sex starved and just needed that dick and would spring on it as soon as it was unzipped and flopping.

Mame as a school administrator was always a sophisticated dresser. She loved the European style of hanging dresses, full under slips, and imported real leather foot ware. In keeping with the European look, she never wore a bra, instead choosing a full length slip or sometimes just a blouse chemise as her undergarment. She loved the freedom and feel of her heavy breasts bouncing or quivering or vibrating in response to some gravity triggering steps, or a bouncy road, or just bending down; it was so natural. The additional plus side was enjoying the embarrassment when she could catch the eyes of a man staring at and taking x-rays of her breasts while focusing on the waves of surface rippling movement through her breasts caused by those vibrations. Almost without fail, the man would timidly avert his eyes. The few more confident other ones would glare back at her and often run their tongue across their lips and lewdly wink. A few would reach down and grab a handful of their crouch and glare at her trolling for an embarrassed response or an invitation, disappointingly, all they got was a cruel teasing and taunting smile.

The only drawback to this natural, sophisticated look was that a chemise under a sheer fabric dress could never hide jutting nipples if they responded by erection to thoughts, passion, temperature or friction. In the all-woman office when it was just the girls it was not a factor of importance. It was only when a man invaded their office that Mame had to cover the tease of the large brown raisin shaped canapes projecting through the fabric of her chemise. Even when innocently out anywhere in public, where her nipples became excited by imagined fantasy or responded to the chill or frigid temperature on especially cold days, she always had a handy shawl to drop over her shoulders to modestly hide her twin nipple peaks. Bob called them the "Grand Tetons", a French term for big tits.

There were no other exceptions, except the lesbian lady whose eyes were always hunting for a sign. The lesbian lady was a sweet soul whose only transgression was to hungrily stare at her nipple projections and smile. Every once in a while Mame wondered if she were to smile back an inviting smile and a wink, what could that lead to. In her college days, she had more than once heard girls giggle that "nobody eats pussy like a woman". But with Bob at home, she had no need or desire for exploration in the mystery of cross gender attraction. Shelia, the lesbian lady would have to be content with an imaginary breastwich with a side of delicious suckling nipple. Mame had Bob to go home to. If thinking about Shelia pearl diving into her vagina brought a flow of excitement to her loins, Mame knew that Bob was there ready to hit the real home runs.

On those few dating nights, when a geriatric date realized Mame had chosen the freedom of gravity and was braless, without fail, it translated in their minds as an open invitation to maul her breasts; after all, was their collective consensus, wasn't she just a horny neglected woman. As soon as they were alone in the car, sometimes after and even sometimes before dinner, they would begin pawing her tits in the townhouse or restaurant parking lot. And the thought of an old man jabbing at her with a wrinkly, floppy cock did not add anything to heighten the experience and was guaranteed to be rain on the parade. Fighting them off while trying to be polite seldom worked, Mame often had to resort to a two handed hard shove or even an open back hand across the face. As soon as they recovered from the shock of the physical rebuke, they became apologetic and promised they would behave the rest of the evening. Mame knew differently and demanded they drive her directly home, if not, she would hop from the car and return to the restaurant and call a cab. They always drove her home, promising they would be good boys the next date. Never with any was there a next date for tit maulers.

With the math problem begrudgingly solved, Mame said "Sonny, let's take a break. I know you're hungry. Go cleanup and while you're doing that I

will throw together something to eat. How does that sound?" "Great, Auntie Mame, you're a super cook and your food is as good as you are beautiful." "Flattery, Sonny will get you everywhere, now go get ready."

One morning while Sonny was eating breakfast and Mame was ironing clothes and getting those skirt creases just right and razor sharp; you know the dry cleaners never got them straight or sharp so a woman if she wanted style had to do the pressing herself, Sonny interrupted her precision strokes with the hot iron. As he was eating scratch pancakes and the bacon breakfast he suddenly blurted out "you sure are a beautiful woman Auntie Mame. Dad says so all the time." "Really, Sonny why would your Dad be saying a foolish thing like that, and I really think you should be dressed at the breakfast table and not sit there in your shorts and tee; do you eat dressed like that at home? "Well, Auntie they don't make me put my jeans on to eat breakfast. They are usually not talking so they don't pay much attention to me. Did you know Mom and Dad argue all the time." "Sonny, all parents argue, it's usually about money or ambition. Bob and I would argue about bills being too much or who should get a better job and earn more money. So, it's a natural thing." "Mine argue about sex all the time. Dad wants to do things and Mom doesn't. Then they start saying mean things to hurt each other. Mom usually wins. Sometimes it's pretty gross, but actually I kinda like to listen and, please don't tell them, but it sometimes makes me feel a tingly but strange sort of feeling but in a good way to imagine them naked and doing those things."

Mama was a little taken back by the subject of her sister and brother in-law actually arguing in front of Sonny about sex. "Well, I can understand how ideas and images can bother you." "No, Auntie, it doesn't bother me, it kinda excites me to think about two grown up people doing those things." Hoping to change the subject and get back to pressing those creases, "Nephew, you need to focus on other things, like your education. People with a good education go places, people with no education labor to make other people rich."

Not to be silenced, as the erotic talk was beginning to make Sonny feel a tingling in his penis and as it was that good feeling again, he pursued the subject further. "You know Auntie, one time Dad and Mom were arguing and I heard Dad say, "Dorris, why can't you be like your sister." "What do you mean, like my sister." "You sure you want to know?" "Just tell me." "Well, Bob got drunk one night and we got to talking guy talk and he said that Mame was a fuck machine, she loved cock. He said that he even talked her into taking it in the ass, said she could suck a golf ball though 50 foot of garden hose, swallow a full load, and she would even let him stick a 10 inch dildo in her anywhere it would fit." Then Mom said "That's terrible to say such gross things, what did you tell him about me, huh, what?" And laughing, Dad said "I just told him we fucked once a week and every time I tried to ass fuck you, you screamed and pushed me away." "Is that all you told him?" "Well no, I told him that you couldn't suck dick worth a shit and you wouldn't let me cum in your mouth." "Boy when he said those things did it ever make Mom mad."

Shocked at what she just heard, but like a cheap erotic novel, Mame just had to know the rest of the story, "What did Sis say then?" "Mom started crying and yelled, didn't you ever wonder why on our wedding night your dick slipped right in my pussy. It was like a fist in a bucket, wasn't it. Aren't I right, remember that night asshole? It didn't even bang on the sides. You want to know why? Remember the guy I dated before you, Timmy Seval, he stretched it so big he could push his hand in it, that's why. I used to suck his thick 8 inch cock and swallow his cum every Friday night in the drive-in. I loved sucking his dick and especially the feel and taste of his hot cum as it flowed across my tongue and down my throat. Sometimes I even let him ram his big cock in my ass. Now fuck you, you asshole 4 inch dick excuse for a real man. Tim could really fuck and ate pussy good, I mean real good; not like you with your poor excuse for a tongue lapping. I often wonder how the fuck I ended up getting stuck with you. Fuck you, you midget dick mother fucker." "Good for her, for some reason, I always liked

Timmy and now I know why. He was never the asshole that Ted was." Mame thought.

"Is what Uncle Bob told Dad about you true, Auntie, are you really good at all those things?" "A nephew does not ask an Auntie a question like that plus that is none of a young man's business." "Sonny, I really need to get back to this pressing and you need to finish your breakfast, OK?" "Sure Auntie, anything for you."

All morning Mame was haunted by visions of her brother in-law trying to force his cock into her sister's ass or of Ted kneeling, face pushed into the oasis at the junction of Dorris' legs, his tongue busy doing up and down laps on her clit and labia lips. Mame knew what Dorris was taunting him about; maybe one or two girls can get off having their pussy lapped at like a dog, but only a rare few. Men that use their tongues like a spear, a curler, and a twirler can get most women to that special place; men that use it like a paintbrush don't. "Hmm, Bob was good, really, really good and he enjoyed it so much." Now Mame was being chased by carnal thoughts of the most distracting and most difficult kinds to erase. Mame also was aware of a slight wetness creeping in her vagina. "Damn that kid" she thought.

That night, as Mame was occupied in her thoughts at the electric four burner kitchen range and was turning several of her famous golden brown pork chops, she suddenly became aware of a presence behind her and trespassing hands creeping upward and reaching under her arms and gently settling and pressing upon her breasts. Unless there was an intruder in the house, and as it was not likely any intruder could get past the security alarms that Bob paid so much money for, without doubt, she immediately knew it had to be Sonny and immediately knew this would be the watershed moment that destiny had brought them both to. The suggestion and then images all morning and afternoon of Dorris and Ted fucking and sucking were baying at and tormenting a beast silenced and

neglected far too long. "Damn, the kid couldn't have picked a worse time to play mind games" she thought to herself.

Talking over her shoulder in a voice a little bit deeper and a little bit smokier then normal and without pushing his hands aside, Mame said "Sonny we can't do this. It is against every morality in every society. Aunties' do not let nephew's explore their bodies. Young men must learn love from young women. Please stop, remove your hands from my breasts and leave or I'll be forced to tell your parents." Her objection did not stop or slow down Sonny as his fingers ever so gently massaged her soft globes, "Auntie I know I can make you happy while you teach me the things a man should know. It's not wrong; it's going to be beautiful. You are the teacher and I am the student. Teach me everything. Please Auntie, everything." With that, Sonny slipped each hand under and up into her blouse. When the heat of his bare hands actually touched her braless bare breasts, she moaned. His hands gently lifted each breast and supporting and curling the bottom side worked outwards until he could capture each nipple between his thumb and index fingers. Another soft moan. She could feel his fingers gently rolling her nipples and she could feel them responding, just like a hardening cock, they were awakening from the self-imposed neglect of a long sleep. This awakening was a pleasure that was forcing her body into shallow panting, a rapid heartbeat, and a rising of her breasts. "Gosh, it feels so wicked and wonderful" she thought.

Mame could feel the nerve centers in her breasts begin to respond to this exciting physical stimulation and the electric of those strong cosmic signals reminding her of her real woman's desires. Long forgotten fire embers flash ignited and started racing through her body. She pushed her hips back into him and could feel his hard cock pressing against her ass. Sonny was very softly massaging each breast. There was electric in his fingertips. She could feel his hot breath on the back of her neck. Mame's mind screamed "No." This was wrong and against every rule and the fiber of every moral she had ever believed in. Her mind was racing. As his fingers ever so

warmly caressed her nipples, huge damning bolts of electric began firing in her body. Her body shuddered. Suddenly Mame could feel her vagina awakening, awakening from a very long ten year hibernation, and after that long sleep, it was a creature that was hungry, very hungry. Here mashed and pressing against the cheeks of her ass was a stalking and ready genuine flesh javelin, not a counterfeit plastic, do it yourself, lifeless cock.

"Sonny, what are you doing, tell me. This is wrong and you must stop it now." But Mame made no effort, like she had so easily repelled and controlled those geriatric old shit groper dates, to repel them with a two hand push or a back hand face slap to stop it and destroy their dreams of warm pussy or vacuum lips. "I can't stop thinking about you and your body, Auntie, I want to love you so badly. I can't think of anything else. I can feel the heat of your soft wonderful breasts and how your nipples are popping out wanting the attention of my lips and tongue. I want you to tell me where to kiss you. I want you to teach me what to do to make us both feel like lovers. Can we just pretend and can't you really teach me love, please I am begging, please Auntie. I swear I will never tell anyone, please."

The tigress beast was awakening and growing stronger by each titillating nerve explosive moment; these incestuous feelings were most wrongful but were most welcomed by her now growling beast. The awakened beast wanted hot, aggressive passion, it wanted the pleasures it once enjoyed but had been denied for so long. Her beast could feel the hotness of his body and the pressure on her bottom of a strong young cock wanting to be swallowed and wanting to plunge and bury itself as deeply in the warm passion passage as its owner could drive it. Her neglected beast now was a slave of its feelings. It was swimming in the warm flow of the streams of that natural vaginal fluid that would welcome and allow that strong young cock to glide past vagina lips that hadn't know this pleasure and passage of a man for many years.

Mame knew as with Bob, his technique of foreplay being a copious producer of natural lubricant, there would be no tissue resistance and so little friction burn that the pleasure would arrive solely by the force and depth of the penetration. The beast was freeing itself, the wings of the dragon were unfurling. During these few moments, his hands and fingers had become keys and begun to loosen the locks of her self-imposed chastity. Mame could feel those warm and delicious juices of her passion wetting her vagina and seeping into her underwear at a flow rate she had not experienced since the last time she and Bob made love. Her recent play time with the sex toys were marginally satisfying but produced so little response in her biological receptive response, she had to use shaving cream lubricant for penetration. Mame was wet, and Mame's resistance was collapsing.

Every single breath of his on her neck was an undercurrent against her objection. She could feel the tip of his tongue tracing back and forth beneath her ear. She tensed when that tongue found its way into her ear and began rolling and curling. "Damn it, Sonny please stop it. We can't do this." The boy had apparently done his homework well and learned not just the lessons from those school primers, but learned more erotic ones from those fuck books he kept hidden beneath his bed. Mame knew Sonny was obviously executing a rehearsed fuck book seduction plan. "So simple, so gross, but damn it, it's a great seduction plan" she thought.

Each firing neuron of the promise of a pleasure teasing desire of carnal reward was taking control and Mame knew it was growing stronger than her will and her power to defeat it. He was defeating her and her weakened defenses were dissolving. Desire was a hungry tigress. She bit her lip. The gentle teasing of her nipples was melting her soul. She felt herself falling into the lust pit that had been denied her for so long, now it was time, now it was time to hunt and find prey. Now was the time of the tigress. She could feel the growl growing.

She turned the burner off and pushing the skillet to a side burner, she slowly turned to face him. She captured his face with her two hands and looking directly into his eyes, softly whispered in a deep smoky seductress voice "school begins now." With that she pushed her lips to his and forced her tongue past his lips and began teasing his. It took but a few seconds for him to realize what his response needed to be. As their tongues danced together, Mame allowed her hand to drop to his shorts. His cock needed no prodding; it was straining to escape from the confines of the thin fabric of his underwear. She touched it lightly and allowed the back of her fingers to tease it with a slight up and down touch. "Go easy" she thought, she didn't want him to squirt before she had her pleasure.

Grabbing his dick she led him from the kitchen to her bedroom. Pushing him down on the bed, she placed one hand against his chest and she grabbed the waistband of his underwear and ripped his shorts down his legs, over his ankles and free of his body. Mame was surprised to see the size of his cock, if Dorris was telling the truth about Ted's 4 inch cock, Sonny must have inherited his 7 inch cock from some long suppressed family Neanderthal gene or maybe, just maybe Dorris and Timmy had a secret. Bob's cock was just under 6 inches, but thick on the stem. At first it wasn't easy getting that length and thickness past her tonsils without gagging or chucking, but Mame many years past eventually learned the OHIO trick from an old spinster at the bridge party. It always made Bob a very happy satisfied, drained and soft dick camper.

Many years ago, during the weekly card session and between hands, after listening to the younger girls talk about the kinky things the group always talked about, the older greyish woman who hardly ever said much, blurted out "my husband, rest his soul, had a 9 inch penis. It was always hard and he was always ready. Each time we made love; he had to force it into my vagina and after months of enduring pain, had gradually stretched it big enough where it didn't hurt so much. He came home drunk a few times and with something different in mind, he flipped me over and tried to push

it in my behind. It hurt so much I had to fight him off. He almost succeeded once and got it in about half way, but I screamed and fought until he gave up. When he realized that I was not going to tolerate him jamming his big prick up into my bowels, he switched targets. After giving up on my ass, he started jabbing his dick in my face. Sometimes I would wake up and he would be standing by the bedside, dragging his dick back and forth across my lips. How would you like to wake up to a cock toothbrush, I mean a big cock, trying to push past your lips and blow a load down your throat? He was relentless. Once in a while I would give in. After those couple of times, he became a blowjob maniac and constantly begged, pleaded and schemed for oral. I loved him and to make the sacrifice, I really tried to do oral but I gagged and choked every time, until one day I was complaining to the doctor and the doctor asked me if I knew the "OHIO" way to do oral. Naturally I said no, I had no idea what he was talking about. The doctor said you take his penis and press it against your lips, then you open your mouth and as wide as it can open saying "OHIO." It not only opens the mouth but it puts your tongue in a position that allows his penis to slide past your tonsils without triggering your gag reflex. Girl's it works. It really works. Made me a cocksucker from then on and kept my pussy and asshole from being sore." With that said, the little old lady went back to quietly shuffling cards. Every lady bridge player was shocked and speechless that here was this little old, matron grandmotherly lady who looked like she had never even seen a dick, was actually telling them how to deep throat a huge cock. Once the sweet old lady had blurted out her tale, there was little concentration devoted to the card game that afternoon, and without exception, every woman, including Mame, were, with a smile on their face, thinking about that word, "OHIO".

Stepping back Mame's eyes locked onto his and she said "Sonny if you ever betray us and tell anyone what we are about to do, I will never allow you back into my house, I will lie to your parents about what happened, and I will cut you from my will. You don't know it but your Auntie sees a great

future for you in this world, and I have left you my life insurance policy and a small piece of land and house that my husband's Uncle Buck owned in the middle of a private forest, it all goes to you, the farm and all $550,000.00; but if you peep one word or even hint about this, it's gone and you are out. Now do you understand?" "Yes, ma'am, this will be our secret forever. You are so beautiful and I want you so badly and forever. There are so many things I want to learn. Please teach me and don't get mad if I am a very slow learner, and we have to do it over and over again" he laughed.

Mame was really surprised when after this first bout, Sonny pulled his cock from her and shuffled up to her face and aiming his prick inches from her lips, continued his passion and jacked off. Mame being so familiar with this finale, (Bob liked to finish with a tongue cum shower) parted her lips and rolled her tongue out as a magic carpet for the head of his cock. Holding onto his thighs, she could feel them tighten and knew he was about to explode. With a moan his cock began jetting squirt after squirt of hot cum on her tongue, on her lips, across her face, and in her hair. "This kid is a milk wagon" she thought to herself. When she saw that the stream of cum began reducing she pulled his thighs toward her and swallowing that mouth full of creamy semen, she seized the tip of his cock with her lips and sucked as hard as she could to empty his pipes. When the tip of her tongue no longer harvested golden drops, she pulled away and looked up at him and smiled. Sonny just moaned and almost fainted; his first real piece of ass and blowjob and he got them from his Auntie. "Auntie, you are the best and I love you so much. I would kill for you. You are so special, I never want to leave and go back home." "Sonny what we are sharing is wrong, but so good. If you ever tell anyone, we both will be in big trouble. For sure your parents will never let me near you again. I will never tell anyone, so if there is anyone that can ruin this it is you. You must forever keep this a secret. I enjoyed this too. We can have so much more of this but you

can't tell anyone, your buddies, your parents, the priest, anyone. Understand." "Yes, Auntie, forever a secret I promise."

Mame knew that one reason Sonny could launch his semen with so much force and trajectory was that Sonny was still a very young man, and his urethra tube and the opening port in the head of his penis was basically still a tiny, tight muscled fleshly nozzle. With age the opening would grow larger and while Sonny would still produce the same amount of sperm, the enlarged penis nozzle would have a less jetting effect on the ejaculation. She knew that as a man ages the jetstream would eventually be reduced to a dribble like melting ice cream trickling down the side of the sugar cone. No matter, whether his cum was a spurter or an ouzer, she still savored every drop.

CHAPTER SIX

Beginning that afternoon and continuing with several more carnal sessions Mame taught her nephew everything she could think of. Sonny learned how to fire up a woman with foreplay, many, many coital positions, how to eat pussy and what to do to make a woman push your face in farther while at the same time trying to buck you off, how to play with a clitoris, anal sex, titty fucking, rimming, and even how to slurp up his cum as it dripped from her vagina. During a short interlude of rest in that first session, Auntie Mame told Sonny "You are sampling a lifetime of carnal knowledge; I intend to make you a master of the sexual arts. You will know every part of a woman's secret places; you will know how to play a woman's vagina like the finest musician entices the sweetest symphonic notes from his musical instrument. I will teach you the difference between the mons veneris, the hood of clitoris, the clitoris, the vestibule, the labia major, the draperies of the labia minor, and a very special spot, the perineal body, and we must not forget the secrets of the anus. Each spot demands different techniques from its lover. If you master these spots and

learn how to tease, titillate and tame them, you will have a lifetime of women begging you for more.

Auntie Mame even promised to teach Sonny the "straw" and "anteater" two very special technique moves that Bob used to explode her pleasure sensors off the charts. School was in session every weekend; academic education first, then carnal school. Sonny got straight A's in both.

Sonny was fascinated with the mystery and intricacies of the vagina. He could not explore it enough, with fingers, tongue or cock, the softness, wetness and warmth tracing those captivating and challenging folds, wrinkles, and hidden secret depths. He loved the smell and taste. He felt especially accomplished when during a dedicated and serious tongue expedition; Mame body's would suddenly and without warning explode in violent response to the hunger of her silent beast. He knew he had released her passions when she would force his face tightly against her body, arch her back and begin, softly pushing back against his face at first, and then gradually accelerating to a buckaroo rodeo force bucking her vagina against his conquering lips and tongue. This was an exercise they both enjoyed and that always left them both, after only five minutes of such intense ecstasy, exhausted, panting and breathless.

"Sonny, you have graduated primary sexual education Magna Cum Laude, it is time I introduce you to finishing school, are you ready?" "Auntie, I am always ready, I can't wait to learn anything you will teach me, so let's get it going." "Sonny, your Uncle Bob was a very sensitive person, a lover of the arts and classic symphony, a true Renaissance man and he strived to experiment with all phases of life and its sciences to increase his personal accomplishment of satisfaction. Bob could take the commonest of things and with his artistry and creativity completely modify and morph whatever it was into another higher level of an especially joyful or rewarding journey or experience. He had the same attitude about sex; he was constantly searching for ways to make sexual relations more special and wonderful. If

you go into his library, you will find a small but interesting collection of sexology books written by both medical researchers and smut authors. It was because of those explorations and imaginations that Bob was able to either invent or improve on two methods of oral sex that if every man would practice, it would make him the master of any vagina he could glide his tongue in.

"Uncle Bob was the champion of the vagina. Your Uncle Bob loved to refer to himself as the "6'er" with no "9'er" necessary. Often as we lay in bed at night, Bob would let his fingers softly trickle across my breasts and gently scrape down my abdomen until the index finger was resting on the hood of my clitoris. Sonny, if you learn the names of all the parts to the girl pussy puzzle, I think it will markedly increase your perception and success with awakening the passion of those sleeping love creatures.. Ever so slowly his finger would begin to trace tiny circles around my clit. That little movement produced some very heavy sparks in my vagina. As soon as I uttered that first moan of passion, his big finger would plunge in and then he would begin rapidly finger fucking me. My passion juice would flow, not just moisten, but actually overflow and I could begin to feel a stream trickling down that so erotic "g" spot between my vagina and anus. As soon as I pushed my hips upward against those magic fingers, Uncle Bob would slide down between my legs and go into his "6'er" mode. He would elevate my legs, use his thumbs to separate the drapery of my labias, and then push his face into my pussy like he was fitting his face into a gasmask. His tongue was like a wonderfully crazed electric serpent. He would stay there doing his tongue massage until I had exhausted my passion and my heartbeat returned to normal. Bob was always in overdrive when he worked the oyster. Many times, once he had taken me to that special girl's place and back, I would say, now it's my turn and your Uncle Bob would just say, 'Put it in the bank, my reward was making you red hot and special feeling of getting off again and again'. Your Uncle Bob definitely was not a selfish man."

"He had developed and had mastered, solely by imagination and library research he sworn to me by oath, two soul draining methods of vaginal stimulation; one he called the "straw" and the other, the "anteater". If Mame knew Bob and Mame did know Bob to the fullest, the only imagination and library research involved was the methodology he developed in college when he was stabbing and curling his tongue deep inside the vagina of a panting and squealing high school or college bobby socker in the back seat of someone's car or on the cheap mattress in a dorm room. Either technique was guaranteed to completely capture a woman's libido and result in a flood of natural fluids and a string of rapid fire, multiple, heavy orgasms that made a woman a slave of fine Cunning Lingus forever. There was one problem. Once a woman became a victim of the "straw" or "anteater", no ordinary man in her life from that point forward would ever be able to fully satisfy or take her to the wonderful and fulfilling heights that the "straw" or "anteater" produced.

"Once Bob introduced my vagina and brain pleasure center to those nerve ending and neuron exploding sensual electric signals, I became a slut slave and would beg him to never stop. As everyone knows, we were both a relatively conservative couple. The oral methods were so effective on my vagina that Bob and I wondered if it was just my hungry vagina or would they deliver equally on someone else's. On a whim, and I have to admit that it was something that I had in the back of my mind for years but was too timid to suggest, we had a very frank and outspoken professional friend that had on several occasions, given us the signals that she was an open invitation and ripe for a tryst. We sort of during a light afternoon lunch engineered the subject to a three way bundle affair, describing it as an experiment in pleasure. Her name was Sofia, she was a lawyer by profession. Our lady friend was intrigued and very eager to continue with the thought and possibility of something new. Sofia was an orgasm hound. The discussion was similar to an interview but with very personal and embarrassing questions for all of us. No one held back on the questioning

about each other's' personal sexual habits, likes, dislikes and limits. She was very candid as to her experiences with men and, to our surprise, a gaggle of women that had routinely and apparently very pleasurably eaten her pussy. Sofia told us that it was just something that she let her boyfriends and girlfriends do as it was as a matter of fact expected. We understood. Sofia apparently had a routine of replacing the current lover boys and girls in her life on a regular basis. Being a lawyer Sofia understood the relevance and importance of a Confidentiality Non-Disclosure Agreement and would require each new partner to sign one before Sofia's panties would slide down her beautifully sculpted legs. As with all of humanity, Sofia's dating success was ultimately providing her bedroom friends of the moment a service center and when a service center broadcasts a "no service to you" sign and does not provide further service on demand, relationships move on. Then it was on to the next conquest or affair.

"So once we were satisfied that Sofia indeed had the degree of receiving oral experiences necessary and generally allowed it to a degree rather emotionless charged and less passionately, we completed the interview part of the experiment with she and us then signing mutual confidentiality agreements. To make that first encounter special for all, we booked into a very upscale motel. Sofia had a knock out body, heavy breasts, responsive nipples, and a completely shaved vagina. I envied Bob. Once Sofia was undressed, completely nude and lying on the bed, I spread her legs apart and Uncle Bob went down and started the treatment. He began with the Anteater and after Sofia's body began quaking and climaxing in response to the the technique she started moaning, real genuine, my pussy's on fire, moans, he shifted into the Straw. The Straw did it, Sofia began screaming and bucking. Bob had to stop, we were afraid that the hotel people would think that a murder was taking place. Just so the experiment did not suffer we had to make a small adjustment. With Sofia being so vocally passionate we were only able to continue with the experiment by having Sophia biting

a pillow to keep her pleasure screaming down to a level where the hotel staff weren't alerted to the sounds of a murder being carried out in the room." Based upon Sophia's responses, Bob and I knew that if the Anteater and the Straw could excite into ecstasy and produce a truely fiery string of orgasms in Sophia, then any woman so accustomed to blandly oral efforts of a man's house painter brush tongue lapping would without question deliver without repent or apology a totalistic, never imagined orgasm to any woman with a vagina."

"Sonny, another thing that men do not understand is that a majority of women do not enjoy pussy slobbering by a man who is interested in, whether with saliva or natural colitis secretions, only paving a slippery pathway for their selfish cock. Men are rarely coached in the science and art by women who after years of pretending, realistically see it pointless and wasted energy to encourage and coach a lover into the fine arts of oral stimulation. Many women were forever turned off by the amateurish conceited and boorish attempts by a disillusioned man using his tongue to lap up and down in a most unwelcome and unstimulating pattern on their vagina. In guarded lady conversations, many ladies likened these feeble attempts at teasing an ecstasy to similar to having your pussy licked by a pet dog. The only one who fails to understand the failure is the dog impersonating, tongue lapper."

"I will share another Uncle Bob seduction enticer and something you and I will be doing very shortly here. I have been holding off shaving my white thatched pussy for just this moment. Now I will explain why. Many years ago Uncle Bob was hospitalized for a minor urology procedure. The prep attendant came to his bedside and said he was here to shave the target surgical area as it had to be free of pubic hair. He asked your Uncle Bob if he preferred a "strip cut" or the "cowboy cut". As Bob had never heard of a "cowboy cut" before he naturally asked what the difference was. The attendant cheerfully explained that a "strip cut" was just the removal of a small patch of pubic hair from the surgical area while the "cowboy cut" was

the complete removal of pubic hair from the lower abdomen, the groin, the penis and the testicle bag. The attendant went on to say that the "cowboy cut" was very popular with men, their spouses and the lucky ones that had girlfriends or even penis loving boyfriends. Bob asked how so? Well you see sir, when I remove all your pubic hair, and I mean remove it totally from the lower abdomen, the penis, and completely front and back from your testicle bag you will be cooler, cleaner, more hygienic, more comfortable and your wife, girlfriend, or any other friend will appreciate they no longer have to contend with loose pubic hair on their tongue, will just adore the smoothness and softness of the exposed skin, and the added plus that now they will be able to see and finger trace every wrinkle, cease and fold on your down below parts. The "cowboy cut" is very popular here and I still get an occasional thank you card from my new patients. Depending on individual hair growth rate, there is very little maintenance; a simple shave once per week will keep all those parts smooth and inviting to the touch. Thinking that the "cowboy cut" might tweak our sex life just a little more, Uncle Bob chose the "cowboy cut". The first time I saw Bob's naked balls and cock, I almost fainted; it looked so glorious and tender, I wanted a mouthful of it right away. Since that first experience, I faithfully shaved Uncle Bob's cock every Thursday night. I kinda got a little horny holding his dick or his ball sack in one hand while making sweeping swipes with the safety razor with the other. Once I shaved the down off, I honestly really enjoyed just looking at and tracing all the creases and wrinkles with my fingernails. Bob's cock would spring to attention as soon as my nails sliced into those wrinkles. Bob delighted in and adored a hairless vagina. I know you love my snow white pussy thatch, but I think it's time to upgrade. This will be the one last time will you be able to play with my pubic hair. Once I have finished with this climax tonight, I will get the shaving crème and razor. After I razor my pussy hair off, I am going to give you a "cowboy cut". You might even cum while I am shaving you. I know you will like it because after the first time I drag my tongue up and down your hairless cock and balls and you lap at my hairless

and smooth vagina you will never want to see, feel or taste pubic hair again. So, get ready to plunge that face down there and plow that nose and lips through those white curls, and say goodbye to them, those snowy curls will be extinct after tonight." As always, Auntie Mame was so right!

"Your Uncle Bob held me on the highest of pedestals. He mastered these two tongue exercises just for me. I have thought about this for a long time, even before we became lovers. Bob's vaginal pleasure makers should never be lost and at least one man should be able to continue and practice Bob's legacy. This is so important to me, that I have typed up instructions. Read this carefully and pay attention; once you have read them, I will explain anything you have questions on, and there will be a test. Understand?" Sonny replied "Yes, Auntie, I can't wait to read it and I hope you haven't left anything out and I can't wait to be tested; are you ready Auntie?"

Mame handed Sonny four sheets of double spaced typewritten content. Sonny eagerly took the pages and sat down on the ottoman and with great anticipation eagerly began reading the text. As Sonny began scanning the pages, Mame studied his face to see his facial expressions as he was exposed to the techniques that Uncle Bob could have used to rule the world of the Amazons.

> It began: You must remember several things. *While you are entertaining the your lady friend, you never, never make grunting or slurping noises, you limit the noise to the barely audible sounds of a soft inhaling or exhaling of breath. You are not consuming, you are charming and flooding her most secrets spots with silent sensual waves of pleasure. Trough noises are disgusting and mood destroyers. Think of it like this: If you were to play soft, romantic music as a seduction tool and her body had begun responding and then you were to suddenly switch radio bands to acid rock, how do you think she would respond? If there is to be any noise, it can only*

be the soft rush of your breath and her combinations of moans and words.

Second major point: While you are teasing those wonderfully wrinkled labias up to yet another celestial level of pleasure, you never, never look up and converse with the lady, never. Once you break the trance of the seduction, you destroy the mood and it's gone and not likely to return. As an example, what happens to your mood if a lady friend is kind enough to perform fellatio on you and she looks up and asks you those nine dick killing words; "I'm getting tired, are you ever going to cum?" That universal question has the same cold consequential effect on your mood as if she were to suddenly stick an ice pick through both of your balls. So avoid conversation and stay focused and keep those lightning strikes of pleasure overloading her circuits. Your lady will confirm the success of your talents with the orchestra of her moans and body movement.

Another important point, every vagina will have physical differences; some will puff outward, some will valley inward, some will have large outer labias and some with almost no labia major at all. Some will have droopy drapery for labia minors and some will have barely a wrinkle. Some pleasure canals will be very tight and some will seem cavernous enough to be able to swallow anything. Each woman is a different canvas and a challenge awaiting the carnal talent of her lover. There are as many shapes and sizes of clitoris' as there are women. Within the clitoris lie secret sensitive receptors not much different from the genie in the bottle; just awaiting in a suspended stage for that emancipating touch. Some will be button tops and some will have strong celery like stalks. A majority will be those with a small round flower bud pouting from a one quarter inch of pink stalk. The larger the clitoris head and stalk the easier it is to ignite her fires. Regardless of shape or size,

most women, just as you like your cock sucked, grow wet when her man takes his tongue to it, massages it, gently bites it, vacuums it, and sucks it off just as if he were gay and working his boyfriends dick. A woman with a large clitoris is a super bonus, something you can actually slide across your lips then suck and not be considered queer. The pussy is a playground. A gifted lover, if he teases pleases, and tames her vagina properly, can excite such a volcanic response in a woman, that she will forever remember him and that special place and the height to which no one else had ever catapulted her to before.

Anteater.............As a beginning and to be an accomplished and successful lover you must understand the physiology of a woman's vagina. To most men, it is veiled with mystery; a furnace containing a trapped beast to some while to others it's just a warm hollow sexual release tool whose friction provides a masturbation receptacle. It is so much more than a deliciously warm juicy port to push a cock into. It is like a symphony awaiting the skillful tutorage of the conductor's wand. Each surface, wrinkle, fold, and bump is charged with high intensity nerve endings awaiting an awakening. It can be thatched with a mat of pubic hair, have a simple Mohawk strip of pubic hair, or be shaved and completely hairless; a condition that most men go wild over. The vaginal opening is vertical; at the very top is a tiny fold of skin, the perineum, that hoods and shelters' the clitoris. Beneath the hood is the clitoris, a soft stalk ending with a roundish mushroom shaped head very similar to a man's penis. To each side are the left and right labia major, the outer vertical large often smoothish lips. To the immediate inside of the labia major are the draperies of the left and right labia minor, the inner vertical wrinkled soft folds of skin that close like a purse around the vaginal canal opening. Directly to the bottom of the vagina is the "vee", where the labia major and

minor join together to complete the vagina. Up inside the vagina is a very secret spot known to only the best of lovers; it is the vagina's anterior, upper belly side wall where a curved finger will discover a bumpy surface. Often a fingernail scratched or a curled and reversed upward pointing fingertip rotated across the bumpy surface will put fire in the coldest of women. Every single cell, both inside the vagina and along the wrinkles and folds of its outside surface contains a network of very sensitive receptor cells that lie dormant awaiting a stimulus that will send sensual and cosmic electric signals throughout her body and awaken the sleeping and predatory beast that hibernates and hides in the being and fiber of every woman.

Every man that visits the love triangle honestly believes that he is the absolute and crowned prince of eating pussy. Every woman knows better. Most men eat pussy like dogs lap ice cream cones, slurping up and down or like a slippery viper stabbing their sensing tongues in and out of that sacred vestibule, without any concerned for lighting those long forgotten smoldering embers present in the network of every woman's nervous system. Women all know that no one eats pussy like another woman as women actually understand the sensation and impulse potential of each down below wrinkle, fold, and bump. Women understand the need for the gentle attention, softness, and creative strokes of an attentive tongue applied as an artist applies the strokes of a fine pointed paint brush to a fine canvas work of art. A vagina is but a beautiful canvas that cringes and retreats from the house painter brush slathering strokes of a barbarian amateur or explodes in pleasure and ecstasy at the magic of a true artist's brush stroke. Only those able to connect the electric signals from the tip of their tongue to the surface and inner vaginal ecstasy receptors, can offer an

exciting pathway to heights of oral sexual satisfaction so often ignored by selfish or unknowing lovers.

The "ANTEATER" is a preliminary sexual strategy with the sole purpose of arousing the sleeping beast. The "Anteater" is intended to tease and tout the vagina to an awareness stage heralding an epiphany of the passions to come.

There are a number of preliminary steps to the "Anteater", the first being you purse your lips as if you are intending to whistle. You will be pushing a soft jet of air through your lips onto her body. It enhances the sensation if you hold your breath for a micro second to allow the air to warm inside your lungs before you blow tiny streams of wonderfully warm, sexually titillating air onto her body. In a left to right windshield wiper sweep movement, you ever so gently blow a jet of air into the very top of the triangle of her pubic hair or in the absence of hair a gentle stream across the soft inviting pleasure awaiting epidermal receptors, reversing back from right to left. The jet of air must be soft and with just enough force to move the individual hair strands or cascade against the epidermis ever so lightly. Once you have made the full back and forth sweep, you begin another sweep slightly below the first sweep. Your sweep grid is similar to making garden rows, the warm air jets the seeds you hope to blossom into a passion flower. You make five or six sweeps per row. Once you have swept downward to the top of her vagina, you are ready for the next step.

Additionally, if you are fortunate to discover that your lady friend has shaved all her pubic hair away, then you must use a combination of that jet of air with a sweep of the tongue, the tip of which barely drags across each row. You must devote the same attention and the same number of row sweeps to the smoothness

of her pubic area just as if she had a full thatch of soft curly ringlets.

Your partner should begin to feel the start of an awakening. She may quietly moan, she may gasp, she may begin to breathe a little faster, she may comment; it is important that you do not allow yourself to get distracted or allow her to be distracted.

The next step with hands palms down and resting on the inside of her legs, you use your thumbs to spread apart the vertical lips of the left and right labia major. Once these mounds are apart, you again use that combination of that jet of air and tip of the tongue to baste the labias in a very slow up and down motion. You will begin to notice some slight tremors and uplifting of her hips.

Again using your thumbs, gently separate and spread apart the wrinkled drapery of the pinkish brown lips of the left and right labia minor which will display the now opening and hollow depths of the vaginal canal. Once again you apply that combination of warm air jets and the tip of your tongue up and down the length of this soft yielding tissue. Your tongue will notice a wash of lubrication and taste the super fluid saturation of the inner surface of these pursing folds of body tissue.

Removing your palms and thumbs you reposition both hands by sliding them beneath and cupping the cheeks of her buttocks. With upward pressure, you lift her body to push her vagina against your lips.

Withdrawing your lips from the labias, you must open your mouth as in a wide yawn, wide enough to completely engulf as much of the vagina as possible, and in a deep vacuum inhalation, draw into your mouth as much of the labia minors as possible. Capturing the labias with this strong vacuum suction, in alternate motions you

stretch the labias and then release the labias and use just the tip of your tongue in an up and down elevator movement to baste the labias. Using an index finger, or a wandering tongue, you can search out and tease the pink button hole of her anus. Some women enjoy anal penetration and some do not, so unless you are certain, do not destroy or threaten the intensity of the moment by a rash or rude anal invasion; limit it to a gentle tickling and circling sensual touch. After a series of your tongue up and down tracing within the vertical residence of each labia, you softly push your tongue as deeply as possible into the depths of that pink warm canal. You must curl your tongue along its full length, and while still curved and vacuuming, ever so slowly extract it. Several times you perform the curling which should result in an increase in softer moaning from your lover and possibly a strong arch of her hips pressing and welding her vagina against your lips.

Now beginning at the confluence of the bottom vee, and again forcing apart the draperies of the labais minor, you push your tongue as deeply as possible into the vaginal canal and with an upward stroke you simultaneously begin an in and out, up and down elevator movement, ascending from the vee to the base of the clitoris and then down again back to the vee. At this point, your partner should be moaning, have rapid breathing, and pushing her hips and vagina upwards pressuring your face for more and deeper tongue penetration. Her hands have typically and predictably (if you have performed your duties correctly) grasped the back of your head are now trying to force your face downward to be immersed, smothered and consumed by the welcome hunger of her vagina.

With her body at this height of excitement she is ready for the final phase of the "Anteater". Her breathing has increased, her moaning louder, and you begin to hear one or two word arena cheers

commanding you onward, her hips should be now pushing and arching against your tongue. The vaginal natural body lubricant will be flowing downward, escaping and cascading over the vee and down the inside of her thighs. Backing your face out from the intimacy of contact, purse your lips and several times again gently blow a warm jet of air up and down the labia minor. Immediately on achieving the apex of the upward slide, purse your lips and engulf and capture her clitoris. It is so important to purse your curled tongue to your upper lip, capturing the clitoris, while drawing your breath in and out, to vacuum up and down the stalk of her clitoris. With a slight head movement, gently suck up and down the stalk while the clitoris is completely a prisoner of your lips, use the tip of your tongue to tease its head. You are actually performing a movement identical to the oral stimulation and oral masturbation of a penis. Completing the clitoris masturbation cycle, you have, if your partner has the normal propensity for orgasm, awakened and spurred the ferocity of her sleeping beast. Your partner should be orgasmic ecstatic and achieving a cosmic gratification height that rarely men are able to deliver to a woman. She should have but one word "more".

Once you have mastered and made a slave of her clitoris, her body will be in command of her mind. Your tongue has become a maestro of her orchestra awaiting the next movement of a powerful symphonic conduction.

The text continued: THE STRAW:

Once you have taken your partner to the first pinnacle of excitement, to further stimulate and titillate the sensitive sexual vaginal receptors to reach an even higher pinnacle of screaming ecstasy, you must concentrate on the five areas; the large outside vertical lips of the labia major; the vertical fold and wrinkled

drapery lips of the labia minor, the forward anterior wall of the vagina, the junction at the upper base of the vagina where both the right and left side are joined in that little hood sheltering the clitoris or technically the perineum, and finally, the tip and stalk of the clitoris. Each of these areas requires slightly different techniques. The "anteater" should have released a trout stream of natural lubricant throughout the vaginal canal and should have cascaded downward onto her inner thighs to moisten her anal passage as well. Every part of her vagina should be wet by now. You begin by rolling your tongue into a tight cone shape. Through this cone shape you must be able to draw a vacuum, similar to a soda straw; hence the name, "the Straw".

Using the index finger on each hand you gently spread open the vagina to free the labia major to rest slightly to the side. Now you curl your thumbs up under her thighs and continue the same circular tickling of her anal pink spot with the tip of your finger. Again, you do not penetrate unless she consents. An unwanted anal penetration would completely destroy her concentration and pleasure. You then introduce and place your tongue on the upper part of the left labia major and begin, very gently at first a vacuum suction. The vertical left and right labia major lips usually have large smooth or semi-wrinkled surfaces similar to the lips of a pursing mouth. You then slide your tongue downward on the surface of the labia while at all times keeping the suction pressure on. Imagine the hose attachment of a vacuum cleaner sweeping the adjoining cushions of a sofa. You continue this for five or six slow up and down sweeps of the labia gradually increasing the suction pressure until on the last sweep the soft fleshy surface of the labia is being drawn up into the tip of your curled tongue. You then apply that same technique to her right labia major. Your lover should by now again begin to softly moan and you should notice

the beginning of a slight upward pressure in her legs and abdomen. Placing your first and second finger gently upon the surface of the labia major, you slowly spread them into a "V" victory positon, which further exposes the draperies of her vaginal canal. Spreading these fingers a little further, you are now exposing the smaller more pronounced wrinkled drapery lips of her labia minor. You begin on the left labia and apply a strong tongue vacuum. The soft wrinkles should be trapped in the fold of your tongue. With a release and capture movement, similar to allowing the nozzle of a vacuum to trap and fix to a material spot on that sofa, you allow your tongue to spot anchor on that vertical wrinkled pleasure tab and with a slow and gradual movement to descend the length of the labia minor. You attempt to draw up into the hollow column of your tongue as much of that delicious appendage as possible. Doing this five or six times, you should notice increased breathing and her upward body movement rhythmic pressure on your face becoming more like a heartbeat.

You move quickly to the right and repeat exactly the same rhythmic tease. Once you have completed the seduction of the labias, it is time to move to and focus on the inner passage wall; there are many, many sensitive nerve ending awaiting a knowledgeable lover's tongue and finger tips. Shifting your hands forward and using your right middle finger you slide it deeply into the vagina and turning the palm of your hand upward, you curl your finger facing you until you can feel the forward anterior vaginal wall. It will be either slightly bump covered or be more pronouncedly dimpled or pleated. This area must be stimulated with both your fingernail in a soft gently scratching up and down dragging motion and the very tip of your finger in both a caressing and a side to side and circular massaging motion. While your right finger is so engaged, you again form the "straw" and begin a strong sucking

vacuum and fix it directly to the lower vee where the pink confluence of both vertical sides of her vagina join. This area should be flooded with her natural lubrication. Using your "straw" you slide it in and out of this tiny, but very sensually charged area, vacuuming her fluids out and then with an outward breath through the "straw" replacing them with the new chemistry of a combination of both you and her fluids. After sweeping this area with five or six vacuum drawls and super saturating it with this new combination of body fluids you should feel her hands becoming more forceful in the downward pressure to push your face and tongue deeper into her secret "x" spots. The upward pressure of her thighs uplifting against your face and the increase of accelerated breathing and moans should be increasing in intensity and soft volume as well. The last target of the straw is the hood and clitoris. Keeping the motion of your fingers and the scratching of your fingernail constant on the front side of her vaginal wall, gently lifting the clitoris hood with your tongue, you should immediately form the "straw" and with as much a vacuum draw as possible attack the entire clitoris, imagine a delicious saucy spaghetti noodle and attempt to draw up into your tongue column both the clitoris head and the clitoris stalk. Imagining all the loving pleasure you derived from someone sucking your cock, you apply a repetition of that suction and movement drawing the head and stalk inside the curl of your tongue in a slow up and down masturbation type motion. You make a dozen or so up and down clit massages, then freeing the clitoris you begin a vacuum suction of the clitoris' stalk sides and the edges of its eagerly waiting pink button head. You repeat this motion and as the electric signals of pure pleasure overwhelm her senses, she begins to respond with screams and/or loud moans and tries to crush your head by crossing her legs around the back of your neck. At this height of seldom reached pleasure, she will usually moan something like

"you wonderful fucker, more, I need more, please don't stop, more, harder, faster…" In buckaroo rodeo style, while trying not to cast you loose from your pleasure mooring, she bucks and bucks until she becomes exhausted and collapses, her legs dropping from your neck and her hands releasing your head from the task at hand. If you were successful, your partner should have achieved a series of chain orgasms, the likes and heights of which she may have never experienced before.

"Gee Uncle Bob was some really pussy eating black belt master" Sonny thought.

Sonny was also intrigued by anal sex. Mame again explained that she and Bob had discovered that when it came to tight places, nothing beat the use of simple men's saving crème. It had twice the lubricating power of the expensive commercial tube sex jelly, was cheap and was super for anal sex. Mame demonstrated a very unique method that Bob had taught her. Lying on her back with her legs up in a "v" and a generous glob of shaving crème slathered on her pink buttonhole, Bob would rest the very tip of his cock on her tiny pink anal door; ever so slowly he would begin with gentle pressure to push it very gradually in, frequently stopping. He would take his left hand and place it on her flat stomach, would then push his right hand fingers as deeply as he could into her vagina. Slightly turning his pussy semi-enshrouded hand he would wiggle his fingers until he could feel through the vaginal wall the head of his rectum enshrouded cock. She would feel his fingers massaging the head of his cock, all the while sending bolts of pleasure up into the sexual predator hiding within her. Uncle Bob and Auntie Mame certainly weren't bashful about seeking new and unusual sexual pleasures and were never embarrassed about experimenting with the off beaten path methodology of kinky sex.

Completing his sexual graduate courses in Auntie Mame's academy of incest, Sonny's life took a different twist. In addition to being obsessed

with sex, Sonny discovered that he got almost as much pleasure from hurting people as he did from the pleasure of fucking Auntie Mame's body. Naturally a bully, he would single out the weaker boys and do ugly, corporal things to them, closely watching their eyes as the pain registered on their brains. Being a bully had the social consequence of being friendless. No one wanted to be alone and caught in the halls, classrooms or restrooms with Sonny. They all feared and hated him. This in turn fueled Sonny to seek better ways to punish these effete snobs. One Saturday, surprisingly unnoticed by Mame the fastidious clean one, Sonny was walking around in deep thought with the glare and the glaze still on his lips and chin from eating Auntie Mame's pussy. "Something is missing. It's so much fun and I love every second of fucking and sucking with Auntie, but it's like a hot dog without a bun" he thought. With the thought in mind that indeed his experiences with sex were falling just a little short of where he wanted to be, Sonny began in his mind to connect thoughts of other things that might intensify sexual gratification pleasure to the degree and level the inexperienced Sonny imagined necessary. After much consideration, Sonny began to lean heavily to pain. He began experimenting with Auntie Mame. While either missionary or doggie style, as he was plunging his hot cock in and out of her sweet honey hole, Sonny would suddenly, just before he released his string of hot semen, seize her breasts right behind the nipple and areole and begin gradually pinching the tissue until the pressure and pain caused Mame to scream out. Sonny would not release her tits until his last drop of cum had been pumped in her cunt. Auntie Mame, in pain, would unsuccessfully try to break free. When Sonny did release her breasts, she would slap his hands and remand him for being so cruel and mean to her. But Sonny knew that secretly she enjoyed it; her struggles to free his hands were far too weak to be taken seriously and Sonny knew, despite what she said, it was her welcoming signal to add this kinky element to their pleasure producing workouts. After several bouts with the new painful twist added, Mame wondered why Bob had only slightly explored the effect of pain on sexual gratification. While Sonny's

mind was working out boundaries of what and how much he could subject Auntie Mame to, she was fantasizing about to what degree she could remain comfortable with the deep dark physically hurtful things that Sonny wanted to experiment with. "Ooo that hurts, but please don't stop"; rough sex was a motherfucker and so good, it was at a height slightly below or maybe even equal to the gratification of "straw" treatment. Sonny began to think more and more about Tommy, how much he enjoyed seeing Tommy cringe in pain, and how much fun he had hurting the slight, femininely body boy. Sonny's cock would harden almost immediately when he thought about how he had grabbed Tommy's tiny penis and twisted and pulled it until Tommy almost fainted. Or squashing Tommy's balls. The thought of paining Tommy combining with the soft tortures he was occasionally paining on Auntie Mame, cemented Sonny's roadworks towards a delusional world of barbarism; a world that was like Mame's forgotten carnal beast, awaiting the opportunity for an awakening.

With the half dick hardening memory still fresh in his mind of her having just sucked his cock dry, Sonny could hardly be expected to concentrate on school work. His mind could not focus on anything but those full wet lips squeezing and milking his manhood while her head pushed forward and slowly inched millimeter by millimeter backwards. With those thoughts still graphic in his mind, Mame broke the spell by reminding him it was time to go to the library. Grumbling a little, Sonny said "Auntie, my grades are way better now that I have you as a reward, do you really think I need to keep working so hard on the school work?" "Sonny, you just don't realize yet how important an education is. People without diplomas work for and work to make people with diplomas money. Which would you rather be; the guy that signs the check or the guy that cashes the check? At the end of the day, who do you think has more money in the bank?" "I know you are right Auntie, but I really don't like school much." "Well Sonny, we all have things we don't like but have to do, so make me proud of your next exam and I might show you a special little thing or two. Deal?" "I'm on it

now Auntie." Mame dropped him off at the public library so he could do a little studying and check out several math books she thought would help him crack a few of those tougher geometry problems.

Smiling at the spinster librarian, Sonny wandered through the shelfing aisles and solely by accident discovered a small section on Sadism and Masochism. One book that immediately caught his attention was a frayed paperback; Famous Torturers of the Inquisition. What an authority of pain and such a graphic work. Paging through the illustrated pictures of torture, pain and the devices that produced that pain, he was amazed at the pain people would wantonly and creatively cause to another human being. Wow, he had never thought that there would actually be books on administering pain to others; that morning in a public library, Sonny discovered "Sadism." He quickly found the math books, set them aside, and spent the rest of the two hours flipping the pages of several of the more illustrated torture textbooks. Of course, he chose the two most graphic and also a book on serial killers. With the math books and the three others he approached the librarian to checkout his choices. "My, aren't you a little young to be reading about this perversion?" the librarian coldly asked. Sonny, always the fast thinker, said "Well, mam, my class is doing research on the horrible things that happened in the dark ages in Europe and the teacher said to be able to explain how the ruling class put fear into the peasants, so I thought this would be a great way to do my paper. Don't you think I am on right tract, mam?" "You have a point young man. You have two weeks before they are due, OK?" "Yes, ma'am." Sonny was smiling as he walked through the door and down to Mame's car. The S&M books awakened an evil and cruel devil in Sonny. The book about the serial killers who tortured and murdered innocent victims did more than awaken a devil, it created a need to capture, dominate, and inflict pain. That book was the birthing of Sonny as a future serial rapist and stone cold killer. His curiosity aroused, Sonny resolved to buy or steal the Serial Killer books and the Famous Torturers of the Inquisition book and a

Marquis de Sade book from the second hand book store as soon as he could convince Mame that he needed to buy a used math primer.

During an especially steamy session, while Sonny was stretching his tongue as deeply up inside Auntie Mame's vagina as possible, Auntie Mame, between moans and pelvic bucks, in a smoky whisper said "Your Uncle Bob occasionally liked to play with sadism and masochism, do you know what that is Sonny?" Sonny feinting naïveté, replied "Well I think it has something to do with pain, right Auntie?" "Yes, Sonny it most certainly does. Sometimes, Bob would wrap my wonderful breasts tightly with rope; tight enough to strangle the circulation and make the titties turn a deep dark purple. He sometimes would rubber band my clitoris or place pinch type clothes pins on the drapery lips of my labias. We had so much anal sex that my sphincter muscle would relax enough for Bob to start a wine bottle neck in there and push until it was so painfully stretched that I would sob and scream. He did the same with my vagina, although my vagina was stretched so much over the years that it could almost swallow the whole bottle. When he couldn't get a scream out of me with the bottle, he would lube his hand and force his whole fist up to his forearm inside me and then claw his fingers which would be unbelievable painful. To reciprocate, there was many a foreign object that I jammed and fucked his ass with; wine bottles, huge strap-on dildoes, huge vegetables, all types of appliance handles, and anything else that caught mine or his fancy. I put rubber bands around his cock and balls and would snap the bands hard enough to make him howl. The harder I snapped those rubber bands, the harder his dick got. The important thing here is that we had boundaries and we never crossed those boundaries. We never got into the really nasty and hurtful stuff; we avoided anything that would draw blood. We knew each other so intimately that we automatically knew when the other had reached a boundary limit. We had a special bi-weekly night reserved specifically for light S&M. Sometimes we even wore masks to add a little more flavor to the kinky sex. This type of sex is very, very exhausting and I think if we

enjoyed it any more than every few weeks, it would have accelerated into a dangerous darkness and it would have made it more of a duty than more of a wonderful pleasure. Since I have noticed that lately you have been squeezing my breasts far harder than ever before and biting those breasts and my labias and clitoris until it takes my breath away, I am thinking that you are on the threshold of S&M. Now Sonny, I want to ask you two questions and I want honest answers; one did you buy a book on S&M and do you enjoy giving me pain?"

Sonny lied about the theft, "Auntie, yes I did buy a book on S&M, it even has pictures, and yes I do like it when I can see your face tighten up and you gasp when I do something a little different to you. I would like to do so much more, the book describes all these neat things I would just love for us to try. Can we look at the book together and see the things you would like me to do to you, can we?" "Sonny, I'll think about it, but for right now I want you to give me that book and promise never to buy another one unless I say OK." "Sure Auntie, I love you so much, you have to be the best Auntie in the world." "Well Sonny beginning with your father and mother and then adding 300 million other peoples' opinions, if they knew I was teaching my nephew all about fucking, I definitely would not be nominated as Aunt of the Year; more likely I would be given life imprisonment, that is, if you mother and father didn't kill me first."

CHAPTER SEVEN

At sixteen Sonny was anything but sweet, but the tutorage of Auntie Mame both in academics and sexuality had given him a great deal of self-confidence to the point of aggression. He masqueraded behind "B" grades which kept him in the enclave of the more gentile and studious classmates. Keeping it a secret from Auntie Mame, he had become the school bully especially when he discovered that the academic levels were populated by the cowards and the meek of tomorrow. It did not take the force of a barbarian fist to rule over these next generation wussies, it only took the threat of that barbarian fist to certify the hierarchy. It took but one episode of Sonny slapping an equally sized and muscled but timid classmate to demonstrate who would command the class. Afterwards, a single hard look from Sonny was enough to send any one of them fleeing to the safer haven of a teacher occupied classroom. Sonny ruled. The boys were terrified that Sonny would single them out and with practiced threat he could easily frighten them out of lunch money or favors. Auntie Mame had no idea that Sonny was bullying

smarter classmates into doing papers and lessons for him. Sonny also and quickly discovered that many of the girls would, without complaint, tolerate his rough hands on their breasts and a few, if Sonny could isolate them in a lonely spot, rather than confront potential violence, would allow his hand and fingers to explore the secret within their panties or if he could force them into a date, he could frighten them into doing unnatural acts and favors that their mothers would not even allow to their fathers. Many, but not all, of the most studious girls were also the ugliest however, Sonny quickly realized that an ugly girl's pussy or mouth were just as welcome to his cock as the cutest of the cheerleaders; "dicks don't have eyes". Any port in a storm as the sailors would say. Fear always commands the timid and meek.

Sonny was athletic and had no trouble making any of the teams he chose. Football was the only sport that he enjoyed. The legal battery of body bruising contact was almost sexual in its personal gratification. But the physical contact violence on the athletic field was not enough to satisfy the devil that was incubating in the dark evil core of Sonny's mind. In the beginning with his timid and silent classmates, it was torturing anyone within range with monkey and gorilla bites that graduated into ball smacking, arm twisting, belly punching, face pinching, and thigh kneeing. Out of abject fear of worse, classmates took the abuse in silence. One day, cutting class, when Sonny went to the hideout in the boy's restroom he discovered, as usual between classes, it was unoccupied except for one sole soon-to-be victim standing at the urinal relieving his self. This was a boy Sonny delighted in hurting and tormenting. The boy was terrified of Sonny and always religiously did everything possible to maneuver out of the vicinity and contact zone. Mostly he was successful, but he was unfortunate enough to be on the receiving end often enough to always be sporting fresh vivid bruises of the consequence of capture.

Small framed, small boned, long tresses of blonde hair, a style his mother insisted he wear (Sonny would always embarrass the boy by saying "Hey

bitch, show us your pussy, come on let's see your pussy."), quiet spoken, thick lens glasses with heavy black frames, and in general, the total definition of a defenseless weakling. Sonny smiled and thought, "what luck, alone and in the restroom, no one else cutting class, I got the place all to myself and this little geek asshole." Not yet deciding of an appropriate degrading abuse, Sonny walked up to the next urinal and looking down at the boy's penis, resurrected an idea from the pages of one of his manuals on the art of black pain. Why not grab it and twist, bet that would really hurt. "Don't you dare move or holler, fuck face. Understand? I can't hear you." The boy's name was Tommy. "I won't move or holler, Sonny, please don't hurt me." Sonny laughed. "I'm gonna yank your tiny dick and twist it a little. You better not yell or try to jerk away." Reaching down, Sonny smashed the tip of Tommy's penis with his thumb and index finger, hard, really hard. Tommy gasped as the pain started to spiral up into his pain receptors and he unsuccessfully attempted to pull away. "Please stop, it hurts." With a slow twisting motion, Sonny began to twist and pretzel that little dick into a tightly compressed appendage of pain. Sonny could feel his own dick hardening.

The pain was enough to outweigh the consequence of disobeying Sonny, so as the boy started to scream, Sonny balled up his left fist and punched the boy in the stomach forcing all the air from his lungs and silencing the boy. Still holding on to the penis, Sonny looked around to be sure no one had entered the restroom and with his scan assuring him that no one else was there, he led the boy into a stall. Sonny then commanded the boy to pull down his pants. "I just want to see if you have a pussy hiding in there, or if your cunt hair is as long and curly as your girl's Goldie locks, that's all." Telling the boy if he made a sound or told anyone, Sonny would make him really sorry. The terrorized boy did as told. With the boys' pants and underwear down to the boys ankles, Sonny stared at the boy's tiny, circumcised button of a penis and reaching down and using his index finger pushed and disappeared the tiny cock back into Tommy's groin. "See, I

knew it; a little push and you got a cunt, a girl's cunt. It's making my dick hard. You don't even have pubic hair, just a few curls of fuzz. I had you pegged from the get go, you're more girl than boy, one of those in between cocksuckers. Like to suck dick? I just bet you do and give really good head don't you? We might have to do something about it, pussy boy." Sonny noticed that despite having a mosquito sized dick, the kid had a very large, wrinkled scrotum that hung loosely from his abdomen, emphasizing and further testifying to the miniature size of Tommy's dick.

Sonny, with his sadistically active mind in over drive, smiled as he had another cruel idea. Pulling the boy up from the toilet seat, he reached down with one hand and in one quick movement, wrapped his fingers around the upper part of the scrotum trapping the boy's testicles and began jerking the sack up and down. The tears down the boys' face were testimony to the agony the boy was undergoing. It produced pain but not the level of pain that Sonny wanted. Freeing the sack for a different grip, Sonny closed his hand around both balls and began squeezing. When the boy could barely take the pain and on the verge of screaming, Sonny used his free hand to choke the boy to silence. Releasing the boy's balls, Sonny who just had a flashback to this morning's Auntie Mame session and his cum jetting onto her tongue, "One more thing and I promise to let you go. Now sit back down on that toilet seat and open your mouth." Sonny then pushed the boy down on the commode, "You are going to suck my cock until it cums and you better do it good. If you bite my dick I promise you, you will really regret it. When I start to cum I want you to keep it in your mouth, open you're your mouth wide and let me watch my prick squirt cum on your tongue, and you better not let a single drop of it drip out of your mouth. Understand?" "Please Sonny, I'll bring some money tomorrow and pay you ten dollars if you let me go." "Open your mouth." "Twenty dollars, Sonny, please." "I said open your mouth, you pussy motherfucker." Tommy began crying and Sonny just grabbed him by his nose and pressure pinched it as hard as he could. "Shut up you little queer

motherfucker, you're sucking dick and if you don't stop the sobs, I might just fuck you in the ass for good measure. Now open that mouth and get to work." Sonny then grabbed the boys' flowing golden tresses and pulled his face forward.

If only Tommy's mother had known how those long flowing golden tresses she adored and insisted Tommy wear caused Tommy to lose his gender identity, draw attention to his effeminate frame, attract a demented mind that preyed on the weak, and that same demented person would be forcing Tommy's to allow a man's penis to ejaculate semen onto and past the very lips she tenderly kissed every night goodnight, she would have been rage fully suicidal. Tommy's mother would have been horrified to know that those flowing tresses were a boy rape magnet. Her selfishness and vanity had put poor Tommy on a journey of no return, as the boys in the locker room opined, "suck a dick once and you were a cocksucker forever." In college, was she not a revolutionary rebel and did she not march against the war and did she not accept an older black man activist professor as a boyfriend who routinely sexually abused every single one of her body's orifices. Did she not, on her boyfriend's command, allow his black friends to fuck her and did she not swallow buckets of their hot black man's cum to prove her remorse and offer of reparation for their slavery? Did she not, again on her boyfriend's' command, occasionally be called front and center to entertain the black caucus pot smokers by eating the wiry haired pussy of cold hearted sisters while the dope heads laughed and cheered, or let that repulsive little nigga dwarf with the huge cock fuck her in every hole as every brother and sister in the audience shouted "fuck that ofay bitch's ass harder, we want to hear you make that white bitch scream". And did she not scream as he forced his gigantic prick up into her ass or smothered her screams as he gagged her tonsils as he streamed a pint of his evil, bitter tasting jizz down her throat. Was she not a cool sister of the Revolutionary? Yes sir, she had certainly paid her dues.

Graduating college, she dated a few more black guys and then out of boredom decided it was time to pick a partner to have a family. Not wanting to face the community issues of being in a mixed marriage, she chose to hunt for a weak non-aggressive bookkeeper type. She found Kevin and with a little sex and an occasional blowjob, was able to set the hook. Kevin fit her profile to a "T"; a white, mousy looking Anglo accountant with a middle class, consistent income and on the first date she realized that her meal ticket was a spineless pussy who could be bullied. The cake was not even cut at the wedding ceremony, when she whispered in his ear "I'm in charge and I will always be in charge in this marriage. If you don't agree, then you will be sleeping on the couch for the next fifty years, no pussy, no blowjobs, nothing. You do agree that I'm gonna be the boss, do you not?" Of course he did; here was an occasional bed mate and he suspected that the sex, both vaginal and oral would be severely rationed, but that did not concern him as much as she thought it did. He had no idea that with her dominance, even the occasional blowjob would be off the menu and as rare as rain in the Mojave Desert. Did he not spend most of his time at the office anyway? So why make waves. Plus, he had an effeminate friend and evening visitor to the office that was just captivated by and loved the shit out of his cock.

Afraid to use the office as a love nest, he and Matt did so much enjoy sneaking around for a remote, uninhabited, deserted spot at those once a week rendezvous in the gay part of the city park by the woods, way back of the duck pond. Matt really enjoyed playing with Kevin's cock. Once they found a secluded spot, they would walk hand in hand until Matt's hand grabbed and bunched Kevin's groin. It was a standard practice, almost mechanical as Matt slowly unzipped Kevin's zipper and wormed his fingers pass the fabric opening and on Kevin's hot manhood. Once those fingers worked their magic and Kevin's cock was straining for freedom, Kevin would loosen his belt allowing Matt to slide Kevin's jeans and underwear down. As soon as his prick was stabbing at Matt, Matt would drop to his

knees, capture Kevin's balls in one hand and forced his lips down the length of Kevin's cock. Matt was a very talented cocksucker. Once he had the cock entirely in, his tongue would snake and tickle the base of Kevin's cock. That sensation caused Kevin to almost, every time, immediately ejaculate. Once Matt choked down the love juice, it was Kevin's turn. Kevin could never come to terms with sucking dick, licking was OK, but not sucking; Matt was OK with that. Kevin knew all the sensual artful moves of masturbation and combining his talented fingers with those ice cream licks, Matt was a very happy camper. Kevin's philosophy was; as long as Matt was there, why worry about how often the boss lady would allow him to plunge and plow into her. Treat it as a treat and don't worry about it.

Sexual happiness and the home front philosophy were a different matter. She had control and knew how to use control. How many times had she, a woman of culture and refinement refused to allow her geekish husband the simple pleasure of a blowjob, an ejaculate, a catch, and then a swallow. No routine matter of fact tonsil swabbing in this household; no sir, not on your life with this proud woman; did she not last year march for woman's equality and rights. No disgusting doggie style or face down, pillow biting anal either. No way would she want her sisters of the cause to know she was a lowly cocksucker or hersey ass fucker, not her. Coital contact once every two week, and as a precaution against a lust crazed, wandering penis, she insisted to always be in control, on the top deck, cow girl style.

Reaching down with his free hand, Sonny grabbed Tommy's throat and started squeezing it. "Suck or die. OK bitch, you better suck it like a vacuum cleaner and when it cums to slurp it like a milkshake. Understand fag?" Tommy opened his mouth and Sonny pushed his dick in, all the way in; in past his tongue and in past his tonsils. Tommy immediately discovered something very important to the oral art; he had no gag reflex. Sonny's inexperience did not notice it as he pushed his cock as it plunged without restriction deep into Tommy's throat as far as he could force it. Pulling Tommy's head forward and feeling his lips touching the very root of his

stalk, Sonny paused. With his cock head resting in that special supernova place beyond Tommy's tonsil stem, Sonny felt the swelling and the tingling as his sperm exploded and surged forward to its warm reluctant, throat destiny. It only took a minute for Sonny's excitement to climax in a river of semen. Tommy started gagging, not on the cock but on the volume of cum. Sensing a pull back, Sonny pinched Tommy's nose forcing him to swallow and swallow again until there were no more stings of cum seeping from his dick. "Well, now you are a real cocksucker and with those golden curls you ought to be a big hit with the boys. I don't think you will be telling anyone about this, or you will be spending every free period sitting on a toilet seat doing tonsil exercises with every horny cock in this school. One more thing, we will be doing this a lot more. Now pull your pants up and get to class." Sonny laughed, Tommy turned around and vomited in the bowl. Sonny walked away trying to decide which he liked better, the blowjob or causing the corporal pain.

This was but the first of many blowjobs Sonny forced poor Tommy to perform. Once when Sonny thought they were alone Sonny suddenly noticed the presence of another boy in an adjacent stall and who had obviously overheard everything. When Sonny realized where the intruder was, he pulled open that stall door and dragged the boy out and with fist raised to his face, threatened that if he ever said anything, he would beat him seven days to Sunday. While the boy was cowering, a thought flashed into Sonny's mind. "Jake have you ever had your cock sucked and cummed on someone's tongue, no bullshit, tell the truth?" "No Sonny, not ever, please don't make me suck your dick, please." "Don't worry Jake, today is your lucky day, I have someone I want you to meet, doesn't have a pussy yet, but does have beautiful golden hair and a very warm mouth and loves to swallow cum." Jake knew instantly who Sonny was talking about. A few of the boys were joking about how Sonny and Tommy would suddenly and mysteriously disappear from the school yard and then later Tommy would show up for class just a little paler and red eyed as if he had been crying.

When Sonny left the stall to grab Jake, poor Tommy should have fled, but he didn't; Tommy's big life changing mistake. "Tommy you are going to suck Jake's cock, understand." "Please Sonny, don't make me do that. Jake please say you don't want it, please." Afraid of Sonny and interested in something different then jacking off in his brother's sock or on his sister's stinky panties, Jake said "Gee Tommy I never had a real blowjob before and it sounds real good, sorry." "Jake, pull your cock out and stick it in his mouth. Tommy, I am going to be watching so you better not fuck up." Not surprising, and much to Tommy's despair, Jake flipped out a rock hard cock ready to explore the alternate world. Being primed and sexually charged by what he had overheard and the fantasy of its pleasure, now looking at Tommy's tiny, tiny cock, it took but just a little contact with Tommy's tongue for Jake's prick to explode a half ounce of semen down into the recesses of Tommy's throat. Jake paled as he spurted his semen, and almost fainted. Gasping, he managed to say; "Gee, Tommy that was really great, I never imagined a guy could do that. Thanks Sonny for making him suck me. It was really great, and he swallowed all of it; not a drop on my pants or underwear. Can we do this again? Sorry Tommy but you can really suck dick good, if it's OK with Sonny I'll pay you or Sonny two dollars next time. I can't believe you actually did it and the way you used your tongue to tickle the tip, primo."

Jake was a talker, so by the close of the school day, Sonny and Tommy's secret was out. By the end of the semester poor Tommy with the long golden tresses had sucked more dick and swallowed more cum than the girls' choir and cheer leading team combined. Tommy was even sucking his geek buddies cocks. Tommy cried rivers of tears and hated his mother who he blamed for the root cause of his transformation. The girls, who were also very much aware of Tommy's new status and popularity, began including Tommy in their group discussions which always centered on their dates and what they did to, and let their dates do to them in that car back seat, at babysitting jobs, or even in the dark corners of the movie theater.

As Tommy came to more and more accept domination and oral turning; he became the "go to person" for the girls to consult with in delivering a puff down. A funny thing, Tommy was enjoying the way the boys would fight over his favors, and with no gag reflex to interfere with the depth he could take the medium and big cocks down, sucking dick wasn't really that bad. The girls with the limited experiences under their belts of the one or two boys they sexually experimented with, giggled and loved his stories of who had big dicks and who didn't and who squirted buckets and who were dribblers.

Sonny reached another crossroads when he met Luke. When Sonny reached eighteen, he occupied part of his time searching for a like person to explore and conquer the world; Luke filled that bill. Luke was an older 20 year old, lanky ex-con and dropout who had found a home in an auto recycling junkyard. To earn room and board, he traded two jobs, a day job and a night job. The day job was rather routine and simple, twice per day he greased equipment fittings with a power grease gun; before the start of the shift he had to attend to the grease fittings on the giant car crusher, conveyor track and magnetic lift crane, and once again repeat the greasing after the operator and his crew left for the evening. At night he kept watch to prevent car part boosters and copper and aluminum thieves from climbing the fence and looting his boss' rusty and accident inventory of driver carelessness. Sonny and Luke immediately hit it off and struck up a friendship. Ten times a day, the owner would say "some fuckin deal, this guy eats ten times more than a watch dog, and I bet he's asleep most of the night while those fuckin thieves are carting off my parts."

Luke was everything Sonny's former non-truant schoolmates weren't. Luke was an ex-con. Luke was no pussy. Luke's fingernails were always greasy and dirty. Luke never uttered a sentence unless it was spiced with at least one curse word. Luke could legally buy beer (but he rarely had the money for anything but cheap wine). Luke had no use for society or its laws. A major plus, Luke had an old beat up semi-faithful pickup truck. Sonny

immediately recognized that Luke could be a teacher of the other things that church and school people warned you to stay away from, maybe even knew a few things Auntie Mame hadn't taught him about yet. Luke was exotic and for sure Auntie Mame would have never approved of any relationship with her Sonny. Once they got to know each other, Sonny discovered that, like him, Luke really enjoyed and got turned on by stories about murders and murderers. From Luke's looks and vocabulary, Sonny could not believe that Luke had ever read a single book much less several of the stories of the Inquisition. They would spend idle hours discussing the methods these inhumane monstrous animals used to trap their victims and the horrible and beastly things they did to them afterwards. Luke loved to recant the story of the fuck that led to his incarceration. Over and over again he talked about how super it was to have a woman completely in your power, just as powerless as a prisoner strapped to a third world interrogation table. Once when Luke was rubbing his cock retelling how dead that drunken bitch was, Sonny asked "Luke would you fuck a dead body?" "Depends on how long it's been dead and what it looks like. In the pen, there was a mortician that got caught stealing money from the boss. His job was cleansing and prepping the corpses for embalming. He claimed that once he washed them off, if they were good looking enough, he would smell their pussies and if they smelled fresh he would lick them to lube them, then climb up on the trolley and fuck them. Said you couldn't cum in them, but you could cum on them. Cum was evidence, you know. Said it was the best pussy you could ever ask for. He said he fucked old ladies, young ladies and even kids that just had their tits popping out. I think he was telling the truth, cause he could go on for hours describing their tits and pussies and what a cold pussy tasted or felt like on your cock. Could you Sonny?" "You know, I'm not sure but if times were hard enough, I think I could, but what really turns me on is a bitch tied up so you can do anything you want to her warm body. I would prefer something breathing versus something not."

One story that Luke shared over and over with Sonny was about the time when Luke was a teenager and got a job working at a gay club as a towel boy. Management had very strict rules about gay patrons and towel boys; absolutely no physical contact with the minors while they were on the property. Any transgressor would lose club privileges or possibly membership. Towel boys did get to see lots and lots of guy on guy make outs. Being a club and protected from police raids, everyone was open and it was no surprise to see kneeling guys gulping cock or guys power driving their cocks into welcoming assholes. There was no shame or embarrassment in the club. Luke had learned a lot about the gay world.

Luke had thought that his experiences would help turn Sonny and help Luke get his cock into Sonny's mouth or ass. "Sonny let me tell you about true friends. One afternoon as I was working in the club sauna, there were two gentlemen in the sauna, and while the back and forth conversation was going on, the one on the lower tier would suddenly begin sucking his buddy's dick. I thought that was one hell of a friendship. After a suck or two, the guy doing the sucking would jump right back into the conversation. Curiosity got the best of me. I just had to ask." Luke just knew that gays liked to share intimate personal stories and get horny all over again. Plus Luke got a boner listening to those intimate tales of seduction.

"I mean no offense Sir, so please excuse my curiosity but I could not help but notice that you and this gentleman appear to be friends and as you sit on this lower tier and talk, you occasionally break off your conversation to him, turn to him pushing your face between his legs and then suck his penis for several minutes and then with no hesitation, pickup up the conversation where you left off. Your friend sitting on the upper tier and smiles but makes no overtures to reciprocate. Is it you alone that brings the pleasure to this relationship. I would just love to hear your story?"

"Young man, normally I would tell you to mind your own business, but my friend Tom is smiling and nodding so I am going to explain our relationship. Tom and I have been friends since grade school. Tom was the jock and still is a very handsome example of an athletic man. I being a rather plain faced guy with little athletic talent, decided to become a book jock and instead of the athletic field, attack life with good grades. In high school, Tom had been screwing two girls; one was a pig that everyone with a kind word and a hard cock could fuck in the back seat of their daddy's car. The pig would let you fuck her pussy or jack you off, but drew the line at blowjobs. Bad for a girl's reputation she said. I never approached her, for I had no interest in fucking someone's worn out, semen filled, oversized cunt. The other was a petite, cute cheerleader. Tom had been fucking the socks off this cheerleader's ass since the sophomore year and she loved it; but as desperate as he begged and pleaded, he couldn't get her to suck his dick. She kept telling him that there was no way she was ever going to let someone push their cock in and out of her mouth and then squirt that nasty sticky cum on her tongue; no way ever! Tom became obsessed with the idea of getting a blowjob; hardly did we ever have a conversation without him bringing up how great a blowjob would be, if only he could find someone to suck his dick. Several times I thought to myself, I wouldn't mind trying a blowjob either, but one difference, I would be the one choking on Tom's proud cock. I kept my desires to myself, as for sure, I didn't want to threaten our friendship. Maybe, just maybe, there would be a right time."

"On weekends, Tom and I hung out whenever he didn't have a date with Sherry. One night I was sitting in teen town bored to death watching the girl's dance, when Tom came in and said, let's take a drive. As we walked to his car, Tom immediately began complaining about Sherry just cancelled his date, something about a sick grandma. As soon as we got into the car, Tom started whining about how Sherry was a selfish, spoiled bitch and he was so horny he could fuck a hand full of roofing nails. She knew his balls

were in knots and needed to be plunging into her, and still she cancelled the date. The bitch! Got the story right so far, Tom?"

"Yeah, pretty much so Ben, but I'll tell the rest of the story from here. Well I drove Ben to my special secluded hideaway spot; it was so remote off the beaten path, that once I pulled the car into the spooky old barn no one ever thought to look for lovers there. I bet I fucked Sherry a thousand times in that barn. I have no idea why I drove Ben there, I had never brought him here before, but here we were. Anyway, Ben and I were sitting in the front seat and I was bitching about her cancelling the date and never willing to give a simple blowjob, looking up I noticed that Ben was staring into my face. I almost jumped out of my skin when I felt Ben's fingertips on my neck. Was Ben firing on me? A guy I had known for at least ten years, is Ben a secret fruit? Then I thought back about how when we were standing at the urinals, how Ben would always lean forward, turn his head and look down at my pissing dick. Several times I thought I could even hear Ben's breathing speed up as he eye groped my dick. But I never paid much attention to it; everybody knew that gays didn't hang out with jocks. Well, I'll be damned, maybe Ben was one of those closet gays; shit, I can't believe it, I thought as close as friends as we are, that I would have known, there would have been some kind of signal, or he would have said something before now. Ben had plenty of opportunities to grab my dick but other than sneak stares at it, he never made a move."

"So I had to ask, Ben what are you doing, are you queer? Well Ben said, 'Tommy I think I have always had a guy crush on you and tonight I want to give you an early birthday present. Just close your eyes and pretend I'm Sherry.' As soon as Ben said that, he pushed his hand onto my crotch and began massaging my dick. It got hard very, very fast. It was frightening to think that well maybe I'm queer too. I could feel him unbuckle my belt and slide my zipper down; I had to arch my hips for him to pull my pants down my thighs. His fingers crept into the fly opening of my underwear. When the tips of his fingers touched my cock, it was like electric rods, the heat

from each finger made my dick scream for more and it absolutely took my breath away. Sherry's fingers were always cold and like claws when she rolled a rubber down the shaft. She acted like she was grabbing something that was venomous and she had to avoid getting bitten. Five jerks and she was ready for me to make the plunge into that hairy thatch between her shapely cheerleader legs; six to ten stabs in her hot cunt and I filled the rubber. But Ben was different; he wanted it. When he freed my cock from the underwear and it was poking straight up he began to lower his head into my lap. I could feel him blowing a stream of warm breath onto the tip of my dick. I almost blew my wad when I felt the tip of his tongue tickle the head and his lips slowly close onto the shaft. My asshole puckered like someone had shoved a popsicle up my ass. With a grunt Ben began sucking up and shaft sliding down until he reached that gag point where he couldn't force any more cock into his mouth. I put both hands on the back of his head and began pushing to the rhythm of his sucking. It didn't take but a minute or less before, like a runaway locomotive, I felt the squirt fighting its way towards Ben's tonsils. When my dick started cumming, Ben tried to back his mouth free, but I forced his head down. In the very end, when Ben was pulling away, one last huge squirt sent a string of cum to rest on his eye glasses, his nose, and his cheek. Ben was a good trooper and though he gagged a little on that frothy, floaty load, managed to swallow it. At that point, I was surprised when Ben grabbed my neck and pushed his cum dripping lips on mine. He even tried to French me; but I wasn't ready for that at all. After that first blowjob, I became Ben's secret lover and to this day, occasionally I do reciprocate a blowjob. Ben gives fine head; intense and so satisfying. That about all of it Ben?"

"Tom that is pretty much it. I knew I loved you and when we were together that night in the barn, I could not stop myself; I had to have you even if it risked ruining our friendship, I had to know. I did give you a pretty good, award winning blowjob for a fellow's first time giving head. Tom didn't say and always forgets this part, but after I smeared that cum

on his lips, he licked his lips and smiled. Another part of the story that Tom always and I mean always forgets, after I had sucked his cock, swallowed his cum, and put some of his hot cum on his lips, Tom reached down and grabbed my cock. Within ten seconds, he had my cock out of my pants and was jacking it off so hard that the friction made it hurt. When I climaxed, my wad shot up his arm, on his shirt, on his jeans, on the steering wheel, on the dash board and all over my pants. I took one finger and wiped some of the goo from his arm and in a quick jerk, smeared it across his lips. I thought that he would explode in anger, but he surprised me, didn't you Tom, he grabbed my wrist and actually sucked the cum from my fingers. He let me finger swipe the cum from everywhere and as fast as I could scoop it up, he licked my fingers clean. While Tom was not a cocksucker that night, cum slurping put him on the road to be one. Right, Tom?"

"So, you see. We have remained best of friends through several marriages and divorces, careers, middle age, and now as we are in our fifties, look forward to the pleasure of each other." "That truly is a hell of a love story fellas, thanks so much for sharing it."

Luke had other history, stories that he didn't delight in telling; at least not right away. As an ex-con Luke had real life experiences behind those cold bars. It didn't take Luke long to discover that even hard asses, unless they were gang connected, could become victims of lust in the penitentiary. In the drunken girl incident, Luke drew a state pen, two year sentence term for drugs and contributing to the delinquency of a minor. Luke narrowly evaded a 10 year statuary rape charge and child molestation charge when he bought beer for two minor girls, invited them to his apartment to a smoke and beer party, partied with them, and then when one passed out said "let's play a joke on her; I'll put big hickies on her titties and tomorrow when she takes a shower she will be pissed but not sure how they got there. Wadda think?" The other drunken girl thought it hilarious and slurred, "Do it, it will be really funny when she calls me tomorrow and asks what happened. You don't have any balls unless you do it." And with the

one girl egging him on, Luke pulled up the passed out girl's sweater, lifted her bra up and sucked a huge passion mark on each tit. As soon as Luke began licking the unconscious girl's nipples, her friend drunkenly screamed "stop that right now motherfucker, tuck 'em in and pull her sweater down before I make big trouble for you. End of joke, it's over, understand?" Luke did, and did as commanded. After she calmed down, they laughed about it again. Luke could see the obvious effect of the alcohol kicking in. The big mouth agitator girl was slowly yielding to the power of alcohol. When the big mouth girl muttered "I'm getting dizzy, I got to lie down." Luke smiled as he led her to the bedroom, where she too, as soon as she hit the mattress, slipped into a drunken coma and passed out face up, without further comment or grunt. "My turn, for your turn, motherfucker" he thought.

Testing to see if there were any human responses, Luke, flopped on the mattress and squeezed one of her breasts really hard. There was no response; she was definitely out to the world. "Why not bitch. Let's put some lip brands on your big tits." Luke unbuttoned her blouse and pushed the soft panels over to her sides opening a full view of her bra corralled titties. "Whoa will ya look at that, they're huge, this girl could be in a pinup magazine. I know I could jackoff looking at a page full of these tits." Rather than roll her over to unclasp her bra hooks, Luke just pushed up her bra over the tits and rested it on her neck. Out slid two mega huge soft breasts, breasts that you only saw in nasty fuck magazines. The saucer size of the rosy areolas were shocking, they almost covered the entire front half of each breast. The nipples were the sunken kind and when Luke squeezed the tip of each breast, out they popped, like wrinkled little soldiers out of a foxhole and ready for hand to hand combat. This was a sight that Luke would never forget and there would be countless times with an animated image of those tits that Luke would mercilessly beat his prick to climax, his cock staying swollen and tender from the abuse for days.

Luke could feel his cock harden as he played with her nipples. Lying aside her with his lips attached to and sucking her tit like a Hoover vacuum, his right hand glided from her breast on down her hard stomach. With no movement besides breathing, he knew the corpse would not be grabbing his hand and saying "No." It was open season, beaver time. Unzipping and opening her skin tight shorts, he let his hand slide deep inside her shorts and inside her panties. He could feel the gentle slope of her body as his fingertips encountered the beginning of her soft pubic hair. His dick got even harder. Slowly he pushed his hand a little further until his fingers could feel the moist top of her vagina. A little further and his fingers were cruising up and down the moistening labia lips. Back up and slightly hidden in her love crevice, his fingers discovered her clitoris hood and clitoris. Pushing the meaty hood flap aside, he discovered a clitoris head and stalk, big enough to match her big tits. It was thick and it felt an inch long. For a brief second, Luke's mind flashed to "is this one of them shemales, that the guys always joked about; discovering a cock when you were expecting a twat?" Luke's fingers started moving up and down the clitoris. "I didn't know that girls could jackoff, but with a clit that size, why wouldn't they. You learn something new every day." he thought. Switching the three fingers back to her pussy, Luke was greeted by a flood of woman lube. The three fingers slid so easily in there, Luke added a fourth and it too was received without issue. There was no protest either from her or her vagina. "Shit this bitch must be fucking horses" Luke smiled. A beckoning from his loins reminded him that he too had something that wasn't going to be ignored any longer. Luke's cock was impatiently straining against his underwear screaming for that plunge. Luke thought "Why not, the bitch is out of it and will never remember."

Convincing himself that this was an opportunity that no normal man would pass up, Luke peeled her shorts and panties down to her ankles, freeing them from one leg. He crawled up between her legs and slowly used his fingers to first use one, then two, then three, then four to again penetrate

her treasure pot. "This is wonderful, absolutely no resistance, none at all. She's a juicy Lucy. Shit if only I could chain her to the bed and keep her here forever," he thought. Feeling the wetness, Luke used his thumbs to spread the draperies of her labia lips wide enough to push both of his lips in and stab his tongue in as far as he could extend it. Luke always liked the foreign taste of pussy. He had eaten four girls and each pussy tasted different; one was pissy; one was metallic, one always tasted like her strawberry douche, and the other tasted sweet. He loved the flavor of all four. What will this one taste like? As soon as his tongue rolled up past his thumbs and began its snake dance, Luke decided that this pussy had a different flavor; it tasted like a slightly salted peanut. When the flavor settled on his palate, Luke's tongue began excavating and siphoning as much of that love cocktail as he possibly could. Luke stayed busy eating her out for at least five minutes until he remembered, he had a little friend that needed a reward. Rolling to the side, Luke unbuckled and pushed his pants and dirty underwear down until his cock was free and quivering for that reward. Luke rolled back onto her and speared his dick in as far as he could push. For three minutes he fucked that pussy hard, as hard as he could pile drive it. He suddenly remembered that if he cummed in her she would immediately know someone had for sure fucked her. Feeling the jizz about to erupt, he jerked his cock free and jetted his load on the inside of her thigh. "Damn, that was good pussy. I wish every girl was as dead as that. For sure, I gotta get the phone numbers and party with these bitches again. Better clean her up and get both of them out of here" After wiping the cum from her legs, he pulled her panties and shorts back over her ankles and realized how difficult it was to dress a girl that wears skin tight clothes, especially one that is passed out and dead weight. He didn't think he had that much trouble getting them down her legs but he sure as hell was having trouble getting them back up her legs. Luke would have probably gotten away scot free, had not the other girl awakened from her alcohol nap, wandered into the bedroom, and while still in a funk immediately realized that Luke had been fucking her unconscious

girlfriend. "What are you doing you mother fucker? You fucked her didn't you, didn't you?" Luke trying to think on his feet blurted out "she had to piss and when I came in here she had her pants off and I think she pissed on my floor." "You're lying you no good trailer trash asshole. Now here is what you are going to do, you're gonna help me dress her, carry her to your truck and drive us to my apartment. You're gonna carry her up to the bedroom and gently set her on the bed. Then you're gonna get the fuck out of our lives, scumbag. Understand?" Luke was relieved, as the way he interpreted the last part of her statement it appeared that as long as he disappeared, it ended.

Five days later, Luke answered a knock at the door and there were two detectives with an arrest warrant for statutory rape, child molestation, and several other less serious felonious charges. Seems someone changed their mind about how funny a passion marked titty could be. "Fuck those lousy no good bitches, a guy does them a favor and next thing he knows he in jail." With no means of support Luke qualified for a free public defender. After interviewing the girls, the public defender knew their testimony potential and pointed out to the prosecutor that being drunk the entire time, both women would be horrible witnesses. With the prosecutor agreeing, the public defender was able to plea bargain down to contributing to the delinquency of a minor, plead guilty, accept a bench sentence and do two years in the state pen.

Luke wasn't in the pen for four nights, when he was caught by three billboard tattooed and heavily muscled Hispanic gang members. He was pushed in a cell, held in a choking headlock, stripped of his uniform pants and underwear, and ass fucked by the two of the three. When he refused to suck the third ones' cock, he was beaten and lost two lower teeth. When the guard eventually found him, unconscious and bleeding on the cell floor, he was rushed to the infirmary and treated for mouth and head contusions compounded with a slight concussion. After spending 4 days in the infirmary and released to the general population, Luke had a

welcoming committee in his cell. Not only did he suck one dick, but as a welcome home present, he was presented with two other very hard and erect Spanish cocks served with a warm creamy penitentiary salsa. For the balance of the eighteen months and time served, Luke was a punk and bitch to anyone who was more terrifying then he. Prison lessons are hard and without mercy.

Luke had other motives as well. He saw in Sonny someone that he might be able to turn with gentle persuasion. Luke constantly talked to Sonny about how nice it would be if Sonny was nice to him. In prison, Luke had witnessed a number of the older, less violent inmates who, gradually, with sweet talk, were able to convince their younger cell mates, that for friendship and sometimes protection in the prison a little more was expected than things in common, a joke or two and a pat on the back. "After all, who would know that you were sucking cock, just the two of us and we won't be talking, will we. And this is prison, things are different then on the outside, no one in here is gonna smell or lick pussy till they get paroled, so it's a cockwich or nothing. There you have it, be nice to me and I got your back. Right? So what's the harm and you do want to be my friend, don't you. Think about it, if I wanted to force you, I could invite my one of my friends over and for argument just say he jumped up and grabbed you in a headlock. I could pull your pants down and ass fuck you. That would hurt a lot, wouldn't it? And, then it would be my friends' turn. Not a pleasant thought is it? So what will it be, do you want to be my friend or not? That's more like it, I just knew I could count on you being a good friend" as he lower his zipper and flipped out his dick to cement the new friendship. Luke sure wished he had a gentle protector, those bandana wearing spics face fucked hard and without mercy.

Luke suspected that Sonny might be weakening. One afternoon, after they had drank a few beers, Luke put his hand on Sonny's shoulder and said "You want me to teach you all about stealing. I can do that. You are my friend. But even friends have to sometimes pay their teachers. In prison, I

had a cellmate and he was my friend. He taught me a lot about stealing and burglary. But he had a price. Naturally I wanted to know how many cigarettes he wanted. Mario said, no cigarillos, just suck. Well, Sonny I had a problem. I didn't want to suck a guy's cock, but Mario was a really good burglar and I really wanted to know what he knew and almost everyone in the pen fucks, sucks or, if you are the lowest, takes it in the ass. So, I just asked him, how do we do this? Mario surprised me by reaching down and grabbing my groin and then pushing me back on the bunk, pulled my zipper down and reached in and pulled out my cock. I thought that I had misunderstood him and that maybe he with his bad English meant he wanted to suck my prick. What happened was he jacked me off till I blew cum all over his hands and my clothes. I thought it was over when, he unzipped, pull out his cock and stuck it in my face. "You turn, gringo bitch." So, after paying tuition every night after lights out, I got a Master's degree from Mario U. Sounds bad, but sucking cock isn't really that bad. But every ex-con will lie to your face and swear on their mother's ass that they never bit the tubesteak. I would really like us to be close like me and Mario was; I will play with your dick if you're nice to mine. Whadda say?" As Luke was seducing Sonny, he reached down and started rubbing Sonny's dick and Sonny's dick immediately went into a granite erection. Luke thought he had reached home plate, when Sonny said, "Maybe someday we can do that, but right now I have an idea. I know a cocksucker that will suck both our dicks. He is thin, wears thick glasses, has long golden hair, looks pretty much like a girl and will suck, catch and swallow. We can drive by the junior college campus where he hangs out, and if we see him tell him that after class we want to party. I guarantee, you'll love the way he will roll his tongue on your dick and gulps down that jizz. I make him twist his tongue up like a hollow little cum tube and when I blow my wad I push the head of my cock on the tip of his tongue and shoot that hot cum down that tube. Makes me so horny just thinking about it. Whadda think?" "You're a terrible man, Sonny, but count me in. Shit my dick's getting a little hard itself, let's vamos."

They were lucky on the first cruise by, Tommy was curbside chatting with the girls, "probably talking about the cocks they had sucked or fucked last nite", Sonny joked. Sonny had Luke pull up curbside then getting Tommy's attention, motioned for Tommy to come over to the truck. "Hi bitch, after class, how would you like to take a ride and meet my friend Luke? I've been telling Luke all about you and he's excited to meet you. You can see the cool crib where we hang out, and we'll drive you back to the campus or drop your off at home. OK?" "Sonny, I really don't want to." "Tommy if you're not standing here at the curb at 3:30 I will find you and beat the shit out of you, understand cocksucker?" "OK Sonny, but you gotta promise not to hurt me and bring me back to the campus after we see your house?" "Just be here you ass wipe." At 3:30, as commanded, Tommy was waiting like the fear chained slave he was, at the exact spot. Luke's old beat up chevy was a front seater with a bench seat. The kids that witnessed the truck were all similarly thinking "Tommy's mom sent the gardener to pick him up", until they saw Sonny get out and push Tommy in. They knew that sweet Tommy was shortly going to be dining on the weinerwich with a side of hot, creamy gravy. As Luke put the truck into gear, Sonny said "Tommy this is Luke and Luke likes girly boys that can suck dick real good. I told him that you sucked like a Hoover vacuum. I told him how I taught you to roll your tongue over the head and to spear that tongue into the tip. I told him how you gently drag your teeth on the cock as you slide your lips up and down. I told him how I like it when you open your mouth and let me see you gargle the cum before you swallow it. Luke wants it all. You better not make a liar out of me, understand?" "Yes, Sonny."

When they got to the junk yard, several of the workers were still moving wrecked cars to the crusher line or were busy stripping the newer ones for the high aftermarket dollar parts they contained. Luke knew a place in the back that had had been stripped over so many times that there were no parts worth retrieving and with no money sitting on the tree, no one ever had a reason to go back there. Driving down a row of stacked wrecks, the

truck stopped in a dead end lane, walled in by old rusting wrecks with an area just wide enough for his truck to turn around in. Sonny opened the door, hopped out and grabbed Tommy by his thin fragile arm and dragged him across the seat and down to the weed covered ground. "Get all those clothes off, you little queer cocksucker." "Please Sonny, no and you said you weren't going to hurt me." "Strip down or I guarantee you will be sorry." Terrorized of the consequence of disobeying, Tommy dropped his pants and underwear. "The tops too." Off came his shirt and tee shirt. "Look Luke, you ever see a dick that small? It's gotta be a record. Someone would have to jump up and down on his ass if he ever wanted to fuck a woman and for her to feel it. I can almost see tiny titties growing, look, his nipples are hard. Now, Tommy I want to see you jackoff." Tommy was surprised; Sonny had never asked him to beat off before, why? Trying to avoid violence, Tommy gently began pulling and pushing on his micro cock. Sometimes at home, he fantasized at mouth fucking and gagging his overbearing mother or fucking that cute girl Laura who was always nice to him and never taunted or made fun of his problems with the boys; or of Tony the boy with the long thin dick. Tommy wished that the other boys would leave him alone and he could just suck Tony; Tommy really, really liked Tony. Tony was so kind and he always was polite when he asked if Tommy could fool around and Tony never made fun of him or hurt him. Thinking again about how nice it would be to fuck Laura or to suck Tony, Tommy's cock began to rise. "Look, Luke the little fuck is getting a hard on. He must be dreaming about my dick. Maybe he could use a little help, what do you think Luke?"

Luke smiled at Sonny and walked behind Tommy and reached around and began playing with Tommy's nipples. On a lark Luke, reached down and pushing Tommy's' flogging hand aside and just using his thumb and index fingers began to play with Tommy's' little cock. "Damn it, it's really getting hard, look Sonny the little bitch is getting a genuine diamond cutter hard on." Luke worked those two fingers rapidly back and forth and with a

moan, Tommy's infant size penis shot a singular jet of cum 2 feet into space. "Well, I'll be damned; the bitch actually had a wad to shoot."

"Now, Tommy watching my friend play with your cock gave me an idea. Instead of doing one at a time, you are going to do two at a time; one in your mouth and one in your asshole. Has anyone fucked you in the ass yet, tell me before I get mad." "Sonny that tattooed Mexican, the JC campus maintenance guy caught me sucking Joey in the shed and ran Joey away and that Mexican said that if I didn't want him to tell the Dean and my parents I had to be nice to him. He took me in the maintenance room, locked the door, pulled my pants down, put vasoline on my ass and his dick, and stuck a rag in my mouth. I almost died, the pain was so bad. He just grabbed my hips, put the head of his big dick on my ass and jammed the monster into me. He wasn't gentle about it and didn't try to softly slide it in, he really jammed it in. That was so painful, it hurt, I was crying it hurt so much. I think I fainted, because when I came to he was just pulling his cock out of my ass and I could feel his cum dripping down on my balls. From that day, every time he got a chance he would drag me in the shed and do it again. He fucked me a lot since then. Once he fucked me twice in the same day. After a dozen times, my ass got bigger and it didn't hurt so bad. Whenever he said 'tamale time' I knew he wanted it. I did get even, one afternoon after he had squeezed my nuts so hard I could barely walk, I went to the pay phone and reported him to immigration. The next day a van showed up and three guys handcuffed him and threw Mr, Lopez in the van and he hasn't been back since. The new maintenance man, Mr. Singh is bi-sexual and actually sucks my dick once in a while. I like Mr. Singh a lot."

"Tommy we're gonna introduce you to a threesome. Know what that is? Well, here's what you're gonna do, first you're gonna bend over and take your hands and spread your ass cheeks and I'm gonna slide my dick into your asshole, second you're gonna lean forward and take Luke's cock in your mouth. Every time I slam my cock you're gonna slide your mouth

forward on his dick all the way to his belly and every time I pull backwards, you're gonna slide up to the head of Luke's dick. Each time you fuck up I'm gonna squeeze or smack your balls, got it?" "Honest, Sonny, I'll do my best, please don't hurt me." With that Sonny lunged forward and could hear Tommy gasp, but fearful of the consequence, Tommy pushed forward engulfing the total length of Luke's cock." Luke came first and Tommy forever fearful, allowed all Luke's semen to collect on his tongue, and once Luke's well was dry, looked up at Luke, opened his mouth, gargled the cloudy cream colored protein, and gulped it past his tonsils. "Damn he's good Sonny. You broke him in good." Sonny meanwhile was hanging onto Tommy's hips and driving his dick in and out of Tommy's entrails. With a loud groan, Sonny pushed forward hard enough to push Tommy's face into the ground. "Fuck that felt good. Luke you gotta try it, this little fuck machine has still got a pretty tight asshole and it feels like its massaging your cock, squeezing your cock, forcing the last drops out of your cock. I think I can understand some of that prison talk now."

After Tommy had cleaned all the spent jizz from the two dicks, as he was putting his clothes back on, Tommy said "Sonny you promised to drive me back to the campus. Can we go back now, please?" "Sure bitch, now hop in the middle." As they started towards the highway, Sonny had an idea. "Tommy, you're not done yet. Pull your pants down, now." "But I just put them back on Sonny." "Shut the fuck up and do as you're told, your cum hungry bitch." One look into Sonny's eyes and he knew if he hesitated Sonny would really get mad. Complying, "What do you want me to do, Sonny, tell me what and please don't hurt me." Luke smiled and was just as surprised as Tommy when Sonny with a sudden movement punched Tommy in his balls. Tommy just moaned and tried to bend forward. Sonny pushed him back against the car seat and grabbed one of Tommy's balls and squeezed, then crushed it in his grip. The pain was so intense that Tommy could not scream, just moan. Sonny grabbing both balls with his right hand and Tommy's little dick with his left, began a clockwise motion

twisting the balls in the ball sack and a counter clock wise motion twist with the dick. Tommy had no idea that pain could be this bad. When the Mexican groundskeeper raped him first semester, he thought that was terrible, but that was nothing compared to this. The pain was so great, he couldn't even get the beg words out. "You are one cold motherfucker, yes sir, a cold motherfucker" Luke laughed. Releasing the captured balls and cock, Sonny reached beneath the seat and pulled out a broken floor shifter stalk with an ivory oval phallic shape shifter handle. "Motherfucker, this is going in your ass, now scoot around and get that ass up." "Please Sonny you already hurt my ass bad please don't push that in me, please." "Do it" snapped Luke. Forcing Tommy's head down on the floor board, and pulling back and up on his balls got Tommy's lily white ass bent at just the right angle. Spreading the ass cheeks with his left hand, Sonny began shoving and forcing that thin, oval handle millimeter by millimeter, into Tommy's protesting rectum. Tommy began screaming, really screaming. Luke took his right hand from the steering wheel and in a hammer like drive, hit Tommy on the back of his head as hard as he could, mercifully knocking him unconscious. With Tommy out, his sphincter muscles relaxed, Sonny was, after a number of hard thrusts, able to completely push that shift rod into the bowels of Tommy's lower abdomen. "Little cocksucker deserves it, don't you think Luke?" "In prison the little punk would have had barbell rods pushed up his ass so many times, he would have hopped around looking like a popsicle." "You know, Luke, I really liked hurting him; that was sorta fun." "Sonny, pull it out and let's drop him off in the first alley we come too. The ghetto boys will know exactly what to do with him when they find him, wadda say? Don't forget to grab his wallet." "Let's do it."

Tommy was discovered, still partially unconscious, by a patrolling police unit and an ambulance was called to convey the bloody ass young man to the hospital. The cops didn't think too much of it; "another honky down here for dope got caught out of his car and the home boys done stole his wallet and his car, then showed him an ass party. Least they didn't cut his

white ass throat." Tommy survived, was taken to the emergency ward for surgery, the cops finding a ID in his front pocket, notified his mother, and had his mother by his side holding his hand for the five days that he spent in the recovery room. When Tommy was released, she couldn't get him away from that hospital fast enough. She knew what the nurses and doctors were smiling about. Her poor little man had been raped by animals and they joked about it. It could happen to anyone. Her precious, sensitive little boy was defenseless in a world of predators. When she had first found out exactly what the circumstances and nature of what the injuries suggested, she refused to accept the obvious, decided that it would be best to ask no further questions and remain silent. After she had put it all together, she thought it was so smart of her little boy Tommy to tell the police that he was grabbed from behind and never saw the thugs who abused him. After she picked him up, she drove him straight back to the safety of the sensitive bubble civilization in their home.

The stiches were removed one week after the surgery. It took Tommy two weeks to convalesce to a point where he could return to and function normally on campus. The word was out; the girls treated him special, the professors with a smirk, made a special effort to see he was not bullied, and the new dick sucking janitor, Mr. Singh, was especially kind to him. Tommy could not wait to get away from all these hypocritical motherfuckers, that either were forcing their cocks down his throat, laughing at his effeminate curse, or was using his balls as a handle to jam their cocks deeper in his ass. Tommy prayed for Sonny and Luke's death. He had been so disappointed as he looked so forward to the start of his sophomore year and so forward to a fresh start on this new university campus with the new faces, only to discover that rumors and reputations often precede people. Had he known, Tommy would have been shattered that his reputation had preceded him, and within 24 hours of watching his mother's taillights as she dropped him off and tucked him in, Tommy was discovered by the campus gay bunch. Within 72 hours of that drop off,

Tommy had found a semi-gay, handsome young black man that did so enjoy blasting ghetto cum down Tommy's throat. But there was a difference, Tommy finally accepting his lot and status in life told himself; "here, at least, I'm in control and I'm the one who decides whose cock I suck."

Afterwards for the rest of that sophomore school year, Tommy made every effort to avoid Sonny and tried to hide whenever he saw Sonny or Luke cruising. If they got under Tommy's radar and cornered him, the consequences were a bitch. Luke and Sonny were working on that friendship and raping Tommy was the common cement to that bond. After a few weekend trips where Sonny or Luke would corral and transport Tommy to a visit to the junk yard way back in that part of the yard that even the rats abandoned, and make him pop blowjobs or get ass fucked on the pickup rear seat, the friendship was cemented. Over the months of abuse Tommy seemed to reach a point where he less and less fought the inevitable and would beckon at Sonny's will with little complaint. Sonny even thought that Tommy was beginning to enjoy tube steak and that extra ounce or two of jizz sauce. If Tommy's mother (who refused to believe those ugly rumors circulated by those jealous crude boys) could have been witness to Tommy smiling with cum on his lips, face or golden tresses, she would have just died, for real just died, to know those ugly nasty rumors about her sweet little soldier boy allowing other young men to put their penises in his mouth or ass were true.

The income from a greaser and minder job of a junkyard does not put one into the high revenue stream of the economy. Luke was a very accomplished thief and burglar. Any items that had resale value, especially items that he could sell to the no questions asked, junkyard owner and was easily lost in inventory or turned over at a tailgate sale, was within the venue. Any home that was vacant during the daytime and had shrubbery around its side windows or doors were an open invitation for Luke's screwdriver to jimmy either a slider door or a side window.

The friendship with Luke launched Sonny into a career of criminality. When Sonny saw how exciting B&E was and how easy crime was to commit and how much crime could potentially pay, Sonny drifted to a career of crime. Sonny realized that thieves never got rich, but always scored enough money to pay a few bills and stay in cigarettes and beer (or drugs). His parents were destroyed and Auntie Mame could not understand what caused him to be a one percenter. Auntie Mame had much more patience and hope than his parents and after a series of arrests and police suspicions, his parents had banished Sonny from their house, Sonny was crashing at dear old Auntie Mame's house whenever money was short or he was ducking a loan shark. The sex was still wonderful. Mame was especially good at blowjobs and didn't mind when his cock occasionally lost its way and ended up throbbing deeply in her ass. She worshipped the way he ate pussy, especially when he would suck up her labia lips, sliding his long finger in and out and rubbing her clitoris with his free thumb. Mame would actually grow faint in ecstasy and pull on Sonny's hair for more. The occasional S&M trips were welcomed as a change of pace in their sexual depravities, provided Sonny kept within the boundaries that Mame lined out.

CHAPTER EIGHT

One afternoon, Luke told Sonny that he had cased a cottage and knew that the owner was a hunter and had several guns that they could easily sell and make a few dollars. The backyard had a wooden high fence and the cottage had a set of sliding back doors. The owner was an older single man that generally spent the afternoons down the block at the corner tavern. Luke had discovered this mark from a junk yard friend who occasionally drank with this guy. The friend did want a pistol if Luke did the burglary. Luke said it would be easy money, they would walk the alley one at a time, slip into the yard and with a screwdriver could easily jimmy the slider doors. Once they gathered the guns and any other saleable loot, Luke would get his truck, pull up to the back gate and Sonny could pitch everything into the truck bed and then off to the "fence". The plan went very well; the guns were there and there were also a coin collection, a stamp collection, and three hundred dollars that Sonny discovered in a coffee can. What Sonny and Luke hadn't counted on was an old spinster woman who spent most of her day peeking

out her curtains just to watch and see what the neighbors were doing. When she noticed Luke then Sonny slip into Jerry her neighbor's back yard, she knew they didn't belong and called the police, not once but five times. When Sonny heard the tires of a vehicle crunching the gravel in the alley, he gathered an armful of long guns and when he stepped into the alley, he looked directly into the barrel of a policeman's 12 gauge shotgun. Guilty as charged your honor. Luke had seen the cop car and in a survivor mode, never gave Sonny another thought, adios muchacho.

During his incarceration, he communicated with Auntie Mame's estate lawyer and had arranged for the lawyer to obtain certain things such as get him a furnished pad, with a big screen TV, some clothes, and to stock the refrigerator with the list of little treats prison life denied him. After serving his completed sentence full term, Sonny was interested in two things; a good steak dinner and some wild pussy. Hailing a cab at the prison gates, he headed for the modest condo where he had instructed the attorney to have a late model van parked, gassed up, and Department of Motor Vehicle legal with an envelope with fifteen hundred dollars in twenty dollar bills. Checking in with the condo receptionist clerk, he got the unit keys went to the condo and checked out the wardrobe the lawyer had chosen for him, decided on a nice clean cut pair of dark slacks and light blue shirt, threw all of his prison smelling clothes in the waste basket, and headed for the car. The first stop was an upscale chop house where he ordered a huge rib eye steak, complete with spinach salad, baked potato with all the toppings, and a frosty, ice cold beer. The meal was fantastic. After tipping the skinny little waitress twenty bucks, he hopped in the van and headed to a section of town where he knew for certain the whores would be walking the streets hooking for johns. This being his first time with a woman in years, Sonny wanted to choose someone with looks, blonde hair and big tits. He had to drive around the area for forty minutes before he finally saw a good looking girl in a mini skirt. Pulling alongside her, he powered down the window and said, "you working?" Looking at him through bored

eyes, "what do you think and what do you want?" "How much is head?" "Forty bucks and I don't take off my clothes but you can play with my tits, deal?" "Get in sweetie." It took but two or three minutes of ancient haggling dialogue to quickly discover that she wouldn't budge from her forty dollar quote, before both were smiling as they headed to her favorite hidden john servicing spot. Once she pointed to him where to park, Sonny had barely gotten the van in park before she was working his zipper open and rolling out his cock. "Nice cock partner, for another twenty I will catch and swallow otherwise it goes out the window, you on?" Sonny pulled some folded bills from his shirt pocket and handed her three crisp twenties; "you're on baby, make it good". After being in the pen so long and the only tits and lips he had were hairy or whiskered, it took Sonny but two minutes of her tongue, lips and throat to vacuum a tremendous ejaculation. The girl actually gagged. "Boy that was some load partner, now I need you to take me back to where you picked me up. When you are in need again, ask for Clara, everybody knows Clara."

While Sonny was resting across the bed in his condo scrolling with the TV remote, he was thinking "Great beginning, I only wish I could have tied her up and thrown her in the back for more fun later. Those titties felt so soft, gosh just thinking about them is making my dick get hard again. But good ole Clara drained the oil and that's all I needed now".

The lawyer bought used van ($14,999.00) was a great idea and an important component in the idea he had developed as part of his after prison release plan. It was a simple conclusion to recognize the value of impersonating a police officer and having a convincing enough vehicle to overcome any suspicions a victim might initially have.

Using police TV shows of authentic police vans as the template, Sonny was able to dress up and put together a setting that would likely fool even a veteran cop. Obviously impersonating as a uniformed police officer would be very risky, so he decided that impersonating a detective dressed in

slacks and a blazer would be more convincing and less of an optic flag as he drove the streets on his hunt.

The firearm was a much needed major prop. No police officer would ever face down a suspect without a drawn weapon or at least cradle his hand around the grips. Sonny was a felon. Being caught with a firearm in his possession meant an automatic arrest and ticket back to the big house. Sonny could not work the capture without at least a brief display, if nothing more than the opening of his blazer to allow the target the optics and suggestion of the power of a sidearm. "If I am caught, then likely it will be either for kidnapping or murder, the gun charge will be insignificant and if I hire a good criminal attorney, chances are he can plead it down as the prosecutor will be pushing for a death penalty anyway. The plus side is that I might even need to defend myself if a target goes crazy and berserk on me." It took but two stops in low rent area taverns for Sonny to find a guy with a .38 Special for sale. For $185.00 Sonny bought a five shot, nickel plated, snub nose revolver. A perfect, convincing prop, as it was definitely a weapon that many police detectives carried in either a shoulder holster or in a waist holster. It would immediately ease the mind of a target by connecting the pistol to legitimate police work. Another thought loomed in his mind, what if he stopped a target and that target turned out to be a police woman. A gun would be most handy then. Most police departments employed a number of women, trained and armed them, so the danger would always be there with that next stop, "is she or isn't she".

The van was another big problem, to prevent suspicion and struggles; it had to at first appear to any captive like a police department lockup vehicle. Everybody knew what paddy wagons were. So Sonny devoted extra care in its outfitting. He first had the interior customized with a wide bench directly behind the driver's seat ($455.65), and an expanded steel screen hinged wall ($248.90) between the driver compartment and rear. The bench was where the police always forced the arrested subjects to sit and they almost always with the more dangerous ones, shackled their legs

to the bench. Sonny with an eye for detail, had one inch eye-bolts welded to the steel bench seat frame ($35.25) and others welded and spaced one foot apart on the bench headrest ($42.75). The welder was curious and asked Sonny what the eye-bolts were for and Sonny said "I often times have to haul cylinders and will be using the eye-bolts for tie down points'. The answer was satisfactorily enough for the welder to move on with the work and to satisfy any additional curiosity regarding the project work. After the welding was finished, Sonny added a leg manacle shackle to each of the eye bolts. Of major importance was a red flashing dashboard light ($98.50) and a siren ($76.85) that he could tap the switch to alert a driver that she was being pulled over if she failed to respond to the roadside once the flashers were turned on.

In the reality of his plan, using an extra pair of official looking nickel plated handcuffs ($39.55@) Sonny had the option of using a second set of handcuffs after frontal handcuffing the victim's hands together, to first lock one cuff on the wrist binding handcuff link and then by locking the second cuff to the bench seat eye-bolt further secure any violently struggling victims' hands to the bench. Once the handcuff combination locked the target to the bench, Sonny could apply the ankle shackles. The target was now helpless and completely in Sonny's control. By now the target was suspicious and the questions, demands, insults, curses, and screams would begin. So, to further immobilize and frighten the victim Sonny could use a single short six foot piece of cord, knotting one end to a head rest eye-bolt, then passing and looping the cord tightly around the victim's neck and finally threading it through and knotting to the other eye-bolt. Always use braided cord, his cell mates said. Cord makes very tight non-slip knots, are tough to cut through, are impossible to chew through and are very difficult to abrade by rubbing against any rough surface. Properly tied, no one escapes braided cord. With the cord looped around her neck, any struggling by the victim would naturally tighten the cord enough to partially strangle the girl while she was in the van. This was an extremely

effective and proven silence producing method to keep a victim controlled.

Once the inside welding was done, Sonny moved on with a white spray painting to cover the bench, the security screen, and the wall vans. Sonny was blessed with a learned talent; years ago he did a short stint in an auto repair shop and during the five months he was able to stay employed, he worked in the spray booth. Sonny only needed five hours to completely change the color of a car and he was pretty good at it, no runs or color overlaps. Once all the metal was coated and the coating dried, Sonny ever so carefully applied to the inside wall a two foot diameter police decal ($250.00). This was the toughest item to get. First Sonny had to locate a printer that was willing to cut a police decal without an authorization letter signed by a police chief. Inquiring blindly from printer to printer shop would leave a trail that would lead directly back to Sonny, so Sonny knew he had to find a back door to get the decal. While in prison, Sonny had been told of an ex-con that was working in a print shop. Sonny remembered the con's name, Leo. It was a simple matter to call around until he found a Leo working in the print shop. Luckily on the fourth call the desk girl said yes, they had a Leo that worked there. Using a prison password, Sonny said "Miss would you mind telling Leo that Don Warbler (the warden's name and used as a con password) needed to speak to him about his sick Auntie."

Of course no one would ever deny anyone a phone call if there was the possibility of a sick relative. Several minutes later when Leo picked up the phone receiver and said "I don't have an Auntie asshole, so what do you want?" it was Sonny's turn to gamble that this ex-con was bitter about life and needed to make a few extra bucks. "Leo, my name is Sonny and you and I know the same good people. I need to talk to you and if you can call me after work, I can explain. There's some money in it for your and there's no risk. Can we do this?" So Sonny left Leo his telephone number and at almost exactly 5:30 pm the phone rang. "Is this Sonny and where do I know

you from?" "Yes this is Sonny and no you don't know me, but I know your old cellmate, Wizzer and he told me all about you. I was wondering if you might be interested in making a little side money when the boss wasn't watching." Afraid of a parole officer's sting, Leo said, "I need a face to face before we can talk about anything, OK. I know you understand." Sonny said "fine, can we meet later tonight, say around 8 pm at the Dairy Queen on Main?" "Sure can, how will I recognize you?" "Easy, probably won't be a lot of traffic in the restaurant; I am an ex-con and will look like an ex-con, but if you have trouble Leo, I'm 5'10", no fat, with black hair and will be wearing an old sweater and a windbreaker with the collar turned up. So, Leo, I don't think you will have any trouble figuring out who I am."

When the project was explained to Leo, and that it would pay $250.00, Leo agreed but he agreed to do the job only on condition, just in case anyone got the wiser, that he could alter something in the logo to make the decal less than official. Sonny had no problem with that and specified that a minor change be made in the background of the shield. "I'll have it ready by the weekend, call me Saturday night and bring all of the money, no short stacks OK." "No problem here Leo, talk to you then." It was ready just as Leo said and it was exactly what Sonny wanted. The Plus was that Leo asked no questions, just took the money and walked away. All cons know how dangerous it is to be curious. In the pen, people get shivved every day for asking too many questions.

Sonny decided that a few props would add to the counterfeit stage. He bought a white police type riot helmet ($18.55) that came with the word "POLICE" printed on the front head piece. The helmet he would just leave rolling around on the van floor, just in the spot you were likely to find it in a real police van. A hand held police scanner radio ($29.99) was very, very important both for an audio presence and for Sonny to be able to track area police responses. To add to its value he plugged in a hand held mike ($4.99) into the speaker port. If anyone questioned why there were no police markings on the outside of the van, Sonny was prepared to tell them

that the van was used in undercover and suspect lockup work and it would be rather silly to have a van with the words POLICE on its side while trying to convince a drug dealer to sell them dope. Sonny did not intend for his victim's to get enough time to pay attention to what was or wasn't on the outside of the van. Sonny was ready to rock and roll.

Then there was the matter of the inherited hunting farm. There was very little improvement to do the lodge. The lawyer took care of all the title transfer work, had the electricity renamed to the new trust (the lawyer convinced Sonny how it important it was to have tax deductible trust expenses), hired a commercial cleaning firm and handyman husband and wife team from two hundred fifty miles away and had them purge the rusty water from all the water lines and hot water tanks, vacuum and dust, restock the pantry and refrigerator, and get the TV system reconnected to the local network. With Uncle Buck's careful eye for appointment and the lawyer's subsequent care, the home did not want for anything. Sonny was really impressed with the professional but expensive, charge the client for everything, lawyer. The first night sitting on the front porch, drinking a cold beer, Sonny was amazed as the darkness and solitude; there was nothing out there, nothing but lonely blackness. The dark surrounding national forest would tell no stories about the future sufferings within his den of despair. Sonny smiled, a few more days and it was time to put his plan in operation.

In prison, Sonny had originally and very carefully developed a method of abduction and body disposal that in fantasy even had a few bugs. Uncle Buck's inheritance property overcame many of those bugs. Body disposal would be a breeze with that giant tree limb shredder. Transporting a dead person and/or found bodies with their inevitable clues were the link that usually spelled the downfall of a serial killer. To overcome the shortcomings, he continually refined it and by the fifth target had eventually polished it to such a degree that had over the years it been proven to be so reliable that he seldom if ever was tempted to deviate the

slightest from it. Police impersonation was a guaranteed winner. Young women victims were trained to always heed and follow the commands of a man in law enforcement; decades of exposure to institutional training seasoned them that a police badge meant safety and protection. Few victims would ever doubt the integrity of a man with a badge and van displaying police trappings. All was ready for the stalk and hunt.

In prison, Sonny spent many hours in the prison exercise yard, asking question after question of Vinnie a convicted serial rapist, who was presently serving 55 years for raping and sodomizing a long string of victims. Vinnie enjoyed a long career of victimizing women and had quite an accomplished modus operandi.

Vinnie's preferred method of crime was the residential invasion. His home invasion tools were simple and relatively inexpensive; duct tape ($6.99), several packs of condoms ($6.55) a screwdriver ($2.79), a small, 22 caliber pistol ($55.00) bought from a burglar friend in a tavern, a pair of socks ($1.49), a pair of surgical gloves ($0.79), a nylon ski mask ($0.99), and a small flask filled with bleach ($4.99 and $1.25). As the proverbial saying goes, looks can be deceiving; Vinnie had a disarming looking boyish face, a person that you would expect to see attending church, or a smiling cherubic face center file in a boy scout troop or choir picture. His face was mounted on a 5'6" muscular 165 pound frame. Vinnie had soft brown eyes, eyes that concealed a pure evil devil's mind. In high school Vinnie excelled at the physical aspects of contact sports and was always the one drawing penalties for unnecessary roughness or personal fouls. Vinnie was friendly but a loner, careful never to let anyone get close enough to discover the dark side.

In high school, Vinnie rarely dated, and girls during lunch table discussions of who was doing who, or who dumped who, or what they had let their boyfriends do to them or what they had done to their boyfriends, collectively wondered why a boy so handsome as Vinnie was not, like even

the meekest of the geek crowd, always on the pookie hunt. All he had to do was ask and anyone, from the glamour queen to the official dog, would have jumped at the opportunity to date and explore that Adonis body.

On the few occasions when he did ask someone out, the naturally shared postdating informational chatter was that he was disgustingly polite, kissed like a brother and disappointingly failed to attempt to sneak his fingers into their bra cups or lacey panties like the other sex desperate date animals. Vinnie was usually a conversation date only, he certainly proved to be a passionless stud. Unbeknownst to the dating pool, Vinnie knew that a handful of warm tit or a finger in someone's sweet spot would not even begin to satisfy the desires that smothered so secretly, deeply and intensely within him. These high school girls were minor leaguers and if he ever began to try to initiate them into the levels and acts of sexual gratification and depravity that his dark side demanded, he was sure that there would be big trouble with the girl, her parents and the police. Vinnie had a higher major league level of great expectations; these bitches were all minor leaguers.

Vinnie was well beyond his age in sexual matters; legions ahead of everyone in his age group and legions ahead of even most adults. The acquisition of such knowledge did not come from the cheap paperback fuck books that young boys respect as "how to" manuals, but from real, skin to skin experience. You might actually say that Vinnie had been tutored by and gotten his Masters in a carnality degree from a mistress of the dark arts. Vinnie had and kept a very big secret; he had a very talented instructor, an older cousin, Lacey, a kiss'n cousin that lived just three houses down the block. She was born, like Vinnie, with a damaged gene containing an insatiable urge, a hidden and caged beast, a beast that once unleashed could be very frightening and insatiable. As she got older and her body matured, she gradually became more aware of the dark beast inside her, the circumstances of her birth and sibling and cousin exploitation furnished her the environment and the easy opportune

pathway to discovery, first the more sensual sexual pleasures of normal sex and then gradually lead to the more accomplished levels of deviant behavior. Eventually, there were to be no boundaries in Lacey's thirst for more.

One afternoon, when Lacey was fifteen and Vinnie was thirteen, and they found themselves alone on a very boring afternoon, Lacey asked Vinnie what fun games he could think of. Vinnie spouted "Strip poker, if you have the nerve." "Get the cards and I'm gonna whip your ass naked as a jay bird cousin." After a half hour of serious play, Vinnie was down to his shorts and Lacey only lost her blouse and pants. "Next hand I get to see your tiny dick and you ain't gonna see nothing of mine, loser." "Gee cuz, I really got some bad hands, I don't think it's fair, but deal." Three minutes later, three aces to his two pair, Vinnie started peeling his shorts down his legs. "Hurry, I wanna see what you got in the locker, bet it's as small as my little finger." "Lacey, are you in for a big surprise." With that, he dropped his shorts and exposed a man's cock, way bigger that brother Jake's. Vinnie could almost feel her eyes burning into his flesh. Lacey definitely was looking and maybe, just maybe interested in more than just looking. "You weren't kidding, Vin, how big is it when it gets hard?" she asked. "I need to see too, pop those big tits out I have been dreaming about for years and let's see that puss too." Lacey needed no further invitation. In a blink, she unsnapped her bra releasing both tits to flop and with a little encouraging body twist, do their jello shake. Ogling her gloriously vibrating pleasure mounds, Vinnie's eyes grew saucer large and he started hyperventilating; Lacey thought he was going to pass out, but he managed to strangle out, "and the panties too." As she slowly rolled her panties down her legs, exposing first the top of her bearded oasis of treasure and then teasing and torturing him by slowly exposing the boldness and nakedness of her vagina, she could actually see Vinnie's dick growing. "Now we got something interesting to play with" she thought.

"What do you think, cock boy? We have the house for at least another hour, how about some games that I like to play? Now bring that big dick over her and let momma make a flagpole." Vinnie was in total shock, here he was, standing naked in front of his first cousin, about to get a super hard on and wishing he could suck on her tits, lick her pussy and plunge his cock into that warm friendly honey pot and she seemed as eager as he to explore each other. One embarrassing thing that Vinnie immediately brought up on his personal radar, was that the only sex Vinnie had was TV soft porn and jacking off to girlie magazines; should her tell her, yes or no, he wondered. Lacey suspected Vinnie was a zero in the cock hound department, so she shrewdly took the decision away from him "Come over here, despite all your sex experience, I'm gonna take you through finishing school and teach you everything about sex you ever wanted to know and some things you never even heard of, now get that dick over here and let's get the school started." Over a period of several weekends, they covered all the standards, and expanded the curriculum to S&M, little ouchies at first and gradually, when they both had a greater appreciation and tolerance for pain, into some pretty major league stuff.

Lacey loved to experiment with sex and the dark side and never ever said no to anything Vinnie suggested they explore. Many, many times she was the lead. Lacey even bought Vinnie two, one dollar and fifty cent S&M paperback fuck books to spice, entice and spur the yearning in his loins. Lacey was fifteen years old, was big breasted on a small and slim frame. While not beautiful, she was cute in a pixyish way. She was as street smart as a whip. Lacey could easily be labeled a "nymph" the vision most young men often dreamed about in their solo sex hours under the blanket and as their cocks jetted streams of semen into their sibling's sock or sister's panties. Lacey had in turn been taught by her off the norm bubble, older brother, Jake, who, when not awake, in school, or otherwise physically occupied, existed in a fantasy world of sex trash magazines and fuck novels.

It took very little convincing for big brother Jake to open the frontiers of fornication. Being two years older than Lacey, and they being turnkey children, it was but little conquest dominating his younger sister. It began by simple steps, first the shower; when Lacey was taking her shower Jake would find some reason to enter the bathroom and remain there talking about silly things and then jokingly refusing to leave when Lacey was ready to towel dry. Lacey did enjoy the way Jake would stare at her body with those laser beady, staring eyes. At ten, Lacey had breasts that most teenage girls would have given fortunes to have. Lacey did enjoy the pleasure sensation when her breasts would respond to gravity motion by sending waves of sensuous vibrations throughout the soft tissue. Occasionally she would exercise naked in the front of her bedroom mirror. The flops and ripples in her breasts were just wonderfully stimulating to look at and it took very little for her woman lubricant to start flowing and creating that special feeling in her vagina. Once the beast awoke, Lacey was almost powerless to resist its demands that usually took a furiously vibrating thumb and probing finger to quiet it, satisfy it, and return it to its hibernation.

Being the child of a swinging couple, Lacey had a kick start in the sexual awareness and sex ed department. It began when Lacey was ten; her mind was matured far above the normal level of a ten year old girl. At ten she had witnessed many times her parents thrashing on each other's body, over heard all the lurid commands and requests, and had actually seen both engage in oral sex. One night when she was supposed to be staying at a neighborhood friends' sleep over, she got bored and snuck back into the house by an overlooked unlocked kitchen door. She almost blurted out in surprise, when hearing the obvious sounds of a loud party in the living room, she realized mom and dad were in the middle of a swinger's party. Quickly she hid beneath the skirting of the old style kitchen sink. She kept the sink curtain skirting ever so slightly opened and was able to observe all the naked bodies as they wandered in and out of the kitchen to refresh

drinks or grab a snack. She was shocked to see a teacher from school come out in the kitchen with a man and allowed the man to push her onto a table and begin to orally explore her vagina. Several other people wandered into the room and watched. When the teacher climaxed, several applauded and joked about the man's unique technique applying a tonguewich to both the teacher's vagina and anus. After the kitchen emptied her mother led the neighbor from down the street over to that same table, pushing him against the table, she dropped to her knees and began to swallow his huge cock. As she was trying to drain him, daddy walked through the kitchen door with a man she had never seen before. The man steered her dad over to the table and pushed him next to the man mother was still trying to suck dry. Dropping to his knees, the man began to suck daddy's cock. Lacey could not believe what she was seeing, a sex party in her house and people getting off on the very table the family had meals at. What a terrible thought forward. As soon as the kitchen emptied, Lacey crept out of the house and ran back to the sleepover, wisely choosing to keep what she just saw a secret, telling everyone that she had just needed a little walk. The sights she witnessed intrigued her and on a dozen or so more occasions, Lacey was able to secrete herself beneath the sink and casually observed the sexual frenzies happening on that table.

At twelve, her body had also developed large breasts and her vagina now had a sparse but healthy growth of soft pubic hair. Lacey was now at the threshold of womanhood. One afternoon, after helping her brother cut the grass, Lacey decided to do a shower. When she finished rinsing the soap and shampoo from her body, she slid the glass shower door open and not that surprised to see her brother sitting on the toilet seat watching her body like a cat eyes a mouse. Naked and dripping water she grabbed for a towel and quickly covered her breasts. "Did you get an eye full Jake?" "No, I didn't and I want to see just a little more Sis." With that he suddenly reached out and grabbed and stripped the towel from her body. She screamed, "I'll tell mom." "No you won't cause I know what you and that

asshole you been playing with have been doing. I watched you let him play with your tits and I saw you rub his cock. You think Mom would be happy about that, to know her twelve year old daughter was touching someone's cock, huh?" "Fuck you Jake." "Damn those are great tits and I got a hard on looking at your hairy pussy, Sis." "That's all you ever gonna do is look, asshole."

From the narrative of that first shower episode forward, Jake was like a hound baying a rabbit; relentlessly and at every opportunity, he brushed against her breasts and behind. He never missed a moment to suggest nasty things they could do together. He put fuck books under her pillow. One night out of boredom when Lacey was reading a particularly juicy part of a brother/sister incest novel, Lacey noticed that her vagina was especially afloat with lubricant. She was always surprised that the beast would find stimulation in typewritten words. Touching herself, she really enjoyed how nice her finger felt tracing up and down the wrinkles of her twin labias. She also noticed that her body and mind had a craving and a finger or two were not always going to satisfy the creature that she had awakened. Maybe Jake had the right idea, and besides who would tell. Mom would pitch them both out of the house if she even thought they were thinking about mutual sex, much less discovered that they were having an incestuous affair. If Lacey weakened and allowed Jake to seduce her, forever forward they would have to be very careful lovers and guard the secrets of that sex.

Jake made a habit of wandering into the shower as she soaped and washed. He would just sit on the toilet seat and make very lurid comments about what they could do together and where he could take her on the passion road. After the fifth or sixth shower, Jake grabbed the towel and refused to give it to her and insisted on drying her body. While drying her body, Jake's fingers would slip from the towel and slowly drag across her nipples or slide up and down her vagina. Lacey was discovering an unknown heat in her breasts and vagina generating from his fingertips and

a sudden overwhelming desire for more. Her body welcomed those tiny electric pulses and she wanted, no needed more of those forbidden sensual feelings. She became aware of an unusual amount but so familiar wetness in her vagina, a wetness that felt so good. Once Jake finished drying her body, he asked her how she liked it and maybe, if she did like it, just maybe there were more things that he could teach her. Lacey confessed that it was fun and she did like it. With their parents due home from work in a half hour, Jake said that tomorrow, if she showered after mom and dad left for the evening, he might teach about some other fun things. When Jake left, Lacey put her finger to her vagina and was surprised at how easily it slipped in with the lubrication up and down over her hymen. Lacey not only thought of those fingers and those touches burrowing in her body and the feelings that they ignited, but dreamed about it that night as well.

Lacey was so eager for that shower that she realized her vagina was flowing again with the slippery natural body lubrication that Jake's fingers had created yesterday. Jake knocked on her door and said "shower time if you are game." Like a shot, Lacey was there and pushing Jake aside, laughed as she entered the bathroom. She turned the shower taps on. She was always careful to get that special temperature so the water had to be just right, neither too hot nor too cold. Turning, she was aghast, Jake already had his blue jeans and shorts off, and was pulling his dick up and down.

She was no stranger to Jake's dick. Over the years, whenever he had the chance, Jake would flash her. Usually, as he ran around the house, just like dad, in his underwear, sometimes he would pretend he wasn't trying to attract her attention and he would sit positioning his leg just so, that his cock and balls hung freely out of the open leg of his boxer shorts. With his hanging dick and balls exposed, he would try to catch her eyes (that was never a problem as she would always look) and smile, shifting only if anyone else entered the room. She had never seen his dick in a hard

condition. Today she was looking at a man's erection. Jake was blessed, just like dad and grandpa, with a bragging size prick. The average man's dick is between 4 and 5 inches; his inherited family jewel was 8 inches and thin, with a large mushroom head that almost leered at her whenever it was free of his underwear.

Jake commanded her to remove her night clothes, piece by piece and slowly. Lacey slowly unbuttoned her nightie top, button by button, until she got to the top button and then, enjoying the theatre, slowly opened her top and slid her arms out. She did something that she had seen movie stars do, she flexed her arms backward and jutted out her breasts towards her brother and shook them. Jake moaned. She smiled. This was her first discovery of the power she would later use in life whenever she wanted control or needed something from a man. Lacey then untied her rope string belt for her nightie bottom, she let it slowly coast down her legs. She then put her hands on her hips with her feet apart to display in all her pre-womanly splendor and grandeur, her breasts and vagina with its inviting prepubescence downy hair. Jake moaned again, and was actually stoking his dick. "I'm jumping in the shower, what's next Jake. You said you were going to teach me something, well, big man, are you or are you not?"

It took Jake but seconds to slip out of his tee shirt and push into the shower with her. "When do we start?" "Right now sis, I am going to soap your entire body first." Jake began to slide the soap over her back and down her buttocks, where he slid his fingers through and between the cheeks of her ass. When he got to her anus, she suddenly felt his soap lubricated finger gliding into her rectum. "Oh, Jake that hurts a little, it's so tight there." "Sis, in one minute, after I get some more soap there, it's gonna feel fine." Jake reached over to the soap shelf and grabbed his father's shaving creme; he sprayed a pillow of white foam on his hand and then pushed it against and into her ass. This time with the super lubrication of the shaving creme, his finger, in fact two fingers plunged with no trouble or pain as

deep as they could into her ass. "How's that feel sis." "It doesn't hurt and it feels strange, real strange, but I kinda like it."

Lacey began to feel an almost electric charge igniting and racing through to her mind, her nipples, and her vagina. After finger fucking her ass for several minutes and with her beginning to make small moaning sounds, he gently pulled his fingers free and then grabbing and holding her by her shoulders, mindful of a slippery shower deck, carefully turned Lacey around, face to face. "Look at my cock." She did. "That's a lot bigger than when you let it hang out of your underwear. Why do you do that, show me your dick?" "I like to see you look at it Sis." "Yeah, I've seen it a thousand times, so what does it do for you, really?" "Well, this is kinda embarrassing, sis." "Tell, me, please." "Well, after you look at it, it starts to grow and get hard and I come here in the bathroom or my room and jackoff. Do you know what jack offing is?" "Yes, I do, one of the girls at school has a brother that jack offs all the time, she has seen him. She told us, he gets a nasty book or dirty picture and pulls his dick back and forth until it shoots out something she called jizz. She says it smells and is slimy. Does you dick shoot out jizz too?" "Well, sis that is something you are about to see." "Go ahead and touch it." With that invitation, he glided her hand to his cock where, like a magnet to a metal bar, her fingers tightly wrapped around it with a death grip. It was hard and it was hot. She really liked the feel of that cock, the way the looseness of his dick sheath skin allowed her fingers to slide up and down. To increase the fun and expand the lesson, she traced her fingers around the tight and stretched head and then through the little slot at the bottom that leads to the tiny spout opening. This was something that she wanted to do more things to. Taking her hand from his dick, Jake told her to place both arms around his neck. "Why?" "Sis I have to remove something that will forever prevent you from really being a woman and from experiencing some of the things I want to teach you. There will be a little pain, but I promise you that you will never, ever regret it. You game, sis." "Full speed ahead, this is so exciting I can't wait."

With that being said Jake again went to the shaving creme can and sprayed a blob of soapy creme onto his fingers, he spread the white lubricant over her pubic area and pushed as much of it as he could into the folds of her vagina. "Ready sis?" "Let's do it!" Grabbing her behind her lower back with his left hand, Jake used his right hand to jam two fingers into her vagina as hard as he could. He could feel her body tense up and push back against the digital invasion. He immediately felt the hymen break as his fingers plunged into a never before explored space. "Ouch" she blurted out, "that hurt a little, but the pain seems to have almost disappeared now and it just burns a little. I'm bleeding a little but nowhere near the flow that happens when I have my period. Am I going to be OK now?" Retracting his fingers, "you sure are, never again do we have to break into your vault, now it's whenever you want to let somebody or something poke inside you, your pussy is ready to gobble it up."

In that single two hour late night bathroom session and long before their parents returned home, that incestuous brother and walking encyclopedia of sex, Jake, introduced his equally and eagerly incestuous sister to getting her pussy eaten, missionary fucking, dog style fucking, tongue rimming the asshole, anal fucking, blowjobs, catching (getting the whole stream of jizz in the mouth), bubbling (opening the mouth and gargling the semen) and every man's delight, smiling and swallowing that oozy mess of pale protein. Lacey knew from her first taste that she could matter of fact and without reservation or a single gag, take that salty protein down in one welcome gulp. She also discovered, a surprise to Jake as well, that she could take the entire length of Jake's cock past her tonsils and deep into her throat without gagging. Jake made a point of explaining that if she swallowed a boy's cum she would never need to worry about becoming pregnant. He even explained the danger of anal ejaculation, as when the boy was backing his cock out, a string of cum was likely dripping from his dick and could slide down to her vagina and swim its way up to her egg. Better safe than pregnant. This was but the first of their afternoon sessions. Lacey

went to bed that night with some slightly sore portals, but with a new creature prowling her thoughts and dreams. The lessons of lust never closed for the pair. They preferred sex with each other to sex with inexperienced classmates or girlfriends. Even during her periods, Jake always had a Plan B, mouth or ass, either of which Lacey had no objection to whatsoever.

By thirteen, with a woman's body, full boobs and a vagina surrounded by a full forest of soft pubic hair, Lacey and her brother could put the Kama Sutra to shame. Brother Jake was a cockhound first class and could never get enough of his sister's body. Jake had a cock that was always ready. Jake joked one time "sis you know when you cough it makes my dick hard." That was almost true. Lacey giggled and imagined that if that wasn't a totally true statement, it was close, very, very close. It was always play time especially on weekends, whenever their parents were making the rounds of the gin mills or swinger parties, Lacey and brother Jake had the house and the privacy the house provided completely to themselves. As a special erotic joke, they would use their parent's bed as their stage, just careful not to overlook and leave body fluids or toys in the sheets. Exploring her parents bedside end table, Jake discovered a pink 10 inch plastic dildo and as a bonus, in a big brown envelop, dad kept a collection of Polaroids of mom and he at redneck swinger parties. Wow, and Jake thought their parents were so square and here they were, just like their bored partners, fucking and sucking other people at suburban swinger parties. Lacey had religiously kept her parents secret and never shared with Jake what she saw from beneath the kitchen sink curtain skirting that one weekend night and the many times afterwards. Both laughed at the thought of their parents naked and doing sex with other middle aged couples. There were photos of women and men in the most compromising of positions. Lacey recognized one woman, Mrs. Thelma Boister, the mother of one of her classmates and president of the High School PTA. So here you have it, Mrs. Thelma Boister was not as pious as classmates and other parents thought;

here she was with her eyes closed and her lips tightly locked around a very long prick. There were other photos of mom sucking cock and dear daddy ramming other women; one even with mom sucking someone's dick while daddy was fucking her from behind and waving to the camera. There was even a surprise photo of some guy sucking daddy's cock while daddy was eating some lady out. Jake was really as surprised as Lacey had been, as he surely thought daddy hated homos. You just never know about people, especially family people. Lacey's educational tutorage would continue with Vinnie and accelerated when she and Vinnie discovered the pleasures of S&M.

One afternoon, while she and Vinnie were laying stark naked on the floor sharing a cigarette when she got the idea to see what would happen if she touched the lit end to Vinnie's chest. Naturally, Vinnie howled and jumped away from the pain. "Well, cuz, that was a little test. What would happen if I touched the cig to your balls?" Vinnie, still a little taken back by the surprise attack said "how 'bout I touch the end to your cunt? That really hurt, so now it's your turn." "Here's the cigarette and you know how to find my cunt, so let's see what happens." Vinnie took a draw from the cancer stick, blew off the ashes from the end, captured a fold of labia skin and slowly applied the hot end to her skin. As he slowly pressed the searing end to her most sensitive parts, he was aware of the slight odor of her skin roasting and charring. He was so surprised that while she grimaced in pain, she didn't fight the hot tip burning into her body. Pulling the searing tip away from her labia, "damn, didn't that hurt?" "Yes, it did, but I really got off on that pain. I think that we have fallen onto something. I have an idea that we can experiment with that won't leave burn marks. You're gonna be first." Hopping up from the floor, Lacey went directly to the closet and rooting through her mother's sewing basket, found the straight pin cushion. Returning back to where Vinnie was still laying on the floor, she held up the straight pin and smiled, "This is gonna be fun, time for a different type of prick." Dropping to the floor she pushed Vinnie

backwards on his elbows and facing rearward she straddled his stomach. Lacey grabbed his ball sack and began stabbing it with tiny, tiny jabs. Each time she punctured his skin, Vinnie ouch'd and bucked a little. After a dozen or so pricks, she asked "well, what do you think? Did you get anything out of it cuz?" "You just know you are one sex crazy bitch. Look at how hard my cock is. I can't believe that I liked that, I did actually like it a more than a little. Now, it's your turn." Pushing her back on her elbows and sitting across her stomach, Vinnie pinched together with his thumb and forefinger a mass of wrinkled pussy lips. Holding the straight pin at a slight angle, like threading a piece of meat on a kabob stick, he pushed the steel pin completely through the labia. Damn, he could feel his dick getting hard again. She grunted and bucked, but it was not a buck to free herself, but maybe more of a buck to meet the next needle prick. He realized that he enjoyed doing this pain thing. Sensing that just maybe, this was something, that if they were careful, they could take turns with this new pleasure. By the end of that afternoon deviant session, Lacey with a pussy that looked like she got too close to a sewing machine, and Vinnie with a cock and balls so full of holes that it looked as if they had been quilled by a porcupine, made a mutual pack for more exploration inasmuch as S&M was something missing from their sex escapades. Vinnie knew that while the pain part was a bit much for him, he was willing to make that sacrifice so he could get the pleasure from and be the one dishing out that pain to his dear cousin. Damn could she take it, and boy did he love to give it to her.

The several years of Lacey's tutorage in pain and hurt codified the fact that Vinnie would forever be a pussy hound in need, and in need of a special type of sex. Simple relationships would fail as soon as Vinnie would begin his aggressive and often times painful domination of his partner. Never were there many who would tolerate the degrading, painful and humiliating acts Vinnie would force on them. Vinnie realized to satisfy his desires he would have to drift beyond the dating circuit. As a beginning,

Vinnie waited in the shadows and attacked young college girls walking the dark streets off campus from a late class or gathering. The timing had to be prefect. A far easier target when he discovered the after hour drinking haunts of young people to be especially victim rich, for at closing time there always seemed to be that one self-confident, independent young woman that drunkenly braved the darkness on the walk back to the dorm or apartment. As there were many souls also walking these streets. Vinnie needed a method to prevent his victim from screaming and attracting attention to the fact that Vinnie was abducting her. On his first victim, he had very little planning, in fact it was a more spontaneous act. As he was walking past, he spied a very cute co-ed leaving the bio-building. He stopped and let her pass and then followed discretely as he tried to formulate an attack plan. He knew the campus and off campus very well and knew she was headed towards a commercial section where there was a trucking drayage company that had had a large lot with no fence and did not have a night watchman. He was sure of this as he had cased the property many times on those nights when he got cold feet and aborted his abduction plan. He would run to the east then run up north two blocks which would then position him to be walking directly towards her and interdicting her at the trucking lot right where all the shrubs sheltered that side of the truck bays. Tonight, as with every night, he had two six foot sections of rope, a large heavy bladed chef's knife, four dime store six inch knitting needles, a pack of condoms, a small roll of duct tape, and gloves.

As he walked south he saw her approaching and had to speed up a little to be sure that they would reach the truck lot with enough time to be spontaneously walking towards her; women were far less suspicious of someone walking towards them and less likely to be defensive. As they were crossing paths, Vinnie punched her as hard as he had ever punched anyone, directly in the midsection. She gasped and doubled over. Vinnie hit her again on the side of her face and then pushed her into the shrubbery. Once inside the shelter of the shrubbery, Vinnie wrapped the

rope tightly around her neck. "No noise, no one saw" Vinnie muttered to himself. First he ripped off a piece of duct tape to tape her mouth and to silence her. Then quickly Vinnie tied her hands together with the piece of rope which he also looped it around her waist; and with the other section tied around her neck, it would allow him should she struggle to give it a hard yank that would cause a constriction and straggling of her air passage. She moaned and in a panic, Vinnie punched her in the temple. She was then very quiet and very still. Vinnie then pushed up her light sweater and rolled her bra up and over her breasts. He gently touched them and bent over and kissed and licked her nipples. Grabbing her left breast, he rested the tip of a knitting needle right behind the side of the areola. He began pushing and realized that the blunt end was not going to be conducive to an easy piercing. Applying more pressure it finally punctured her breast. He continued the pressure until the knitting needle point broke through her skin and appeared on the other side, completely skewering the breast. It surprised him as very little blood seeped from the piercings. Admiring his work, he squeezed the right breast and skewered it in a similar manner. The victim, still very much unconscious, softly grunted each time the needle pierced through her skin. Vinnie smiled but wished that he had her captive in a dungeon and could see the fear in her eyes and hear her screams and cries for mercy. Arching her legs, he then pulled down her skirt and using the knife cut off her panties. He carefully tucked the panties into his pocket as a souvenir of this conquest. Combining the fear of being caught committing a criminal act with all this sexual arousal raised that special exciting feeling he only felt when he was in an overpowering commanding situation over someone defenseless and helpless. His cock was screaming, it was now hard, diamond hard. Freeing his penis from his jeans and rolling on a condom, he dropped to the ground and pushed her legs apart. Directly his cock to the opening of her vagina he jabbed and pushed. This first assault he discovered that trying to force his dick into a very dry vagina was more difficult than he ever imagined. Spitting on his fingers and slathering her vagina, the combination of the lubrication of the

condom and spit made penetration just a little easier. Even so, her vagina was still very dry and Vinnie had to push and push till finally there was a little release of her body lubricant and with a sudden plunge Vinnie could come to fucking terms as he shoved his cock as deeply inside her as he could push it. Grabbing onto the knitting needles for anchors, he savagely slammed his body against hers. Rape was a lot harder then he imagined in any of his fantasies. It took but the little friction of a few plunges before Vinnie ejaculated. After withdrawing his penis from her still unconscious body, Vinnie suddenly realized that he had no exit plan. Stripping the condom from his now retracting and rapidly shrinking cock and aware that a condom full of cum in a rape scene area could likely convince a jury to give a person fifteen to twenty years in a not so homey jail, he carefully and swiftly knotted the condom end and tucked the condom and its slippery cargo in his pocket and doing that then pushed his penis back into his pants and zippered the closure shut. Sterile disposal of the condom would have to wait for later.

With his sexual gratification satisfied, the reality of what he just committed set in; he was almost in a panic, what now were his options? Should he just walk away and chance that she wouldn't remember her attacker as the man who in full view walked towards her? Should he carry the crime one big step forward and cut her throat, forever silencing her testimony? Leaning heavily to the second option, Vinnie was drawing the knife from his pocket when a sudden shift in the circumstances made the decision for him. He heard a group of drunken college kids laughing and cavorting, likely looking for a secluded spot to smoke their cheap dope. Possibly they had smoked at this site before as their pathway was heading straight towards him in a route that would take them within 15 feet of this crime scene. Panic ruled. Vinnie could only think of one thing; escape. Returning the knife to his pocket, he crouched and ran along the truck bay walls until he could exit the lot between two staged tractor trailers. Peering in both

directions he noticed no one; the students had all entered in the woods and would likely in seconds discover the girls' body lying there.

Vinnie briefly wondered what they would think when they saw the needles stabbed through her tits or if any of the boys would get a hard on and wished that they had found her body with no witnesses along and what would any of them really do if after looking at her exposed titties and her inviting pussy still gapping open from Vinnie's assault; Vinnie smiled, probably just say "sorry, bad luck bitch", or "not your lucky day, now it's my turn". Snapping back, he knew he had to put his feet in motion and distance himself before the police responded. As he reached the street he heard one of the girls scream a piercing scream; that could only mean they discovered his victim. Tonight, only by a thread of luck did Vinnie escape being caught in the act. Who knows, if he had been seen, maybe one of the young men had enough hero in him to have chased and tackled Vinnie and held him for the police. Vinnie vowed that he would never again put himself in such a risky situation. That night Vinnie began writing out a tactical plan that over a period of two months he wrote and rewrote and even did several dry exercises to make future crimes as risk free as possible. All criminals are not creatures of compulsivity; many have the intellect to plan to the very smallest of detail, the most heinous crime of their choice.

Vinnie's victims ranged in age from ten years old to one eighty seven year old matron, the majority, in fact his specialty, were old forgotten retirees. Vinnie's was now a planned opportunity rapist, a very careful calculating rapist; never a rapist of compulsivity. Any woman not individually targeted by the plan, was a woman safe from Vinnie's cock. When he had felt the symphony of the urge he would between the hours of 10am and 3pm, begin cruising the downtrodden neighborhoods, the museums of the wrinkled retirees, looking for any signs of an occupancy that could produce another victim. Vinnie was the definition of patience. His patience and craftiness for detail kept him out of prison and off the police suspect radar

for eleven years. However, one simple and careless little oversight led the police to his door step; after raping and torturing a 56 year old widower, he overlooked a single piece of duct tape that he used as a blindfold. On the duct tape was a partial thumb print, resulting from an unnoticed tear in a surgical glove that allowed his thumb to leave a very clear thumbprint. Vinnie's military prints were on file. It took the detectives 14 months to make the match, too late for five other rape and sodomy victims, but a case closer none the less. Once in custody, and with positive identification by 8 victims (32 were unreported and another 6 refused to step forward in the investigation), it was a case that prosecutors in the District Attorney's office dreamed of and fought over and a case in the Public Defender's office that took drawn straws to assign a reluctant defense attorney to.

Vinnie had a method and a very precise check list that he would case residential homes for victims. He was never a street or alley animal, a lesson long ago learned at the trucking facility; there was always too much chance of some bubba hero or someone with a concealed weapon permit coming to his victims' aid, plus his style of a home invasion had so many benefits; privacy, rooms of his choice and furniture (Vinnie often liked to blindfold his victim, tape her hands behind her back, and force her forward over a chair or table for his choice of which up or down portal for his doggie style, rear entry),

On Vinnie's home invasion, he spent hours deciding on whether a house provided enough of the insufficient risk for him to be the chosen one. He looked for a driveway that had no parked car, frilly curtains on the windows, an uncut lawn, a trash can close to the back door (women disliked walking any distance with bagged trash), a few old newspapers that were thrown off the mark and too unimportant to retrieve, flyers stuffed in storm door handles, the little things that telegraphed that an elderly person resided there. Low income, blue collar transition depressed neighborhoods were less likely to have nosey neighbors. This was a special factor when it was necessary to park and sit or to walk and gawk.

He would cruise by the target house at different hours over a period of three days. Cruising would tell him if it was a woman that lived there, if she was elderly, if she was married, if she had kids, if she worked or stayed at home during the day, if she walked for exercise, if she had a dog (and how big was the dog), the types of windows, if there was a sliding patio door, were there concealing bushes along the house, the closeness of the neighbor's home, did the neighbors have a noisy outside dog, were they likely to be home during prowl time, a slew of small facts that converted into a big picture. Often Vinnie admitted that he wasted his time because at the last minute he would notice something that increased the risk of apprehension, but Vinnie was successful enough to always believe that his rape plan was foolproof and he was smart enough to plan around any new small risk while being exposed to any larger risk.

Vinnie always carried several lost dog posters. If a cop stopped him and asked questions, Vinnie would flash the lost dog poster and say "Gee officer my kid's pet got out last night and my kid hasn't stopped crying, if you see this dog, I would appreciate you calling us, no matter what time." Twice when Vinnie was cruising a likely target and was pulled over by the area patrol car, he used this dodge to escape the embarrassing questions by the police officer and twice it worked. It also was handy if Vinnie noticed some neighbor staring at him. The dog scam was very effective to dispel any suspicion. The only negative being that once Vinnie used the dog scam, he had to completely abort and abandon that particular stalk.

A key to Vinnie's string of rape success was the U S mail. On the first go around and an important leg of the plan, Vinnie had long ago stolen a Social Security check. The check inside the envelope wasn't the key element; it was the official government envelope that the elderly immediately recognized as the envelope containing the monthly happy money. If the opportunity safely presented itself, he would late at night also steal any mail to get the name and then check whether it was Mr. & Mrs. or Ms. Once he could pretty much confirm that it was a single woman

living there and Vinnie had a name he was pretty much on the road to a successful home invasion. This was his door key. He could without fail count on whether a person had just received their check or not, that the social security money envelope would grab their attention, especially if they thought it was in the form of an additional social security check. Once the target was confirmed, Vinnie would knock at the door and hold the check up to the door peephole, always moving the envelop to keep the victim's focus on the envelop and not on his face. When the woman answered, Vinnie would say "Hello Ms. Mayberry, my name is Percy Eater, (he loved that play on words) I just moved in a block away and the darn postman delivered your mail to my house. It looks important like a government check so I thought why take a chance on those people mis-delivering again, so I decided to personally deliver it to you Ms. Mayberry." The woman obviously seeing what it was and had the comfort of the man knowing and using her name, naturally and reactively would open the door to get her bonus social security check and to thank the kind man.

Once she had the door open, and the woman was busy trying to look at the envelope, Vinnie would quickly scan the inside for visitors and if he was reasonably sure she was alone, he would craftily maneuver his body into a position where he could deliver a hard punch to her stomach. The woman, having the air knocked out of her could not scream and being bent over could not fight. Vinnie would then grab her by the hair, push her head further down, pull her away from the door, close and lock the door and still pulling her by the hair, guide her to the first room away from the windows. Rotating a hand hold of her hair to force her face out and down with her hips to him, Vinnie would then use his free hand to first slip on the ski mask. If he couldn't initially maneuver into the striking position, Plan B was to pretend to hand the woman the envelope and drop it where it fluttered behind her. Once she bent over to pick up the envelope, Vinnie would wrap his arm around her neck in a side choke hold and then pull her away from the door. The shock of being choked was usually enough to

incapacitate his elderly victim. If not, back to Plan A, a hard punch to the abdomen that would suffice to put his plan back on track.

With the woman still partially incapacitated, keeping her bent where she could not straighten up, he would twist first one hand behind her, taping it, and then would twist the other hand so he could tape it tightly together to the first hand. Every criminal knew duct tape made super handcuffs. Next was the blindfold. Vinnie knew that while he was standing at the door she was more interested in the envelope in his hand then in detailing his profile. To help with identity confusion, Vinnie always put a band aid over his left or right eye. Victims always focus on that band aid, and when trying to describe their assailant to the police, they rarely got past a general description but could with great definition tell the police investigator the color and brand label of the band aid. "Officer I was so scared, all I can remember is that he was a white man with a band aid over his right eye and once he got inside he had a ski mask and then he blindfolded me with that tape that tore my hair out when it came off." The next step was stuffing the cheap sock into her mouth and placing tape tightly across her mouth to prevent any screams. Once he had his victim secure he would push her to the floor and walk the rest of the home to be certain no one else was in present in the residence.

Old women were wonderful play things. Most had not had sex in decades and he was always either guaranteed a very tight vagina or one so loose it was like sticking your dick between two slabs of round steak. Some had dentures, and when he made them remove them, the dragging friction of ancient gums on his dick were a special bonus. Seldom did he encounter a virtuous old bitch, almost every single one, at one time or another had sucked more than an occasional cock and had engaged in other techniques of the back seat arts. Once he removed the gag and told them simply "I am a sex hound. If you are a good girl nothing bad will happen to you. If you fight or try to scream or try to hurt me, I will have to do very bad things to you. Do you understand? Do exactly what I tell you to do and how I tell

you to do it and we will get along just fine. Some things might hurt a little, so when I am ready to let you do those things, I will put the gag back over your mouth. Now, which will it be, a fun afternoon of fucking and sucking or an afternoon of the most terrible things you can imagine? Shake your head yes or no." Never did one of the desperate old ladies shake her head no. "Good, now we can begin. I am going to remove all your clothes. One of the things I love is an old wrinkled pussy covered with white pubic hair. I hope we are going to see snow on those pruned up pussy lips. Oh, one more thing, I like it a lot when you say things like "fuck me harder, or your cum tastes so good, or gosh that's a big prick", you know erotic little things, think you can remember to say those things. Shake your head again, yes or no." Naturally, the frantic old woman motioned "yes."

All were terrified, although a few of the more resistant he had to slap around a little. Most had flat saggy breasts that hung straight down their chests. Vinnie loved to squeeze and twist those soft bags, some he was even able to twist tightly liked dough. Occasionally, he would use his kntting needles, he loved to hear the muffled screams as he pushed the metal rods through their flat and wrinkled breasts. As another fun thing, on those with flat pancake breasts he loved to wrap rubber bands (he usually carried a dozen of the big brightly colored art project ones in his pocket) or duct tape tightly around them to see them swell and turn purple. Anal was usually not of much interest as the old matrons over years of sphincter atrophy enlargement offered little pain to them or pleasure to him, but occasionally when the wild hair struck, it was into the hersey way. It was always so entertaining when an old bitch feebly fought to keep his spear from ramming deep into her bowels. These old play things were never disappointing.

The next stage was a very special part of the rape; Vinnie fed off the terror in their eyes, the more pain he was able to inflict the more their eyes would burn with the horror of what such a cherubic looking man was doing to them. The most dependable methods to put horror and pain in their

eyes was the knitting needles through the breasts; or grasping those old worn sagging and bagging labias and skewering them with the needles; or stretching them in a tightly twisting motion or grabbing those purple tits and squeezing one as tightly with his fists as he could while pretzel twisting the other in the most painful of contortions. He also enjoyed using a thumb and index finger to pinch over the nipple slight behind the areola ring with as much gripping pressure as he could leverage. The pinching seemed to consistently produce the most pain. He often remembered that one lady who instead of screaming began moaning and shouting "harder, make it harder"; Vinnie put in overtime at her house. The last extreme was the thumb and forefinger crushing of the clitoris and its stem. Sometimes these old matrons fainted at the pain; a few slaps, a little cold water or an ice cube pushed up their ancient twats always revived them. No fun if you can't see their faces and eyes. These tortures he would alternate between cock plunges.

The afternoon was filled with every deviant thing Vinnie could call up. The poor woman was tortured and raped again and again. Vinnie knew that he could only cum twice, so to stay alive for the finale, Vinnie would pull out of her vagina and rest his penis just before it exploded. When he did reach a point where he was ready to conclude the captivity, Vinnie executed the last phase of his plan. If the mouth gag was still in place, the gag was removed and Vinnie would force his cock as deeply past the tonsils as he could, almost always causing a gag and immediate choking. When it came time to cum he had a rehearsed finale, on the tongue and across the lips, commanding them to swallow or lick the shiny dribbling cock globs with their lips and tongue. After the finale, he would replace the gag, and then remove the blindfold, knowing that he would remain safe from identity as all they would be able to see exposed by the mask was his lips and eyes.

Once Vinnie was ready to leave, he would slowly walk throughout the invasion and rape scene with his eyes scanning from side to side carefully checking for any overlooked item that would be the evidence to lead the

police to his door. As a last measure he would squirt bleach on and into the woman's vagina and anus to destroy any molecules of semen that might have somehow escaped from the condoms. As an existing remark, Vinnie always reminded them that if they contacted the cops, the next time he would make them really suffer. He also asked them if they had a fun time (shake your head yes or no) and if they would like him to return (again shake your head yes or no). No a single old spinster ever shook her head no.

Vinnie was an excellent tutor. During the stay of his prison term, Sonny was able to incorporate many, many of Vinnie's tactics into his own personal abduction and hostage plan.

Sonny knew from interviewing prison yard kidnapping experts with decades of experience how to craftily lure a lone woman into the van. He also learned in prison that patience was the key to success. Sonny had served one five year term for burglary and had been refused parole thrice; so Sonny ultimately served his time in full. Sonny had learned a lot in prison. Fellow convicts gave lessons in defeating locks and alarms; how to kidnap victims; the latest in crime scenes and evidence retrieval by police technicians; the best drugs for recreation or seduction; how to choose targets; the quietest way to kill; how to dispose of a body; and the most important two rules of crime: patience and attention to detail. Prison was a finishing school for those who preferred high jacking the wealth and sanctity of others as their career road of self-achievement. The modus operandi was simple, he would select his cruising area from two geographical categories; a neighborhood of low income renters where people avoided the streets after dark; and neighborhoods where high end middle class or upper middle income residents neither cared naught about or observed neighbors. He further defined his strategy to center on America's 24/7/365 shoppers' Mecca, the convenience store. Rarely were the Muslim clerks interested in anything beyond the next sale. These isolated convenience stores were prime hunting grounds flush with late

night shoppers needing just that one little thing that they forgot to get at the supermarket or had depleted at home. The majority of his victims had stopped and shopped for milk, bread or cigarettes. This last need was the thread that connected and introduced them to a painful and a untimely bloody destiny.

He would spend hours sitting across from a convenience store casing patrons for his next victim. Sonny preferred young attractive girls. Occasionally he would choose a slightly overweight middle aged housewife. It often took days before he zeroed in on the chance prospective victim of his choice. Sonny had infinite patience and knew historically that any haste on his part would lead to an eventual identification and arrest. Being caught, arrested, and prosecuted as a societal monster did not fit in Sonny plans, so patience definitely became a virtue.

CHAPTER NINE

While lying in his prison bunk and later after his release, Sonny dreamed of methods to produce various levels of pain upon these imaginary victims. These dreams were fantasies fueled by stories or actions of the cruel and heartless psychopathic criminals who glorified in recounting the torturing of their helpless victims. These dreams became Sonny's passion, and in his mind he inventoried a glossary of methods he would inflict on his future prisoners. The glossary started with the mildly uncomfortable and rapidly escalated to the severe bloodletting. During an exercise yard session, a convict that had mastered rope binding, explained to Sonny that if you very tightly wrapped cord or the big rubber bands around a breast, it would first turn a brilliant purple then have a somewhat numbing effect whereas he would then be able subject each breast to the most horrible of puncture and penetration tortures. Sonny liked the idea of tightly roping the breasts so the constriction would darken and deaden the breasts so he could experiment with pliers, pins, nails, electric shock, fire, and clamps.

But, himself a prisoner to the plan's pattern, it all had to start with his calming of the victim, by explaining the pleasures of his cunning lingus talent to the fearing captive. This was a part that he enjoyed and he just loved the way that the anteater and straw would awaken a victim's passion that ruled her body and defeated her fear. Even the most rebellious and aggressive of women had lost out to the talent he had learned in the schooling Auntie Mame provided. He was a master at it and every vagina became a hungry instrument of passion and want. After Sonny had finished with his tongue exercises on the victim's vagina, he would accelerate to minor levels of pain. Perhaps it would be the dripping hot candle wax on the tender labia minor and clitoris which would at first be a minor discomfort, the hot melting wax only slightly painful or maybe he would chose to start with the electric rodeo. Then again, maybe he would begin the pin punctures of each breast, or tongue clamps, of vaginal insertions (he did love the frozen bottle vagina expander), maybe fish hooks through the nipples with weights or tension stretching the nipples to extreme elongated shapes, maybe super glue the eye lids open, a spoon to torment the tonsils, maybe a wire piercing or a vice clamp on the tongue exposing the tongue to other ingenious prison conjured pains, a piercing of the nose septum or the red hot tip of a good cigar applied to the nipples, tongue, clitoris, anus, nose or anywhere sensitive enough to trigger screams and body thrashing. And he did not overlook a dab of petroleum jelly mentholated athletic rub pushed up into a rectum or smeared on the sensitive walls of a birth canal. Sonny had witnessed this many times in the pen where a convict master had punished his punk slave by pushing the hot searing salve up into the asshole of his disobedient punk. Sonny used to laugh as the punk screamed and clawed at his ass scuttling across the cell floor. One method that intrigued Sonny was the self-strangulation method using a hog tie. One inmate, who had committed many unsolved murders, and was doing ten years for a robbery, vividly described how, of course only someone he vaguely knew, would hog tie a victim and loop the ankle rope from the ankles to the soon to die victim's neck, and sit by and

calmly watch as the victim struggled to prevent the noose from closing his/her air passage. Fatigue was the victim's enemy and sooner or later the exhaustion would rule out and the noose would slowly tighten, the poor soul eventually losing the battle to strangulation.

While victims were random, they none the less were carefully chosen, just as the police had criminal act identification profiles, Sonny had a perfect victim profile. She could be any age. He preferred teens and those in the twenties but found much easier to target housewives in the thirty to forty year old bracket. Sonny did not discriminate, any race would do nicely. He really preferred blondes. Occasionally he would hunt for an old matron, one that likely had not had sex for decades. It was always fun re-introducing them to the steamy acts they had left behind so many years ago. Sonny loved big breasts, and if possible would pass up many opportunities because the woman did not fill up her cups and this definitely did not live up to his specifications and expectations. He always avoided muscular women or heavy weights; definitely a problem if the victim decided to fight. Sonny was coached in prison by an experienced street rapist about "struggle potential". Always be certain to avoid two types of victims; a body toned, muscular looking woman that could fight and possibly escape or injure the abductor, while any woman weighting 250 pounds or more was more likely to be able to absorb a hard punch to the stomach with little affect and many of these heavyweights had the knockout power and aggressiveness of a welterweight fighter.

Sonny learned to avoid the typical pickup area within known prostitute's strolls, where the busy traffic of low income renters and johns would guarantee little to no interest in cruising vans but there was another caution that Sonny learned the hard way; the women who walked the streets selling their wares were always hardened street smart girls who knew police procedures and were often armed with razors or hat pins. In the beginning when he deviated from his prison plan on the spur of the moment and ignored his master and detailed plan of his crusade of carnage

against women, it took a young Sonny only two failed and painful abduction attempts with night walkers to learn that he must stick to the master plan and that street wise hookers were trouble in spades. The first girl leaving a razor cut on his left arm, the second girl driving a steel hat pin in his groin just missing his jewels. Other than complaining to their pimps, neither woman reported the attempted abduction to the police, avoiding any possible extended interaction and optics with the police while chalking it up to a job hazard.

Sonny's third attempt was more successful. Eight months after receiving that hatpin stab that almost kabobbed his balls and cock, as his plan was still a work in progress, he again modified his capture plan and shifted from the obvious prey to a target far less suspicious profile. Driving and scouting convenience store scenes far away from the red light districts, where he falsely imagined every cop car was looking for him, he by chance located a hamburger drive through that did not have a camera and was located next to a bowling alley that also did not have parking lot video cameras recording the coming and going of patrons. Thinking it was worth a target capture try, he once again altered his master plan. By parking next to the shrubbery, he could sit in the van, smoke cigarettes and observe who and how many were in the car going through the drive thru lanes or the pulling into the parking lot. On the first night's hunt and within twenty minutes of parking, he observed a lone young woman pulling into the drive through lane. As she sat focused on the menu billboard he was able to determine that she was likely in her late teens or early twenties, had long blonde hair, looked to be thin, long neck, and appeared to be pretty. The late model car likely belonged to her parents. As she paid for her large soda and began to pull away, Sonny decided that he had to have this one. Once she got off the main road and started speeding down a lonely stretch of farm road, Sonny turned on the police lights and pulled her over. Rightfully assuming she was naïve, he said "Ma'm two things; we just had a robbery not far from here; a young woman had robbed an elderly lady of her purse

and you were speeding away from the area that the crime was committed in. I am going to have to take you into custody. Please turn the ignition off and step out of the car and with your hands up, move to the rear of the car." His observations were not far off; she was a teenager, long neck, thin, tiny tits, and was very cute. She was not so terrified that she was going to a police station inasmuch knowing that she was innocent and did not commit a crime and would be immediately released; she was more terrified that she was going to get a ticket that would really piss her parents off and lose car privileges.

While she was walking to the rear of her car, she explained that she went to Supra High School was an honor student and would have never hurt an old lady. She also explained that she had daddy's car and would get into lots of trouble if she got a speeding ticket. Apparently not worried about the felony, she immediately began pleading with Sonny not to write her a ticket. "Miss, we can talk about the ticket at the station, but, and I am sure you understand, for your safety and mine I have to put you in handcuffs and secure you in the lockup van. This is going to happen so please do not make trouble for yourself." In consideration of the degree of criminality of the crime, she was very surprised that he didn't pat her down and try to get a few cheap feels in. She smiled with the thought that with this copper's relatively relaxed attitude, she could have cut his throat with a razor blade had she one hidden in her bra like all the colored girls talked about at school. Thinking that sucking up would go in her favor after they realized she was not a robber; "Officer I do understand and I promise not to make any trouble. Do you think I can get by with just a warning on the ticket?" "We will see, but first things first." Handcuffing her hands behind her back he led her to the van side doors. "Watch your step, please." When she had settled down on the bench, he chained her legs to the bracket. With her legs now secured to the bench brackets, it was time for Phase II. Suddenly when Sonny grabbed her by the hair, she started screaming; "I didn't do anything officer, what are you doing." Sonny

slammed his fist into her stomach, incapacitating her. He then quickly duct taped her mouth and placing the pillow case over her head and with a few loops of a cord he secured it around her neck. Locking the van door he ran over to her car, removed her purse and phone, locked the car, looked in both directions for potential witnesses and seeing none hopped in the van, keyed the ignition and pulled away from the crime scene.

"Listen you little daddy's girl. You are going to be my love slave for the next few hours. I am one horny fucker, I plan on fucking you everywhere. When I speak to you, you will answer and always, always address me as Master, you only talk when I ask you a question, and you do exactly what and how I tell you to do things. Obey these simple rules and it will be fun for both of us, violate them and the nasty consequences will be your fault. Shake your head if you understand." She shook her head and he could hear her sobbing under that hood. Two hours later when he pulled into the farm driveway, he unchained her legs and pushed her through the doorway. Leading her over to the OBGYN exam table he pushed onto the cold cushion of the stainless steel frame. Seizing her ankles he forced them into the stirrups and secured them with the straps. Pulling her up into a sitting position, he spoke "Bitch I am going to un-cuff you, if you try anything funny I am going to hurt you really bad." He first un-cuffed the right hand and pushing her back down on the table strapped that to the table frame, securing that, he then repeated it doing the left hand. In prison, they always said when fucking with someone in cuffs or tied in ropes, always transfer the power hand first. Another lesson well learned and now put to practice.

"Honey, now it's time for show and tell. Before I remove the hood and the tape, I going to remove your blouse and bra and once we get that off it's your shorts and panties." In anticipation of the control and the excitement of his first catch, Sonny's imagination was running wild and his dick was granite hard. With the images of so many past daydreams with his imagination going unfretted of the degrading and painful things that

woman deserved and Sonny was the one that was now going to do it, his head was spinning with happiness; a happiness not to be shared with Number One Victim. Cutting her blouse and bra loose, he was very disappointed at the sight and size of her breasts. They were barely formed and the nipples so tiny they were almost flat against her chest. The areolas barely shaded around her nipples, they being the diameter of dimes. Sonny felt cheated. He had planned to wrap her tits in rope just like in that picture that guy in cell 10 had his girlfriend smuggle in. That single photo burned an image in Sonny's imagination that was hard to disregard. The girl's tits actually turned purple from the tourniquet action of the rope. Once he had cut off her shorts and pulled her panties off, he smiled. "Honey, I am the Prince of Pussy and I can really appreciate a work of art. It is a masterpiece that way that you sculpted and shaved that pussy; such a narrow little pubic patch and the way it makes those pouting lips an invitation to a hungry and spearing tongue. We are going to have some fun, I can guarantee that." Unable to resist, he teased and folded open the draperies of her labia minors with his fingertips. Her body recoiled at the touch. "Let's see what we got here, you a virgin or a slut?" He spit on his finger and pushed it up into her vagina, where it immediately encountered the gate guard. "I'll be damned, I never thought I had much chance of catching a cherry girl, and here you are." Undoing the cord around her neck, he slid the hood off and saw the fear and terror in her eyes. That fear and terror was fuel for his deranged furnace. All sadists must have that fear and terror present in the victim for them to really appreciate and enjoy the pleasure of the torture.

"I am going to remove the tape gag, if you get loud, curse me, or scream, I have something a lot worse than that tape to keep you quiet." He yanked the tape to achieve maximum pain to her lips. She began crying. Sonny decided that it was time to demonstrate how helpless and venerable she was; balling his fist up he lifted and held two feet about her mid-section. She was broadcasting her fear and panic in the frantic movement of her

eyes. He liked that and hoped that future victims would also be that afraid of him. It gave him a strange feeling of power and it also sent signals from his cortex to his cock. "What is your name bitch?" Her eyes never leaving his fist replied, "My name is Joan, but all my friends call me Jo." In a hammer like blow, he drove his fist into her stomach with so much force that urine squirted out of her vagina three feet in the air. She vainly fought to double up and fold her body over the collapsed and damaged stomach. Gasping for air, she tried to scream but no words came forth. Tears cascaded from her eyes. "Did I not tell you to always address me as Master and did you not fail to do so? I do not like to punish women, but if you break my rules you suffer the consequences. I think it is time to take a small break to give you enough time to put together you thoughts and amend your behavior. I want to be your friend, but I can't if you keep disobeying the rules. Do you want to be my friend?" Not knowing what the terrible consequences could be if she said no, Jo still unable to speak, shook her head yes. Lighting a cigarette, "Better, now let's take a break and start over in say, thirty minutes".

Trying to rest, the young girl's mind raced with thoughts about how this had to be a nightmare, there were no monsters like this in real life, her daddy would not allow anyone to treat his princess like this cruel animal is doing. The binding straps were cutting into her wrists and ankles. Slowly she tested them for any looseness; they were seriously applied and there was no slack to try to work free. She was helpless and at the mercy of this pervert. She could hear his footsteps returning and there he was, standing beside her. "Well, I'm ready to go, how about you Jo, you ready?" "Yes, Master." "That's what I want to hear, now I have some questions I am going to ask you and if you lie you will be very sorry. Understand?" "Yes, Master." "How many boyfriends have you had and I want you to name them and describe what you did to each other when you were alone." "I'm listening" as he lit a cigarette.

"Master, Bobby was my first real boyfriend. We necked a lot, just French kissing and once in a while I would let him feel my breast. We never went any farther cause Bobby found another girl that he could do nasties with." "What do you mean nasties?" "Well, Master, according to my girlfriends, his new girlfriend would let him feel her up and would let him put his fingers in her vagina while she would squeeze and jerk his penis until he moaned and made a wet spot in his jeans. Eddie was my second and still is my only boyfriend. Eddie is handsome, plays quarterback on the football team. His parents have money and he drives a new car. This is kinda embarrassing, Eddie is pretty aggressive and to keep him I had to do some things that made him want to keep me as his girlfriend. It started with letting him feel my breasts, as you can see they are not very large. Then he kept trying to push his fingers in my vagina and I fought him because I want to be a virgin on my wedding night. One night, when we were really getting at it, he unzipped his jeans and pulling his penis out he forced my hand around it. He kept his hand over mine and started moving my hand back and forth. This went on for a few minutes and then he arched his hips, moaned, and cum squirted out all over my fingers and slacks. He smiled and said I was very good at jacking off a cock. To keep him away from my vagina, I did this on the next few dates. Then one night when we were playing around, he grabbed the back of my head and told me I had to either fuck or suck. I had no choice Master, he pushed my face down into his lap and forced his dick past my lips and into my mouth. He grabbed my hair and pushed me up and down on his cock until he shot his cum. I didn't mind the taste too much, but I hated being forced. After that first blowjob, I had to do him every time we were alone and had the opportunity. When we are alone, he calls me his tiny titted cocksucker. We are still dating and I am still a virgin. That's it Master, only two boys."

"I can tell you right now, you can forget being a virgin on your wedding night and you can forget Eddie's cock. You are mine now and I have lots of plans, actually a plan for every one of your holes." The description Jo had

given Sonny about her sexual experiences had produced an erection and his loins were beginning to feel the throbbing fire.

Sticking with the plan and first things necessarily being first, he soaped her body and purged her bowels followed by a scalding water rinse. All the while he was busy with the cleaning phase, she screamed, cried, pleaded and sobbed. In between screams, tears, and sobs she pled, "Please, please that water is so hot and it really burns inside me, please don't hurt me anymore. Maybe my daddy can give you money. I just want to go home, I won't tell anyone, I promise. Please mister." "Listen cunt, you better shut up, I don't care if it hurts, I don't want daddy's money, you are my slave and I have all sorts of things planned for your body. Keep talking and I promise you something very ugly will happen."

"I do so enjoy eating pussy. You almost fucked up and pissed me off enough to forego something I try always to treat my ladies to. This is my contribution to the fun; once it's over it will be your turn to treat me to all kinds of fun things that you have never even thought about before. But now, it's all about you. It is such a special treat and you really will experience orgasm after orgasm. I hate to brag, but you will be begging me not to quit. Now lay back and relax, it's time for me to treat you to a tongue fiesta.

Positioning himself in the vee between her legs, he unzipped his trousers and fished out his prick. Holding it tightly in his fist he began rubbing his cock up and down her pussy. "Now slave, first is Phase One, where I burn your pooter up with my dick and open up your cunt hole, then its Phase Two, I eat your pooter out; now shut up before I lose my concentration." "Please Master don't do this, my wedding night, please let me go. I don't want to be hurt and it's gonna hurt. Please Master." "Shut up cunt, you are talking out of turn again and when I get done fucking you I'm gonna punish you again. Now be still." Jo felt his dick rubbing up and down her labia lips and then center on her vestibule and could feel it pushing initially

with a slight sneaky pressure against her hymen and the pressure increasing until he with a grunt and a strong stab and instant pain, she knew his lance had broken through her chastity. She screamed with pain, it had hurt but not as bad as she always imagined it would. Knowing that she was about to experience more pain, she began crying and begging. Sonny continued his thrusts until with a loud moan he slammed his hips with a final slam against her legs and she could feel his balls dangling against the cheeks of her ass. With a loud moan he propelled his string of cum as deeply up into her vaginal canal as his cock could penetrate and spew its alkaline signature. He draped his body over her body and when he recovered from the fuck exertion, he slowly withdrew his penis from her vagina. Sobbing, she could feel her vaginal walls collapsing as his penis slowly pulled backwards and the contractions of the muscles within her vagina expelling his warm semen to drip from her vagina and down over the pink of her asshole. "I wish I had a knife and could kill this monster; I know daddy would not hesitate to shoot anyone that did anything like this to me, his little princess." Flashing back to ten years ago when she strayed from her father's view and wandered behind the park pavilion; remembering the pleasant afternoons in the park where daddy would read and momma would crochet and then was that one terrible afternoon and that horrible guy in the park when she strayed off the playground and that man grabbed her, kept his hand over her mouth so she couldn't scream and pushed his callused hand down in her underwear and his finger kept stabbing at her little twinkie and when daddy walked around the bushes, saw what the man was doing, and screamed at the man and how when daddy chased him and caught him, beat him half to death before the cops got there. And when the police did get there, how they then beat the man with their nightsticks and then afterwards, handcuffed, dragged and slammed him into the police car. If only daddy could be here and see how this son of a bitch was hurting my little twinkie, he would fix things in a hurry." She smiled at the thought of that happier moment but then the smile triggered a bolt of pain in her desecrated and abused vagina and

brought her back to the reality of being trapped and in the power of another more heinous monster who daddy wasn't going to catch and wasn't going to save his little princess from.

"Popping your cherry was not as hard or as bloody as I imagined it would be. I did enjoy the tightness, but we will have to work on that, my toys are pretty thick so I think we are going to have some stretching problems. Maybe if we put the pussy hardware on you, it will loosen you up some. I need to think about that. Because you were a bad girl, you won't be getting the Phase Two of pure pooter pleasure; I am so sorry, I know it would have made your pussy sing. Now for your punishment, since you can't seem to stop talking and it annoys me a lot, I will need a way to silence you. The tape gag is boring, but I have in mind a few other ways to shut your mouth." Wiping the blood from his penis, folding it back into his underwear and then zipping up his pants, he went to the prep table and picked up a pair of pliers and a long knitting needle with the tip honed to a needle point. "I read about this in a book on the middle ages. Let's see how well it works." Seizing her jaws and forcing her mouth open with his left hand; he took the pliers and probed into her mouth until he was able to get a good clamp on her tongue. So intense was the pain that she tried to scream but with a pair of plier mashing her tongue she could only make grunting noises and futilely bite down on the metal of the pliers. Once he had her tongue pulled out past her teeth, he slowly pushed the sharpened knitting needle completely through her tongue the knitting needle pinioning her tongue in a stretched extension beyond her lips. She had never imagined pain like this. Her tongue bled freely as the flood of blood reduced her to making gurgling sounds. Lighting another cigarette, he said "Tilt your head to the side or you will drown in all that blood."

Jo being his number one victim, Sonny was ecstatic with the torture things that had floated about in his mind while he sat in that prison cell. "Jo, I have an idea, let's start with that tight pussy of yours. We need to have it a little larger, I have some frozen bottles that I want to push in there and I

don't think that even the smallest one will fit without ripping your cunt apart. So, let's put the vaginal spreader in there first and see if we can stretch it a bit." First picking up a can of shaving crème, he filled her vagina with the white foam knowing from past experiences with his Auntie that it was a super duper pussy and asshole lubricant. Then he reached over to the prep table and removed the spreader. He pushed the cold metal jaws of the spreader into her vaginal canal and forced its tongues apart as wide as possible. He could tell it hurt her as her body was squirming and twisting. Locking the spreader tongues wide open, he said "Now Jo, I have your lips spread as wide as I could get them, unfortunately it isn't very wide. I am going to wait twenty or thirty minutes and then come back and readjust them. We are going to keep doing this until I get your pussy open enough to get my fist in it. Bet when you left home this morning, you never ever would have thought that you be strapped to a table, had a knitting needle stuck through your tongue and after a pussy stretching have a perfect stranger shove his fist up your cunt?" Sonny started with his maniacal laugh. Poor Jo could only moan and sob. "I need a little smoke break, bet you could use a break too."

Ten minutes later, "Time to move on. I just had an idea, I am thinking that a little electric will cause that pussy to tighten up and then relax. Each time it relaxes, I bet it gets a tiny bit looser. Wadda think? I think it's worth a try. First we start with those tiny disappointing washboard tits and microscopic nipples. No wonder your boyfriend wanted to spear your tonsils, I bet his tits were bigger than yours, I know mine are. After we buzz your tits with the electric rodeo then I am going to attach a probe to the stretcher and push the second probe up your asshole. Since we douched it clean, it should conduct electricity fine. So, let's get started." He smiled as he could almost hear the screaming terror leaping from her eyes.

Her nipples were a big disappointed, her body did buck with the higher charges of current, but the nipples never did pop and with her body

twisting the clips kept slipping off. Then with the probe clipped to the metal of the vaginal spreader and the second probe up in her rectum, he discovered a major flaw in the probes: each time he zapped her with the higher current, her rectum's sphincter muscles would contract and the contraction would worm the probe out. The only way he could keep the anal probe in place was to duct tape the wires to the cheek of her ass. Even that was not too effective and to no large degree prevented her strong sphincter muscles from partially forcing the probe out. Sonny knew that he would have to design something that would grab the tissue and defeat the expulsion by the contractions. "Maybe something like a small claw or hook on the end" he thought to himself.

Disgusted that his electric stimulation was not producing the desired effect, Sonny decided to make notes of the failure and remedy that between hunts. Move on to something else, the big question how to stretch those wrinkled lips big enough to get one of his bottles in there. Removing the clamps another idea popped up in his demented mind; "Let's try dildos, we can start with one having a normal cock thickness size and work up to the jumbo, maybe that will work." Back to the prep table he grabbed the shaving crème and spritzed her vagina until it looked like the muzzle of a rabid animal with the white lather overflowing and globs of it slipping and dripping down from her pussy through the narrow crevice of her ass to puddle on the table top. First he chose a dildo slightly larger than the circumference of his cock. "Jo, I am going to push a bunch of plastic dildos up in you and the size will keep increasing until I can get your hole stretched to about four inches. I am not sure how much this is going to hurt, so please be patient. Once you get the big hole, I will have a treat to slide in there." Jo was barely conscious and was beginning to have out of body experiences.

After forcing incrementally increasing sized ones, one after another up her vaginal canal, he finally got to the jumbo five inch diameter size and was able with a good deal of pressure able to shove that twelve inches

completely up her. Additional applications of the shaving crème was necessary to keep the lubricant working, but the last few dildos were causing a red tint to the snow white lathering. Her gargled screams were now barely audible. The relentless torture had Jo in and out of consciousness a dozen times, the pain so intense it caused her to continually black out. Sonny did not care if she was conscious or not, he was only interested in making that warm passage as wide a hole as possible. After several minutes of working the huge dildo like a cannon brush Sonny was finally satisfied that he had created the perfect portal. But she had to be conscious; if she wasn't conscious there would be no terrified looks, muffled screams, or body responses; no rewards for his hard work. Walking away from the table Sonny drew a pitcher of ice cold water from the refrigerator. Back at the table, he tipped the pitcher and allowed the water to trickle over her face. Not reacting fast enough, Sonny poured water into her skewered tongue propped open mouth. Immediately as the water threatened to drown her, she revived, choking, gagging and desperately fighting for breath.

As he was speaking he was also busy douching the shaving crème residue out of her vagina. "Good girl, glad you are back with us. I have worked very hard to get your little pussy big enough for the next treat. Now you will be very, very uncomfortable but I am afraid it's necessary. You see while I was in prison, didn't know that did you, one of my cell mates charged a five cigarettes admission, and we got to watch as he did this to his punk cell mate. For fun, he would grease the boy's asshole with a methylation rub. The methyl would cause the boy's asshole to burn like fire. Then he would get the punk in a headlock and hang on as the punk screamed and fought until the fire went out. We all liked to watch that, it sure cured the boredom for an hour. Now that you kinda know what happening, let's see how you do." With his left hand he smeared the petroleum based methyl charged grease on his right hand. He made certain that Jo could witness the care he took getting the grease spread on each finger and coating the

whole hand. The terror in her eyes and twisting of her body told Sonny he was on track. Slowly he slipped one finger, then a second, then a third. Jo could immediately feel the heat within her abused body as it intensified into a firebrand pain. The fourth finger was more difficult, as many of the stretched muscles, like a memory foam, had slightly contracted and were resisting being force stretched again. With a grunt and a shove Sonny got the fourth finger in and having folded his thumb inside of his palm into a spearhead, he pushed as hard as he could to get that spearhead up to his wrist and inside her. Naturally with the pain and the feeling of burning coals inside her, her screaming faded and she fainted again. Grabbing the water pitcher with his free hand, he again used the cold water to shock her back into consciousness.

"Now Jo here is where the pleasure lies. My hand is deep inside you. I am going to twist the fist and turn it back and forth one hundred and eighty degrees. I am going to push it up into you as far as I can get it to go. We are going to play like I am an engine's piston, just like the little choo choo, in and out, back and forth. After we do that I am going to open my hand and use my fingernails to claw your insides. Damn my cock is sure getting hard. The burning heat of the grease and the motions of my fist and fingers inside you, I guarantee will take you to a place you had never imagined before. Once I finish the swabbing, I will pull my fist out and it will make a popping sound. By then I will probably be ready for two things; number one to shoot a hot load of cum down your throat and two, another cigarette and maybe a cold beer break. When the break is over then it will be time to play a game with your tiny pink asshole and once I get bored stabbing things in that, we can move on to the bottles. Sound like a plan?" Jo did not hear most of what he said as the pain from the fisting and the hot salve kept her thankfully between a state of semi-consciousness to absolute unconsciousness.

Fortunately for Jo and disappointing for Sonny, poor Jo died while Sonny's fist was in- exhaustingly pumping hand signals inside the depths of her

never to be used, birthing canal. Poor Jo's abduction and death served many purposes: a) Sonny would never skewer a tongue again, too much blood, too many gurgling noises and it lessened the sounds of victim pains, instead he would always use a set of lock grip pliers, the locking jaws gripped the tongue well and the weight and size of the pliers kept the tongue extended out of the mouth; b) never target a flat chested woman again; c) he needed to get a source for chloroform to sedate the more aggressive ones; d) he needed to work on a design for his electric probes so they would stay in place ; e) he needed to add a cattle probe to his inventory; f) he needed to park the shredder closer to the tank so there would be less activity when he fed the shredded body to the hungry fish; g) he needed to buy a lot more of the cheap shaving crème, it was a super, super lubricant; h) maybe buy some cigars to touch to the nipples; i) larger and more sturdier candles, and j) a larger transformer to boast up the current on the voltage adjustment dial.

In the penitentiary Sonny had conceived a plan that while exposing him to minimal risk would use the power of an ingrained societal respect for authority to subordinate a victim. To achieve success, it required but two things; choosing and isolating a victim and a low traffic road. Once he chose a victim he would follow her auto for several blocks watching her and also watching for cruising police patrol cars. When he was reasonably certain there was but a small chance of encountering a cruising police car, he would flip his police lights on and tap his police siren for a brief wail to get the doomed driver's attention. Once the driver pulled over, Sonny would turn his police monitor radio on to its highest setting, exit the van and walk up to the driver with his 9 cell flashlight glaring first into the side view mirror and then as he got closer shine it blindingly into the drivers face. Sonny would then shout to the driver "Police, please turn your vehicle off, face forward and exit the vehicle with your hands up". Sonny learned years ago if you dressed convincingly enough as a plain clothes policeman, dark slacks, sports jacket, and flashing a dime store badge on a

chain around his neck, there were few questions or suspicions, just curses about bad luck and denials of wrong doing. He made certain the woman could see him and see his drawn revolver. Sonny would shout police orders; "Stay calm, no sudden or jerky moves, keep your hands up, walk backwards to me to the curbside until I tell you to stop, Do not talk." Once the frightened driver complied, Sonny would grasp her left hand, twist her arm behind her, march her to the side of his van, and push her body to a leaning position against the van. The terrorized driver would naturally try to explain she was just buying milk and hadn't done anything wrong. Then Sonny would say, "I am sorry for this inconvenience and I would like to believe you, but we just had a homicide where a woman driving a vehicle of your description killed a man. Calm down, take a deep breath and if you're innocent we can get all of this straightened out by the desk sergeant." Sonny knew that his plan allowed for eight minutes to have the victim exit their car, get cuffed, get the pat down, get shackled in the phony police van, retrieve their personal belongings from their car, lock up their car, and pull away on his way to the compound; just eight minutes.

Naturally the woman was begging to be let go. Sonny would say "lady I got a job to do and if I were to let you go and you turned out to be the killer I would be sitting in handcuffs and kissing my pension goodbye, I hope you understand." Usually this calmed the soon to be victim down. And usually the woman would say, "I understand officer." Sonny would then tell her it was police department rules that all suspects be handcuffed and pat down searched. Like the good sheep she was conditioned to be, the woman followed the order. Once Sonny had the handcuffs on, he would say, "I have to frisk you and because this murder has everybody in the district out looking, there will be no police women available for the next few hours, so if you want to sit here for 2-3 hours and wait that's fine but if you want this to be over quickly, then I'm the one who has to frisk you. But I have to do it before I can drive you in to the station. What do you want to do; wait or get it over with? Also if you want to file a complaint when we get to the

station, I understand." "OK officer, I am OK with that, pat away." The frisking was an important part of the plan protocol; it was expected, maybe not by a male but none the less expected. Without frisking the victim, the woman would become suspicious. That skinny, tiny tit cunt immediately noticed it and it started her processing a panic attack. Sonny had practiced the cuffing and frisking pat down routine and had it down to a science of less than three on scene minutes. The major problem with the pat down was occasionally on a super trophy, Sonny's dick would demand that the pat down fingers linger and explore; it was a curse that he had to fight.

Sonny would then check all the pockets of her winter coat, reach inside her coat and slide his hand up and down her back over her buttocks and down to her ankles. He would then slide both hands up the inside of her legs until he reached her groin. Then changing position he would slide his right hand inside her slacks, shorts or up her dress and creep it up to her panties. Using a finger he would burrow under her panties and slightly penetrate her vagina. Always, the girl would gasp in surprise. As she was beginning to object to the outrage and embarrassing body intrusion, Sonny would again calm her with "Sorry ma'am, this is the procedure." Rotating her body slightly he would then slide his right hand down inside the back of her slacks, shorts or skirt, trolling his fingers down the buttock crevice and slightly pushing it into her anus. Then Sonny would place both hands on her collar bones and slide them down to her breasts, over, around and beneath her breasts and back down to her groin where he would wedge his open hands upward in a slight push. It was as professional a pat down as expected by the woman and actually did more to calm and override the woman's instincts. "Now that wasn't so bad was it lady? Time to load up and go to the station." "What about my car?" "After I load you into the van, I will lock it up and give you your car keys. Understand that the police department does not provide taxi service, so if everything you are telling me checks out, when the desk sergeant cuts you lose, just ask him to call

you a taxi. Any problems with that?" "No officer, you have been very kind and professional."

Walking to her car Sonny grinned, "Damn these women are so stupid. Let you feel them up and even stick your finger in their pooter and still don't complain. They all love it and I am just the one that is going to be giving her a lot more than just a friendly tit hand slide, finger tuck and pussy bump." As she was being half pushed, half shoved into the van, it suddenly occurred to her that this police officer had not asked for an ID. "Officer, don't you want to see my ID, why didn't you ask for my ID and you didn't wear sanitary gloves when you frisked me?" Sonny pushed her onto the seat, pulled a chain up from the van floor and locked her cuffs to the chain with a padlock. The woman was becoming suspicious. "Officer I demand to speak with your supervisor and I am not going anywhere with you until I speak with another policeman." She had heard about police brutality and had several black friends that claimed to have been beaten and left in alleys, but always when you got into questioning the details they got very vague and could only provide weak and elusive answers. Their encounters of cop brutality rarely would hold up to questioning and most listeners just blew it off as fake attention getters. Everybody loves to be a victim, real or not, it is the best way to grab attention, and if you are a black hound on the prowl it was a proven and guaranteed white cootchie getter. So she thought of another angle to let this cop know that there were eyes everywhere. "My cousin is a major in the Chicago police department and I know he won't be happy when I tell him about how you scared and hurt me. I will have you fired and charged for false arrest and sexual assault, Mr. finger in my cunt and asshole man."

Sonny hopped from the van, slid the side door closed and climbed into the driver's seat, started the van and off Sonny went to a special destination known only to him and would be briefly known to his victims. Throughout the one hour drive the woman pleaded and threatened constantly. "Why is it taking so long to get to the police station, where are you taking me?"

"Listen lady, the holdover is filled, which is good for you and you won't have to wait. They gave me orders to drive everyone over to the county jail where the victim is waiting to see if you are the perp. So, just let me do my job." "Girl are you about to get a big surprise" he thought. Not satisfied with his answer, her complaints continued. Midway to his special hideaway, Sonny pulled over onto a lonely gravel road, parked the van, and hopped from the driver's seat and walked around to the side door. Opening the door he looked directly into her fearing eyes, "I am so tired of listening to your fucking complaints and moaning, time to shut you up. Oh, by the way in about another hour you will doing a different kind of moaning." With that said, Sonny started laughing a maniacal laugh. Suddenly this victim had a major revelation and realized she was not in police custody, this was not a police officer and "My God I am being kidnapped, but why, I can't pay a ransom, I have no money, I'm a nobody, why would he choose me? There isn't a soul that's gonna miss me for weeks. Life can't be anymore fucked up then this." "First missy, you get the car wash and hot rinse. Then I'm gonna eat your pussy and take you to plateaus you never ever imagined. You will reach orgasm after orgasm and shout and scream for more of my serpentine tongue. Once the pussy fiesta is over it will be your turn and I will be jamming my hot rod down your throat and after a stroke or two or three, I will be swabbing your tonsils with cum gravy.

The woman instantly feared for her life, and as the danger she was now in began to become clearer, she began to scream "help, someone help me, please help me." Was he going to kill her, what was he going to do? "You make way too much noise, so for both our peace of mind, I need to gag you. Your screeching noise isn't doing my cock any good. When we get to my playhouse, you and I sweetie are going to have fun. I have a playroom filled with toys that you're gonna just love." "Please sir, (she lied) I have three small children, please let me go, I promise I won't tell anyone, please." This was a part that Sonny savored almost as the pain part, the

begging and pleading part. In desperation she thought maybe I can bargain "Sir, I will do anything, anything if you release me, I'll suck your dick, you can fuck me, anything, anything, and I promise never to tell anyone about this, please just let me go." Sonny teased her "will you wiggle your tongue up my asshole?" "I'll do that right now if you just release me. I promise I won't say anything to the cops, I promise mister." "Fuck you bitch, you will be doing more than rimming my asshole, I promise you that."

Sonny smiled and with lightning speed drove his fist into her stomach, a punch that drove her body hard against the metal frame of the van. If she had any doubts, there were gone now. She was in a serious life and it was a situation where she had no control, no bargaining chips, no nothing. He hit her so hard so she a bladder release. As the impact shock of the punch drove the air from her lungs and caused the collapse of her solar plexus paralyzing her, and she could feel the warm urine soaking her panties and slacks, she began to cry. Damn that was the best advice professor Vinnie in the Prison Cell Abduction 101 course ever gave; it never failed, a quick punch to the stomach gave him complete domination and control, it never failed. "Got anymore demands, bitch?" Gasping and folded like a jack knife from the trauma of that blunt attack, she sputtered "who are you? What are you doing, please I have some money in the bank, just drive me there and it's all yours, please?"

While Sonny was busy forcing a sock into her mouth and duct taping it in place, he noticed the urine dripping from the bench seat. "Pissed yourself didn't you bitch? Don't worry, when it's time to run you through the body wash, I have a hot stream pressure hose that will squirt that piss away and make that pussy rosy pink, fresh and sweet again. I really like sweet pussy, have you ever tasted sweet pussy? You do look like a girl that has sampled an oyster once or twice, huh, well have you?" Raising his hand as if to strike her, she again the girl frantic to avoid being struck again, grimaced and nodded "yes". "I just knew it; knew it!" Once Sonny had her feet duct taped together and was satisfied that the gag tape was secured, he allowed

himself a little test squeeze of her breasts and through the flimsy fabric of her bra and blouse he could tell these were very soft breasts and soft breasts were so much fun and held so many promises, there was so much you could do to a mass of cells with a jello like consistency. Smiling as he could see the fear in her eyes and that fear was something that fueled and fed his dark beast, he whispered to her "I am going to take your passions to places you could have never imagined you would ever go. You will beg and plead and call me Master." Now quiet down, unless you would like some more punishment."

The van bounced over several more miles of really rough unimproved road, finally making two brief stops while Sonny jumped out and opened and relocked security gates. In a very short drive from the last gate, the van finally stopped in a glade surrounded by tall pine trees. This she could see from her seat. Parking the van, Sonny jumped out and walked around to the side of the van, opened the van door and in a very normal voice said "Welcome to my castle. We are deep in the woods. The nearest road is twelve miles and the nearest neighbor is 23 miles due south. I inherited this land and customized this fortress all by myself five years ago. Nobody even knows it exists. You are welcome to scream all you like, the only things that will hear you are critters that prowl these woods and they aren't going to help you. If you try to escape, I will find you long before you reach the road or any person. I do not like to hunt escapees, so I am warning you only once. When I catch you, and I promise I will catch you, I will first beat you, then like the Indians used to do to their re-captured fugitive slaves, I will first tie you to a tree, you will be naked, I will dribble honey on your pussy, finger some inside your pussy, and the dribble a little trail of it down your legs. Ever hear of fire ants? They are nasty little bastards with an extremely bad attitude. The ants will find you within 4-5 hours and first begin biting and stinging your legs, then the outside of your pussy, and then the more aggressive ones will get inside that warm honey hole and the pain will be something you could never imagine and will never

ever wish for. You will scream with the pain and beg me to help you. You will beg me to kill you. How do I know this, you are thinking, well over the years, on two different occasions, two dumbass girls thought that I was kidding about escaping. Both discovered how much ants love to bite and sting. I never had any trouble with those two again. They actually begged me to kill them. Understand? Shake your head yes or no." She quickly nodded "yes".

Taking a few quick moments, Sonny emptied her purse on the console. He was looking for her driver's license and any photos so he could verify her name, marital status, and family. In addition to her wallet and the usual clutter in a woman's purse, found a six inch sharpened spike woman's self-defense weapon. "Hmm, something to fight off a mugger. Not a bad idea, but it didn't do her any good, like a gun in a night safe, if it's not conveniently handy and immediately assessable, it's worthless. So glad she didn't get her hands on this, she could have put a world of hurt on me" he thought.

I am going to remove the gag, and if you are a good girl, it'll stay off. Are you going to be a good girl?" She again nodded "yes". Sonny removed the gag and asked her what her name was. "My name is Monica. I have three small daughters to take care of. Please do what you want and just drop me anywhere, I really will tongue your asshole if that's what you want me to do. I can make you cum like you never cummed before. I swear I will never tell anyone or go to the police, please." Sonny smacked her across the face. "Listen, Monica, I just asked for your name and you started carrying on. We have rules, simple rules that you are going to obey or be punished. First rule; always call me Master. Number two; only answer my questions, nothing beyond. Number three; always do exactly what I tell you and how I tell you to do it. Number four; never, never try to hurt me; I haven't forgotten about that spike you had in your purse and would have stabbed me with if you had gotten the chance. Never hurt the Master, never. A long ago girl bit my dick a little too hard. She really needed to be punished

so I pulled out all of her front teeth. Damn that was messy but once the bleeding stopped; I sure enjoyed sliding my cock back and forth over those gums. Number five; always tell me how much you love what I am doing to you regardless if you like it or not or if it's painful of not. Are you OK with these rules?" Monica in a trance like reaction to what she had just heard responded, "yea." Quickly Sonny slapped her across the face again, "Are you deaf slave? Did you not hear what I just told you, you call me Master every time you address me? Let's try it again." Smarting from the pain of the slap Monica blurted "Yes Master, yes." She wisely decided not to beg or plead; instead her tactics changed from pleading to waiting for an opportunity to grab some type of weapon and kill him.

Sonny then grabbed her ankles lifted her legs and began pulling and cutting her slacks off. While stripping her slacks down from her legs Sonny thought of something she had earlier said. "Three kids, how old and what are their names?" Quickly, making it up, she responded "Debbie is one; Karen is four, and Carrie is six Master." "Monica, that's a good thing to know, I'm sure they will be happy to see you when this is over, won't they?" "Yes Master." Always give them a flicker of hope, Sonny smiled.

With him yanking on her slacks, the woman really panic'd now thinking, "he's out of his mind and is going to rape me, so she screamed, Please someone help me." The louder she screamed the louder Sonny laughed. "Guess what, no one is going to hear you, we are out in the sticks so far they have to cart in sunlight so your wonderful beautiful body and everything that goes with it are mine for the time being." Sonny laughed at his joke. With her slacks off, Sonny pulled her panties down and off. "I guess that you are not a beach fashion girl; looks like you haven't trimmed your bush ever, it's very overgrown down here but we will take care of that a little later." With a forefinger and his thumb he pinched a tassel of pubic hair and pulled until he saw pain register in her eyes. Smiling at her, he released the tassel and gently touched her vagina with his fingertips. Watching the fear grow in her eyes he wet his fingers in his mouth and very

slowly pushed them, one at a time past the drapery wrinkles of her labias and as deep as he could into the warmth of her vaginal canal. In a falsetto voice he jingled "Somebody's been here before. Judging by the ease my fingers got swallowed, they been here before a lot, haven't they?" She groaned as the penetration, while not exactly painful, was uncomfortable. Forsaking her kill him plan, she reverted to pleading "Please Master let me go, anything you want I'll let you do to me, anything but please don't hurt me. I won't tell anyone about this, I swear, just let me go, please Master." "Are you stupid? Seems like right now I can do anything I want to you without letting you go. I love big pussies and you got just what the doctor ordered. A fellow can push all kinds of big things in a big loose pussy. I think that you will like some of my play things. Do you like to have your pussy eaten? Well, that is something I am really a Master of. Just as I promised, when I put the "anteater" and the "straw" on you, you're gonna beg me to keep that fire burning. It will start on your pussy lips and by time I get to the "straw" your juices will be flowing like water from a water facet. I have never had a woman fail to get excited to the max when I eat their pussy, never. So, instead of thinking of ways you'd like to kill me or ways to escape, just think of the best sex you have ever had and triple it." "Please, Master I am sure I will love it when you do those things, I am very good at oral and will give you the best blowjob you have ever had; all you have to do is to let me go. Everyone has always said I give the best head. Honestly, I am really, really good at it. Right before you cum, I will take my lips and suck real hard at the tip of your cock and get every drop of your cum. Please, Master just let me go free."

"Shut up bitch, I'm getting tired of listening to your whining." Picking her panties up, he rolled them into a ball then forced her mouth open and jammed them in. She started gagging. Holding the panties in place, Sonny reached for and pulled a roll of the criminal's friend from beneath the bench. Duct tape is used just as much in criminal actions as for handyman fixups. Tearing at the roll with his teeth, he managed to strip off a long

ribbon of tape free from the roll. Using his right hand he smashed the tape across her mouth securing the gag in place. With both hands now free, he placed more several ribbons of the grey tape over her mouth.

Releasing the lock on the floor anchor chain, Sonny grabbed Monica by the arm and dragged her from the van, across the yard and pushed and pulled her through the doorway and into the playhouse. When he opened the door he closely watched her eyes. This was another exciting part of the ritual, seeing the desperation and fear in their eyes when they first see the room setup with all the torture devices. There was no mistaking the purpose and intention of this room. Entering the room, Sonny was not disappointed. Monica was so frightened, she had another bladder release. When Sonny noticed the urine dripping from her naked vagina, he spun her around, and brutally tore the gag from her mouth. Grabbing a hand full of hair he pushed her face downward and forced her to her knees. With her face now inches from the urine puddle, "you made a mess in my beautiful playroom. I think it's only fair that you slurp and lick it all up. What do you think Monica?" Knowing that there would be no choice and if she refused more hard slaps, Monica said "yes, Master, I'm sorry". Sonny forced her further downward until her lips were submerged in the arid puddle. "I want to hear you sucking. Ever suck up piss before, Monica?" "No, Master." "Begin now." It was probably the nastiest thing she had ever been made to do; the fact that it was from her body did not temper the disgust of it. After several minutes of this improvised floor cleaning, Sonny said "Good job, piss sucker. A little later I'll give you some mouth wash to get the nasty odor off your lips and tongue. I have lots of other plans for those lips and don't want a pissy odor to throw my mood off. You even looked like you enjoyed it. Did you?" Monica thought why take chances with this lunatic, play his game until I can get a weapon in my hands, "Yes, Master, I love drinking my piss." Pulling her up from the floor he pushed her over to the cold stainless steel OBGYN exam table.

"Not a very good first impression Monica, but welcome to my playroom. The interview will begin once I get you nice and comfortable. Sit on the table and take the examination position and lift your legs and place them in the stirrups. If you try to kick me, I will beat the shit out of you. Now do it." Monica tried to come up with a plan to kick him in the throat but her tormentor was smart enough to stay to the side and the configuration of the frame of the OBGYN exam table prevented any opening for levering even a feeble kick. And to think about all those hundreds of dollars she wasted on Karate lessons, "Women, be able to defend yourself and repel attackers" the ads said." "Bull shit" she thought "Fuck, if he were only a bag dummy and her handsome instructor were here to yell out the numbers, she would kick this perverts' ass, real bad." Drifting for a nano second, she remembered how that handsome Karate instructor fucked, he did that by the numbers too and she never even climaxed once during all those sweaty after hour private lessons.

Strapping her ankles securely in the stirrups, Sonny commanded her "You are going to extend your arms back over your head and I am going to remove the handcuffs, one wrist at a time. You will briefly have one hand free. You will be tempted to try to strike me. Remember that with your ankles locked in the stirrups, there is nothing you could achieve but to upset me and make me punish you. So if you are a smart girl, Monica, you will not struggle or fight. Which will it be, let me anchor your wrists to the table or fight and be severely punished? Answer quickly." Knowing he was absolutely right, Monica recognized the futility of her situation. "I will not fight, Master." Extending her arms over her head he released one handcuff and immediately secured that wrist to the table bracket. Pulling the other hand towards him, he released that handcuff and secured the last hope that Monica had for an opportunity to kill this monster. With her ankles and wrists secured, Sonny joined the straps of a wide Velcro belt across her stomach forcing and anchoring her torso to the flatness of the cold stainless steel table frame.

Addressing her remaining clothing, "Now Monica, I will be cutting your blouse free to inspect your breasts. My thoughts are they are 36 Ds, am I right Monica?" "36 Double Ds Master." "Thank you Monica, before I do a thorough inspection, I have a question; they appear natural, are they natural or will I be cheated by silicone." "They are real, Master." With a heavy medical shearer, Sonny clipped up the seams of her blouse and with a hard yank pulled at the front popping all the tiny buttons loose. Wadding the blouse fabric in his fist he pulled it free of her body. "Now the bra, this is a most exciting moment Monica, I look so forward to cutting the middle band of your bra and when I separate the cups, seeing your tits roll to each side. Are they soft enough to roll to the side, is this what you see when you lay down?" "They are soft and they are large enough to roll to both sides Master." With that Sonny clipped through the fabric connecting the cups. Setting the shearer aside, he gently took a cup in each hand and slowly tipped the fabric cones to the side, freeing the captive breasts. Each breast then rolled at a glacially pace gently to rest on the side of her ribs. "Magnificent tits, and a bonus, sunken nipples and huge areolas, Monica, you have turned out to be a very special toy. My peter is beginning to harden and perhaps in a moment or two I will be massaging your tits and nipples with it. Would you like that Monica?" "Yes Master I want your cock to rub my nipples and tits." "I have so much fun planned for you and me, well to tell the truth maybe not so much fun for you. Excuse my rudeness, you must be very tired, would you like a little rest before we start the fun?" "Yes, Master." "You have piss breath slave, I don't care to smell piss breath. Open your mouth." Sonny picked up a small bottle of blue mouthwash removed the cap and poured an ounce or so into her mouth. "Swish it in your mouth and just spit it to the side." Monica complied. "Much better now your breath doesn't smell like you were drinking out of a urinal anymore, you smell like fresh spearmint." Then Sonny reached over to another table and grabbed a pillow case and painfully lifting her head by a hand full of hair, he slid the pillow case over her head and with a drawstring tied it around her neck. "Master, please, I am very frightened

and this hood makes me very uncomfortable. I want to see your cock, please Master remove the hood." "Damnit Monica, did I not tell you to speak only when spoken to, now I have to punish you. But you do make a point, plus I think you should be able to see so you can really appreciate the tool that I am so proud of." Sonny then released the drawstring and slipped the pillow case hood from her head. "Thank you Master, I really want to see your big, hard cock." "I love dick flattery, bitch." Sonny then walked behind her and was lost from her vision.

Breaking the silence Monica could hear the sound of water forcing itself through a nozzle. "I always believe in good hygiene and I am going to wash you down. I do this special treat for all my lady guests. This nozzle has a jet spray and it might make you a little uncomfortable, but it will clean you like a shiny new penny." Sonny adjusted the spray head to a normal shower setting and wet her entire body. "I am going to release the waist strap so that you can arch your back and I can get the soapy brush under there. The water is going to be a little hot. I do that to make your skin pink. Any funny shit and I promise, there will be lots of real pain to pay for it. Understand?" "Yes, Master."

After the preliminary washing, the next phase involved a more personal internal hygiene cleansing and purging. Filling a red rubber pharmacy douche bag with hot soapy water, Sonny forced the hot water up into her vagina to flush her vaginal canal clean with the cleansing soap. Monica started screaming. "That soap is strong enough to make the nastiest of cunts smell like a bed of roses. I know it is a little uncomfortable, but I don't want to stick my tongue into anything that's rotten tasting or smells like a garbage can at a fish market. I'm sure you understand." More screams as the caustic soap burned and ate into her sensitive vaginal walls. As the intensity of the caustic soap seemed nothing but madding pain, Monica was so relieved when Sonny flooded her vaginal canal with a douche of cool, medicated rinse lotion.

"Now, Monica, how I do love that name, I am going to fill the douche bag with soapy water and I am going to stick it up your ass. The hot water is going to clean your intestines and you are going to uncontrollably shit all over yourself. I want you to twist your body and try to lie to your side. Do not be embarrassed, the table is over is large catch basin and as soon as you finish emptying your bowels I will flush it all away and you will be as clean and as fresh as a daisy." Finished explaining, he forced the nozzle of the douche up into her ass and squeezed the bag forcing the soapy laxative into her bowels. More screams as the hot caustic, soapy water scalded and ate away at her insides. Within seconds, Monica lost control of her bowels. Once Sonny had washed away the fecal matter, it was time for the body soaping.

With a body brush and a bucket of disinfectant soap, Sonny swabbed her hair, and head, her back, her legs and her groin. Using his hands he soaped her buttock cleavage and anal artifice. "Thank goodness, everything is clean; so many of you girls have nasty asses with balls of toilet paper wadded in there. Disgusting and so unhygienic, men expect their women to be pure of body and yet when you get past the perfume, so many of you have smelly vaginas and stink ass." Shifting to the side he pushed his soapy fingers as deep as they would go into the tenderness of her vagina. With the lubrication of the soap, he discovered that he could get all his fingers and thumb inside her canal. "Wow, Monica, we are really going to have some fun with this. Most girls are so tight that in the beginning I can only get a few fingers in their cunts, but you girl, have a hungry monster. Now it's time to rinse you clean." First Sonny used a white rinse hose fitted with a douche flow head and pushed it five inches up in her vagina allowing the water to flush all the soap residues, cascading it out of her body. Spreading the cheeks of her ass, he pushed the douche head it up in her bowels to flush the soap and any remaining fecal matter free to the floor drain. Changing hoses, he grabbed the one with the long adjustable pressure head. Adjusting the jet to full power, he directed and jetted the painful hot

water from her crown to her feet. Monica screamed as the hot water again scalded her skin and most tender parts. Once he had completely rinsed the entire soap residue from her body and hair, he returned the hoses to their neat little mounting brackets. Sonny then squirted a fragrant douche lotion up into her vagina and into depths of her bowels. Sighing, he said, "I am a little tired, time for a break, say a thirty minute cigarette break. You OK with that Monica?" "Yes, Master, I am your slave" she moaned.

Lying there helpless, Monica's mind wondered how she could have ever been trapped by this monster and subjected to the monstrous whims of his sick mind. Her skin still burned slightly from the caustic soap and hot water, her vagina and ass pained from the stretching and the burning soap, her stomach aching from the punches, and her thoughts racing as to what tortures he had in store for her. There was no way she could have ever imagined being strapped onto a cold stainless steel OBYGN table while a madman was sticking his fist up into her vaginal canal. Why would any human being want to do this to another and worse, why was he enjoying inflicting such pain on her? Would he play his pain games and then pitch her out on some lonely road? No, not likely after he had let her see his face. Maybe if she could bargain with him and promise to be his special cocksucker, he would keep her chained as a fuck slave and it would buy her time to put together an escape plan. She knew that any escape plan would have to include killing him. But how? And with what? If only she could be free of these leg and wrist bindings, there were plenty of sharp or pointed things lying about these tables for her to grab and stab. She would show no mercy and would continue stabbing him until there was no heartbeat or breathe left in that monster body. Beg and promise to be the best sex toy he had ever captured. Plead with him to give you a chance to suck him into putty. Tell him that you know so many special ways for your tongue and lips to make his cock happy. Give him a reason to want to plunge his dick down your throat again and again. Every boyfriend you ever had said you

gave the best head they ever had. This monster is still a man with a dick that wants to squirt, turn the tables and make him the prey. With the martial arts training and the tools lying about, you could easily make this motherfucker wish he was never born. You just need seconds, but you must endure the pain of his toys and hope and beg for an opportunity to cloud his mind with lust for more. If he is a man first over a monster, then his dick will betray him and by keeping you alive, present you a future beyond a fatal destiny this afternoon in this chamber of horrors.

To the second, Monica knew the break was over and he being behind her, she could only hear his footsteps walking across the floor accompanied by a slight squeaking and dragging sound that sounded like the rollers on an office chair. She alerted to a fearful pop of some type of electric spark and could smell an odd sour odor that she just couldn't immediately place.

Sonny walked into her line of vision and lifted his hands to display the source of the sounds and odor. Holding the probes in front of her face he proudly stated "I am especially proud of this device, I engineered it myself. It is an electric current transformer that converts 110 volts into 24 different degrees of live current. For my safety I designed and attached a non-conducive handle to each lead wire. It has two fifteen foot wire leads that are attached to, and end with a special five inch long one inch thick copper probe rod. I flattened one end above the handle of each rod and drilled an eye through it to connect the wire leads. I discovered that I needed to modify the probes, because experimenting on the first several girls I discovered that once I applied a little juice, the muscle contractions on the probes would cause the probes to either slip out or be bucked out of the vagina or anus. So back to the drawing board it went. I then split the non-handle ends of the probes into four tiny fingers. I filed and sand papered and polished smooth the rough edges, after all I'm not an animal, and curled the four fingers up something similar to the feet of a hall tree. When the probe is now placed into a vagina or anus, it only comes out if and when I want it to come out, those little four little fingers really grab

onto that soft tissue. Once I get it inserted in your pussy or asshole, you will feel those tiny, tiny fingers grabbing and clawing at your insides."

"Monica I am afraid it is time for the lesson number two, to start." Plugging in a twenty foot extension cord that was attached to the transformer, Sonny carefully placed the transformer and current control dial device on the prep table. He positioned the prep table close enough to the exam table so he could easily adjust the current control dial. Sonny always liked to start the horrid exercise by standing close enough to the poor victim for her to see the blue spark of electric pop and hop from one electrode to the other. At this point the begging for mercy always began. "Please don't hurt me Master, please don't. Anything you want me to do, I'll do. Anything. But please don't hurt me with those probes. Please." "Now Monica, you have been bad and you must be punished. Just now you again spoke without permission. I just can't allow a slave to misbehave, I am sure you want to understand. Now, I am going to give you a choice; A. the probes or B. I stick that fucking spike up your cunt. Which will it be?" "Master the probes." "Wise choice Monica, wise choice."

All types of horrid thoughts were running through Monica's mind. "What's happening, Master, please tell me. Please don't hurt me." Rolling a chair over and taking an eye level with her vagina, he positioned himself between Monica's trussed legs. "Let's make this educational, OK? Know what you call the bottom and top of your pussy? Knew you didn't, no girl does. The top is called the Anterior Labia Commissure and the bottom of your pussy vee is called the Posterior Labia Commissure. Before I start the punishment, I want you to experience the pleasure that I give to all the good girls. I have mastered the art of eating pussy. I will be using two methods, the first is the "anteater" and when I think that you have reached that special height, I will apply the second which I call the "straw". You are right now thinking you are going to get another dog lapping your cunt, but you are wrong. When I get finished you will have climaxed at least 4 or five times and you will crave and beg for more. Now, let us begin."

Monica thought that like the dozen or so men before him, this pervert would be stabbing, licking and swabbing his tongue in, up and down her sweet pleasure spot. None of them had ever moved her to any sexual pinnacle and almost everyone kept looking up at her from their business at her honey pot asking "am I getting to you?" You always lied.

When Sonny had finished with the "anteater" Monica was bucking against his face. Despite all the pain, this man was phenomenal; she never imagined anyone could cause so much pleasure. During the "straw" when she was at a level of ecstasy she doubly never imagined possible, Monica squirted a long stream of girl juice up through the curl of his tongue, into the back of his mouth and all over his lips. She thought that he would be very angry and was surprised when he said "don't be ashamed, the straw would cause a nun to cum like a circus monkey." He laughed. "After that pussy pleasure circus", she thought, "if he would let me go free, I would be his slave forever. I don't understand why he has to do this to me, when after that unbelievable method of cunninglingus, I would volunteer for anything just to get him working on my slit again."

"As the Chinese say "so sorree girlie, pleasure time is over." With the transformer set on 12, Sonny very carefully touched one lead at the vee bottom of her vagina and then gently pushed it inward to be secured by the muscle pressure within her vaginal canal walls. Monica could feel the coldness of the metal and the probe's fingers grasping at her vagina walls. "What are you doing? Please don't hurt me." "Again you talk out of turn and forget to address me as Master. Consider this a lesson in manners." With the one probe secure and resting in the vee of her vagina, Sonny then lowered the second probe directly towards the button of her clitoris and delighted when a half inch blue bolt of current arc'd from the probe and speared the button top of her clitoris, Monica could feel the current race through the button and downwards on the stalk until it grounded on the first probe held fast by the pressure within her and felt it cruise through her left and right labias. Monica screamed and threw her body upwards in

the pain of the electrocution; her entire vagina was exploding in pain. "Not a nice experience was it Monica, too bad I must do this to be sure you remember when to talk and when to say Master. You know girlie, the more you experience this the more you will come to like it. I enjoy doing this. I like watching what the little blue jolts do to your cunt and those wrinkly cunt lips and how they cycle between contraction and then collapse in exhausted relaxation. Makes my dick really hard, but that fun comes a little later. Didn't piss yourself this time, good girl. Now because this is just a beginning I'm not gonna boost the current above 12. Later if you are still a bad girl, we might even have to take it all the way up to the 24 setting. I know you won't like that, no one ever likes that." "I'll be a good girl Master." "We will see Monica, we will see." With that said, Sonny repeated the electro shocking eleven more times. When he finished, the sweat was pouring from her entire body, her voice was crackly and dry from screaming and in addition to the pain inside and outside of her vagina, all the muscles in her legs, back and arms were exhausted from the involuntary responses to the stepped down but extremely painful 110 volt current.

"Say, Monica, I have forgot what your children's names and ages are, please tell me again." "Fuck", she thought "hope I remember right." In abject panic she blurted out "Master, Debbie is one, Claire is four, and Marcia is nine." "Monica, I really hate it when someone lies to me. This is what you told me "Debbie is one; Karen is four, and Carrie is six Master. There were no photos of children in your wallet or purse; wouldn't you say that was a bit unusual for a proud mother? You're not even close, any real mother would know the names and ages of her children, wouldn't you say so?" "Master, I am so sorry, I was frightened and hoped that you would show some sympathy and maybe just let me go, after of course you did your special treats to me. I am so sorry Master." "No, Monica, you will be sorry, sorry you tried to make a fool of me. For lying I am going to do some very special things that I only reserve for the very bad girls. Now I am going

to take a cigarette and drink break and give you a little time to wonder about the things that are going to happen to you. When you came in, I saw you looking at all my special tools and devices. Which ones will I be using you will be wondering. Well, I haven't really decided yet, but I can guarantee that none will be pleasant for you. I'll be back in a little while and we can continue the interview."

Sonny allowed her to be alone with her thoughts for fifteen minutes. Walking back to the OBGYN table, and looking directly into her eyes, Sonny asked her if she had a pleasant rest. "Yes, Master, it was wonderful. Master I was thinking about how much money I could give you if you just let me go. You can even do the electric shock again and anything else you like, please just let me go. Master I swear I will never tell anyone about this or you, I swear Master." "Monica you are one lying cunt, ten minutes after I release you, you will be on the phone talking to the cops. Now, Monica for thinking I am one stupid motherfucker, I am going to punish you for lying. First I am going to put the dental spreader in your mouth. I don't want to hear any more lies so I think you will not be saying very much after I get it strapped on, well, you won't have very much to say that I will be able to understand. Once that is in, I am going to start on your pussy. I do like bald pussies, they are very much in fashion and apparently you just hadn't gotten around to shaving your cunt smooth. Your Mons Pubis looks like a hairy and dirty door mat and we just have to do something about it. We aren't going to shave though; I am going to pull all your fucking pussy hair, strand by strand, until that pussy is as bald as a cue ball. I think that it might be a bit unpleasant for you, but once I get the yanking done, you will have a pink pussy to be proud of." Sonny then removed a dental spreader from the prep table and using a spatula, forced her mouth open wide enough to get the spreader set on her teeth. He forced her mouth open as wide as possible and then locked the spreader gap setting keeping her jaws apart as far as possible. To doubly secure the spreader, he secured the

Velcro straps behind her head. The dental spreader was only coming off when he decided to release its painful hold on her extended jaws.

Taking a position in the chair and pushing up to the junction of her extended legs, his face within inches of her vagina, Sonny held up a hemostat clamp high enough for her to see. "Monica, at first I tried using simple pliers, but they pulled to many hairs at one time and I just didn't get as much pleasure from it as I thought I deserved, so I looked around and discovered that if I use a hemostat clamp I can pull each hair out individually. It lets me actually choose which cunt hair to pull. Pubic hairs are tough and it takes a bit of a roll like spaghetti on a fork then a bit of a yank to pull one out. You would think that after I pluck a dozen or so you would get used to the pain; but let me tell you, no bitch has overcome that brief but sharp pain so far. It is both a delight and then again so disappointing when I pull down the panties of one of my pets and discover a bald pussy. As much as I love a bald one, I do get so much pleasure from transforming an ugly pubic mons veneris patch into a smooth hairless honey hole. Sorry, Monica but now it's Show Time." Monica tried to speak but the dental spreader prevented any recognizable words from being formed. The only sounds coming from her vocal cords were gargles. As she was trying to beg and plead, she suddenly felt a single hair being plucked from the top of her vagina patch. Then another and another and another. Each time he locked the hemostat clamp on a hair and plucked, a pain neuron fired. They were not strong hard pulls, but a steady instrument rolling motion, winding the hair around the tip of the hemostat clamp and then with an upward lift pulling the hair until it ripped free of its follicle. "Fuck, this really hurts" Monica thought and "how many pubic hairs do I have? That last boyfriend hated my mat and really hated picking pubic hairs off his tongue and even laughed when he said I had a Neanderthal pussy. If only I would have shaved it slick, if only."

It took Sonny almost an hour to remove all the hairs in her pubic triangle. Monica with tears streaming from the pain, had gargled, arched her back

and legs against the restraints, and banged her head on the OBGYN table as the pain was relentless. Especially painful were the short curly hairs sprouting from her labia major, once he got one wrapped on the clamp the upward pulling pressure would stretch the labia until the hair popped free. Finally finished with the hair extraction, Sonny stood up and admired his work saying "Damn that was a lot of cunt hair, you even had a mat around your asshole. Didn't anyone tell you what a disgusting snatch you had? Fuck girl, I can't imagine anyone ever wanting to stick his dick much less his tongue in that nasty crack." Sonny laughed and walked over to the prep table and picked up a large vanity mirror and positioned it where Monica could see her now hairless pubic area. "See how sweet it looks now. Any guy would love to slide his tongue in and wiggle it around for a lap or two. The plucking has made the skin really pink, and those brown pussy lips really stand out now; you ever had a pink pussy before Miss Monica? Now that we have a slick pussy, I believe it's time for us to take another short cigarette break. What do you think Monica?" Monica blinked her eyes yes.

Sonny decided that he would experiment with several torture methods he had read about in the two dollar paperback novels he bought for idea inspiration. "Now Monica, you have beautiful little feet. Have you ever thought about doing the bed of coals where people test their tolerance for fire? Since I can't very well have a bed of hot coals for you to walk, I have thought up another way less combustion hazardous way; see this soldering gun. I am going to touch it to the soles of your feet to see and hear how you react to the tiny hot tip." With that Sonny began touching the red hot soldering iron tip to the soft and sensitive skin of her feet. He pressed it against the tips of her toes and dragged it across the arch of her instep. Monica naturally screamed and bucked against the leg and ankle bindings. After fifteen minutes of horrendous, piercing screaming Sonny decided he needed a cigarette and beer break. Ten minutes later he returned to her side with an everyday wire clothes hanger. "Monica, you ever see how they mark cattle? Well, guess what my bovine friend, as soon as I twist this

wire into a "S" I am going to brand a big "S" on your forehead and on the cheeks of your ass. That for sure will let the world know who this cow belongs to." "Please Master no, the pain from the solder iron was bad, real bad, I don't think I can take much more. Please Master, no that." "Well, bitch sorry but you don't get to choose." With a pliers Sonny bent the end of the clothes hanger into a two inch "S". Wrapping a cloth around one end, he used a butane torch to heat the "S" to a red and then to a white. Holding her head tightly, he placed the white hot "S" against her forehead. And as the hot wire seared the letter "S" into her forehead and the smoke and smell of cooked meat rose to Sonny's nostrils, Monica screamed louder than ever and on a scale of one to ten, easily a ten going on fifteen. The fire had drained from the wire to her body and Sonny had to reheat the wire tip again. Pretty much the same reaction when he branded her ass cheeks. Then Sonny had another idea, and that would also predicate a reheating of the wire. Pushing her body flat against the OBGYN table, he pushed the against her lower belly just above her vagina. Poor Monica really bucked when that wire seared into softness of her shaved hairless flesh. Sonny was quite content with his markings. "Damn Monica, you are one marked and claimed bitch. Now everybody will know who you belong to. Who do you belong to Monica, tell me?" Tears flowing from the pain still radiating from the scorching, You, Master, I belong to You." "That's my girl. But the branding is getting pretty boring and the good spots are used up, so I think it's time to move on after of course we take a little break again."

"Time's up Monica. Do you like to swim? I bet you are a great swimmer and can hold your breath for a pretty long time. Let's see how long you can." "Master, I was never very good at swimming." " Nonsense, Monica. I think you might surprise yourself. Let's give it a good try." "Please don't hurt me anymore Master, Please." From a pail of water Sonny removed a soaking wet terry cloth towel. Draping it over her face, he began to pour water across the towel. This produced a drowning effect in the victim by

cutting off the air flow and allowing water to seep into her lungs as she fought for her breath. Her body went into a fighting struggle mode as soon as it realized it was being deprived of breathing air. After five minutes of her fighting the stirrups and bindings, Sonny said "You know Monica you were right, you aren't worth a shit at holding your breath, actually you are a big disappointment and now I will have to punish you." "Please no more, I can't take no more of this awful pain you lousing cocksucker." "Oops, you should never curse your Master. Jamming a cloth into her mouth, effectively gagging her, "Your noise was beautiful, but it is a little tiresome to listen too so the gag is now necessary and for being a nasty mouth, now you are going to really feel some pain. Sorry Monica, but now you made it personal. First I am going to fill your pussy with hot wax. Then when you think it's over, I'm going to treat you to a fine Costa Rican cigar."

Sonny then forced a set of vaginal spreaders into her vagina and lighting the butane torch, held a large blue colored candle inches from the gaping mouth of her vagina. As the flame of the torch melted the candle it at first dripped then streamed into the secret parts of her inner body. Monica bucked but had little energy left and soon just rolled her head from side to side as the scalding hot wax spilled into her birth canal. After filling her vagina with the wax Sonny then set aside the candle and lit a long, fat aromatic and expensive Costa Rican, hand rolled cigar. Once he had the cigar lighted and drawing, he began puffing it as a blacksmith does to create hot temperatures on his smithy forge. When the tip was a glowing red, Sonny placed it in front of her eyes and as she stared in horror at it, touched it to the tip of her nose. Immediately a small wisp of smoke rose from the searing. With no energy let, Monica could only continue her pain protest by rolling her head side to side. Encouraged by the reflection of pain in her eyes, Sonny then applied the searing cigar tip to her nipples and finally to burn to a char, her clitoris.

Several hours later after Sonny had exhausted all the horrible tortures he had in his inventory of terror he decided it was time for poor Monica to

feed the fish. The execution was the part of the plan that thrilled and excited him the most. Every second of it was designed to prolong the heinous entertainment as much as possible. Sonny even had a special spot; a four foot by six foot, two foot high, elevated stage built directly over a large floor drain and flooded in light by three spotlights. As no mistakes could be made, each step was rehearsed in detail. First he would saturate a rag with chloroform. Placing the rag over the doomed victims nose and mouth he would wait the two minutes before the poor girl succumbed to the conscious depriving vapors of the chemical. When her body went limp, he tested her by lifting an eyelid and placing his finger directly on the eyeball; if there were any reaction he would chloroform her again. He had to be absolutely very careful here, there could be no mistakes, at this phase of the abduction the victim would be the closest ever to freedom and a sudden revival and struggle for escape could ruin the show and put him on death row.

Once she was unconscious, her released her from the exam table and carried her over to the stage. Placing her face down on the stage platform, he carefully tied her ankles together and then carefully tied her wrists together behind her back. Once the hands and ankles were tightly bound he secured her waist to the stage with a large Velcro belt strap. Double testing the knots and the strap and satisfied that they would not fail, he walked to the refrigerator and grabbed a cold beer. Returning to the stage area, he positioned his lawn chair to view her face and body as it slowly recovered consciousness from the chloroform coma. Sitting in the chair, he lit a cigarette and sipped the beer. He enjoyed watching her body go through the stages of recovery. Occasionally, he would lean over and shock her ass cheeks or her nose or the side of her mashed tits with the 9 volt personal pocket, self-defense shocker. He liked to see how the body, although unconscious, would jump when the voltage from the tiny twin prod electrodes sent the message of those 10,000 watts of juice into her receptors. With portly women, it didn't have as much effect, it seemed the

more the girl weighed the less spectacular the response; another reason to be careful in his victim selection.

It usually took twenty or thirty minutes before the girl was conscious of her surroundings and predicament. At this point Sonny would stand and begin the dialogue. "I am so sorry but, as they say, everything must have an ending. Monica, you have provided me with pleasure and entertainment and I to you, when I treated you to the "anteater" and "straw". But we must part now. I would like to hear your last words, but I, from experience, have learned that you would probably just call me terrible, ugly names, so I will be leaving the jaw spreader on. Your body was a wonderful toy and I enjoyed playing with it very much. Thank you so much and it is now time to say goodbye."

Grabbing her ankles he then looped a thin cord around them and pulling them up over her back as extended as he could, he looped a large lasso around her neck in a modified "hog tie". Immediately she realize how she was about to die; she would be killing herself. As her legs became tired they would tighten the cord around her neck, eventually strangling her. Sonny, once he was satisfied the cord was properly connecting her legs to her neck, sat back in his chair, lit another cigarette, and sipped at the now semi-cold beer. This was the finale; this was the part that he loved the most. Sometimes he would masturbate and watch the victim's eyes as he jetted his semen in their faces. Other times he would sit silently and watch their losing struggle against death. Normally the self-strangulation took twenty to thirty minutes, although that one bitch took over an hour and a half; every time he thought she was dead, she would gasp and start the clock again.

After the victim had succumbed to the self-strangulation, Sonny would undo the velco strap and heave the body onto a small cart that Uncle Buck probably used to move boxes of meat in and out of the freezer. The freezer was a wonderful built-in, if the weather was raining or too icy,

Sonny could just store the body in the freezer for a better time. Wielding the corpse about on the cart, he would, using two large drum size black plastic bags and to cover the body, he would slide the top half over the head section then slide the second bag over the bottom leg section. You just never knew who might have wandered onto the property and would become a witness as he moved the body around the outside. Once the cadaver was bagged, he would load it on the bed of the all-terrain vehicle. He would then open the sliding barn door and before he drove the jeep like vehicle out, would survey his property with high powered binoculars. Seeing no one (no one ever had any business on the property and the signs warned against trespass) he would then drive the remains to lakeside where the brush shredder was kept parked. Climbing in the cab of the shredder, he once more scanned the area for trespassers; seeing none, he pressed the accelerator pedal several and turned the ignition key to the "on" position. Sonny was immediately rewarded with the roar of the huge horsepower engine coming to life. Sonny then set the idle and hopping from the cab, he approached the all-terrain. This was the manual part that Sonny dreaded; he had to cradle the body and lift it to the feed belt, a height of three and one half feet. Groaning, he lifted and pushed the body upwards until he had it balanced on the feed belt. Thinking about how unwise it would ever be to snatch an overweight buffet queen, he smiled; another reason to victim shop carefully.

Standing to the side of the machine, he opened the control panel and pushed the "Start" button. The machine bucked and shuddered to life, the interlocking toothed and bladed cylinders began spinning and roaring and the belt started carrying its unfortunate cargo to its destination. In less than thirty seconds, Monica's remains were chewed and reduced into a vapor mist of blood, flesh, and bones and sprayed through the discharge funnel across the surface of the lake. Sonny, ever thoughtful of the value of evidence, had strategically placed the shredder along the deepest shoreline part of the lake making it convenient to aim the grinder discharge

funnel up and out onto the surface of the lake. In the blink of an eye, Monica became a chunky fish slurpee. The fish now long accustomed to the noise of the machine shredding the many previous victims, associated that noise with food. As Monica's remains were sprayed on the surface, the fish raced to the area and began a feeding frenzy, the likes of which are often pictured on nature documentaries on the feeding habits of sharks. With the exception of a few pieces of bone that had escape a hungry catfish and settled on the bottom where likely a carp, turtles or other bottom feeders would eventually find it, Monica had successfully entered into the re-cycle of life. Within thirty minutes there were longer any traces of Monica on this world.

CHAPTER TEN

As sole heir to Auntie Mame's estate, in addition to the $550,000.00 life insurance policy, Sonny inherited a nine hundred and forty five acre hideaway retreat, complete with a catfish stocked five acre lake that belonged to Mame's husband's Uncle Buck. The nine hundred and forty five acres was in the center of a National Forest and accessible at the end of double gated, very private road. Uncle Buck had bought the land from a land speculator and paid a sweet price for it. As an entrepreneur, Uncle Buck had realized its value as a hunting lodge. Uncle Buck had electric run from the main road, a five hundred foot deep water well drilled, and built a three bedroom rustic log cabin lodge to entertain his rich deer hunting friends and occasional paying clients. Buck also built a state of the art abattoir to process the harvested animals. The 30x30 foot abattoir was constructed of local rock and to conform with state health codes, the entire flooring and walls tiled with white glazed Mexican 14x14 inch tiles. Overhead, for ease of handling, dressing and finishing the carcasses he installed racks and conveyors. Buck installed one stainless

steel autopsy table and a stainless steel OBGYN gynecologist examination table complete with stainless stirrups and leg straps that he bought at a surplus auction to use as a deer carcass butcher primary cut and break down cutting tables. Buck even had overhead water lines with pull down retractable hoses and spray power nozzles for washing the blood from the carcasses and off the tables, walls and floors. Buck also had installed state of the art HVAC climate control panels for the entire room; if you wanted it chilled, you could get that temp almost immediately, if you wanted it warmer, and you could do that as well. The blowers on the HVAC were oversized and could flip the atmospheric temperature completely in 25 minutes. For storing meat, Buck installed one walk in cooler/freezer and two chest freezers. The contractor that Buck hired did not overlook anything. For ten years Uncle Buck entertained friends and clients with stories of the wild while they cut and packaged for storage any unfortunate wild game creature they were able to harvest.

After Mame passed, now free from prison, and in need of dependable transportation Sonny had the attorney buy him a late model used van; no sense in burning up that windfall money up yet. On a lark, he decided to drive down and see what the inherited property looked like. He had made his mind up to put it on the real estate market as soon as he surveyed it for any other items of value he could sell. Career thieves never stop equating the opportunity and conversion of goods for the black market demand and instant liquidity of property. The drive took one hour and twenty minutes, not too long or hard on a good running vehicle. Sonny smiled to himself when he thought of the many, many times when Luke's beat up rust bucket truck would stop running or refuse to start. On many occasions, Sonny had to push that damn truck for many a mile to reach the next gas station or mechanic garage.

The directions took Sonny to the general area, and after several drive bys, he realized that the road and gate he was looking for, was for all practical purposes a grassy lane, hidden by underbrush and dense pine trees that

immediately twisted and ran on a diagonal from the county road. The only indication that there was a road there at all was a single tire rut in the 12 foot gap between the leafy walls of the barrier green pine trees. Turning onto the rough gravel lane and driving just a little farther from the county road brought him to a metal pipe gate. Sonny slid from the seat and grabbing the manila envelope the estate attorney gave him, removed a crusty metal key and tried to get it in the gate padlock. With the padlock keyhole corroded, it was obvious that no one had opened this lock for many years. Most people would have immediately thought that a lock smith was the next step. Not so. One afternoon in the general population exercise yard, a "how to" session on old resentful locks was presented by a very knowledgeable thief. This professor of crime also explained the versatility of a lowly penny paper clip how to bend and configure that paperclip into a tool to use it as a key to open a set of handcuffs. Remembering this lesson plan, Sonny went back to the van and retrieved a common one cent metal paper clip. Tilting the lock upwards, Sonny after bending the clip into a straight wire and tee handle, used the wire to scratch away the corroded metal from inside the lock tumbler chamber. Once he got the key in the lock and the lock open, Sonny drove the one mile long lane down to the second pipe gate. Once again, same type of lock corrosion. After Sonny mastered that cranky lock it was down another mile to reach the property improvements. As he was driving down the lane and appreciating the solitude and privacy, Sonny was thinking, "what a perfect hideout this would make. Let's see what the shack looks like. I might just move out here. No nosey cops, no nosey neighbors, nothing but trees and furry little bunnies."

When Sonny reached the end of the lane, he was shocked to see the buildings. He expected a rundown hillbilly cabin or falling apart trailer home and shed; astonishingly what he did see was there were a very nice stone lodge and some type of stone building probably used for a tractor or animal barn. Pulling another set of keys from the lawyer's envelope, Sonny

opened the front door of the lodge. He could not believe his eyes, before him were a well-designed and appointed home, a real home. Not the hideaway beer party trailer trash type of dwellings he was accustomed to, but a really nice home. By the measure of dust on things it was obviously in need of a good cleaning, but that was all, just a cleaning. Flipping a light switch, Sonny was surprised when the bulbs lite up. He did not know that Mame's husband and then the estate manager had kept the electric bills paid and the power on all these neglected years. Walking from room to room, Sonny noticed that the previous owner was a man of quality and did not buy the same cheap garage sale shit Sonny bought for and used as furnishings. Whoever closed the house up when Uncle Buck died did a very good job. Covers or throws were over everything, even the lamp shades had plastic bag covers slipped over them. Turning a bathroom water facet on, he was rewarded with a gush of very rusty water. Trying the hot water side, that too was very rusty. "I bet that rust will clear up when I run the facets for 20 minutes or so to purge the lines." He thought unconsciously. Sonny knew what he had to do and went to the circuit breaker and flipped the 220 circuit on for the hot water heater. After a ten minute cycle, he was rewarded with first warm then scalding hot water. "This shit is great. This place is move-in ready. Plug the frige in, get some food and beer, sweep the floor and do a little dusting and I got a castle that nobody knows about. Thank you Auntie Mame, you are the gift that keeps on giving. If you were alive and here right now I'd give you a hip toss, throw you to the floor, give you a good ole horse fuck and then eat your pussy till your toenails exploded and you begged me to stop 'cause you couldn't take it anymore. Yes sir." he mumbled to himself. In the kitchen someone even had placed balls of odor preventing newspaper inside the fridge and wedged the huge refrigerator door and the bottom freezer door open so the refrigerator and freezer would not get that musty stink odor. The commercial size PL gas cooking range had a large center griddle, two huge ovens and six burners. "A talented chef or even a prison cook could turn out enough food to feed an army with that stove", Sonny thought. In the

main room, there was even a big screen TV and Sonny bet that when he looked outside he would see a dish on the roof. After the inspecting the rooms and closets, Sonny decided to go see what surprises were in the shed.

Opening the door to the abattoir, Sonny immediately thought that Uncle Buck was either a mortician or was operating some type of medieval den of torture. Same thing here, everything was covered or sealed or ventilated as protection against the elements of aging. Because of the strict health department rules, the building to be allowed to commercially butcher meat for consumption had to be drum tight to pass the inspection and get the state health department stamp. There was not a single speck of dust anywhere. Sonny opened every drawer and every closet. He discovered the sharp knives and scalpels, the electric and hand operated saws, the electric leads used to tenderize meat, the meters, the stainless steel meat hooks, the hanging chains and a plethora of small tools and appliances used to breakdown and retail process meat carcasses.

Where Uncle Buck had designed a rail system to move a one hundred pound deer carcass hanging from a pulley, Sonny imagined a bound one hundred pound naked and screaming blonde girl swinging from the hook. Where Uncle Buck saw a bloody two hundred and twenty five pound bear carcass stretched and spread on the autopsy table for breakdown in consumable sized freezer wrapped portions, Sonny imagined a naked redhead tied to the table with electric probes in her ass and pussy. Where Uncle Buck saw a deer bent over the stirrups of the OBGYN pelvic examination table for ease in trophy taxidermy preparations Sonny imagined a raven black girl with her legs elevated in the examination stirrups begging him to remove his fist from deep inside her birthing canal. "I could make this examination table my altar of torture" he thought out loud.

In a third building, a very large pre-fab metal barn like building, upon sliding the barn doors to the side, Sonny was again surprised. Parked on the concrete slab was the big equipment, good ole Uncle Buck had used to contour a lot of the property. Their spotless condition looking as if they had just been driven through a showroom window, he saw a bobcat; a big backhoe; two all-terrain four wheeler, utility vehicles; a brush and limb shredder machine; and assorted maintenance parts and tools. The lawyer said that Uncle Buck had purchased a lot of the bigger equipment at public auctions, the limb shredder being a device that Uncle Buck got for a song and used to shred big alfalfa hay bales to feed and keep the deer healthy and happy residents of the property. To the south of the vehicle building were several one thousand gallon, free standing metal fuel tanks, one for gasoline and one for diesel fuel. Both were bone dry; someone had wisely emptied them to prevent the fuel from aging and going bad. Uncle Buck had considered every contingency and had everything covered. Sonny immediately saw the criminal logic of that equipment; with the heavy equipment he could dig graves and hide victim corpses so deeply no one would ever find them.

Now the next step was to get some fresh gasoline to fuel and start the four wheelers to scout the rest of the property, his property. Days later after returning to the property with two five gallon plastic gas cans he fueled the off road four wheelers and did a fence to fence complete survey the full acreage of the property, Sonny now knew that he several creeks, a thirty acre lake, two twenty five acre open fields, several elevated deer blinds overlooking the open space of those fields, and a balance of brush and tree covered landscape. While driving a four wheeler, Sonny had a sudden but criminally interesting thought, one of the convicts had hinted that he had the perfect way to dispose of a body; push it through a limb shredder. The sight of the huge machinery caused Sonny to pause, "Wouldn't that be convenient if someone were to take a body, push it into the steel shredding teeth of the shredder machine and have the discharge funnel pointed out

into the lake? Would the fish make short work of the tiny shredded meaty pieces, he wondered? A perfect disposal method for an inconvenient piece of evidence. If I follow through with my snatch plan, it is something most definitely worth thinking about. I bet the fish in the lake would just love to have an occasional feast of some juicy protein." Sonny thought. As a later project, Sonny decided that he definitely needed to move the brush shredder lake side and as a test, throw two fifty pound bags of fish food and maybe some beef scraps through the shredder teeth to see if the fish would actually feed on the shredded pellets and meat scraps or be frightened and avoid the area.

Returning to the lodge, Sonny rested in a leather recliner chair as his mind began to enter a zone that few sane minds would ever even dare to penetrate as he envisioned the capture and torture of victims.

Within thirty days Sonny had disappeared from society, the only one with a forwarding address was the lawyer who handled Auntie Mame's estate. He also realized he would need a mailing address to receive personal letters and parcels. For an extra fee, the attorney agreed to allow him to use the law firm's mailing address. He could then pick up his mail once per month or sooner whenever the lawyer would call or Sonny would alert him to an anticipated delivery. He truly needed a credit card to buy groceries, beer, and pay for the endless string of day to day items that popped up. The attorney arranged a card that drew directly from the trust and used the PO Box for an address. A phone and computer was a definite need and by using the attorney's law firm as the purchaser he was able to keep his name off the radar screen. He hired the lawyer to also purchase a late model pickup truck for him, do several contracts (one being an internet provider contract), create an escrow account to pay the utility bills, and asked for counseling on several criminal matters. Another little pearl he had learned in the penitentiary finishing school; once you paid a lawyer his testimony was forever sealed with client attorney privilege.

Using the pickup truck Sonny avoided the two closest towns and drove another fifteen minutes to the county line town of Gilette. In Gilette, with a resident population of over two hundred thousand, there were a number of big box stores, convenience stores and gas stations where Sonny could easily get lost in the crowd. From a long and carefully thought out list, he first bought enough provisions to last several weeks. On his next trip he bought a two hundred and fifty gallon metal gas tank and had it fitted to the back of his pickup truck. No one at the service blinked an eye when he pulled up and began filling the tank. This area being an agricultural one, ilt was quite a common practice for local farmers to do their fueling needs in large, portable fuel tanks at local gas stations and to drive into Gilette to get sale price gasoline.

Having surveyed the property and the farmland neighborhood, Sonny was now comfortable in his new home and now had time to acquaint himself with all the inherited equipment and butcher toys; Sonny was now ready to begin executing his plan and searching that first victim.

His inherited farm's strange slaughterhouse abattoir was outfitted with the standard tools and devices a person would expect to see in either a slaughterhouse or a medieval house of horror. Uncle Buck even had an inventory book that listed each item, where he got each item, and what he paid for it. Uncle Buck was an incredibly detailed man. There were several tables located directly under rafters which had pulleys bolted to them, but Sonny's plan recognized the need for several other things and to keep with the tradition of Uncle Buck, Sonny too kept a log of purchased items and cost. Thumbing through the Yellow Pages, Sonny found a medical supply house that stocked and sold used medical instruments and appliances. With his computer online, Sonny could shop and buy from the convenience of his lodge home; the only inconvenience was driving the one and one half hours to pick up the items at the lawyers office. Adding to Uncle Buck's inventory, Sonny bought several mobile surgical lamps (internet $123.65@) and one large stainless steel surgical prep table (($65.00 at a garage sale).

From the medical supply house he bought various scalpels (internet $9-15.00@), and different types of locking forceps (internet $3.50 – 22.00@) and other surgical tools to mount on that same wall. He had two Dremo drills (internet $18.45) complete with accessories. There were several dental adjustable jaw spreaders (got this idea from a porn movie) (internet $29.50 & free shipping), a large and a small, stainless steel, speculum dilator exam spreader (internet $21.55 & free shipping) and three different sizes of vaginal clamps (internet $19.50 @ plus shipping). On the other wall he mounted numerous tools for penetration; different sized dildos, funnels, even a stainless steel surgical device to force open and dilate an asshole.

Lupie…… *A single, head strong, semi- retired Latina career activist woman, 5 foot 4 inches, 125 pounds, 56 years old, jet black hair, small breasts almost covered with huge inviting, dark brown areolas, protruding wrinkled raisin shaped nipples, and a shapely body that was a man magnet, still attracting the wondering eyes of hopeful wishful thinkers. Lupie enjoyed teasing those serious eyes that begged for just a little taste, maybe a tiny kiss of those alluring nipples. Lupie had just a little bit of wildness in her; her mother used to call her "my little bandida".*

On the last day of her life Lupie had decided to reward herself with a few drinks after work. She knew a quiet little get off the pathway place that served good Mexican plates and great frosty Margaritas. Arriving at the bar she chose a table in a corner away from the drunks and noise of the bar. She ordered an enchilada plate, extra hot and spicy. The cold and frosty Margarita got to the table first. Lupie took one small sip and to appreciate its flavor, allowed the combination of the cold liquor and the salted rim to slowly savor and wash across her tongue. Oh did that taste so good as she felt its coldness elevator down into the depths of her digestive system. Before she finished her first drink the food arrived. As usual the cook nailed it perfectly. It was not the typical wet newspaper tortillas and cheap cheese of the fake Mexican restaurant chains, it was genuine handmade

tortillas and real, stringy and tasty Mexican queso. This was the perfect end to a day that she had looked forward to all week. Finishing her meal, she ordered another drink. Every time she dined at this bar, she ordered the same meal and also had five Margaritas. There was enough potent alcohol in the Margaritas to give her more than a slight buzz. Her apartment was in walking distance from the bar and Lupie always figured that if the drinks started to overpower her, as they sometimes did, she would just leave her car, walk home and return tomorrow to retrieve her auto. Lupie being a regular, the staff didn't worry if at closing time Lupie's car was still on the lot. They knew that once in a while she would leave her car on the lot and she always reclaimed it by noon the next day.

Tonight, the drinks seemed a little more potent than normal, but like any drunk, she did not think that she was that impaired. Wishing everyone a great evening and with a slight stagger, Lupie left the bar. Getting into her car and narrowly avoiding backing into another car, Lupie pulled onto the street. Concentrating on staying within the stripes of the roadway, Lupie did not notice the van that pulled behind her. Suddenly her rearview mirror was flooded with the Christmas tree bright flashing lights of a police light bar. "Fuck, just my luck" she thought, "I should have walked. Maybe I can talk myself out of this." Pulling over to the gravel of the county road, she parked. While she was waiting for the officer to leave his vehicle and walk to her window, she unbuttoned the top three buttons of her blouse. "Maybe if I give him enough of a peek, he will just give me a warning. So glad I never had any use for a bra."

Not wearing a bra had always been a tool that Lupie had successfully used in job interviews, negotiations, and any other matter where a horny gringo would stand on his tippy toes hopefully looking down her blouse to see that hidden treasure, her nipple. They were always rewarded if not with a nipple then with the shadow of her dark areola circling around that biological landmark. If the view did not work, Lupie was ready with the trump card, her ethnicity. At an early age Lupie had learned from her black

activist friend, Tayanta, the power of a minority race. In a lesson in persuasion, her black friend said "Lupie white motherfuckers are afraid of people of color. When you reach a stalemate, you need to pull out the race card. It will never fail you. I never say that they are prejudiced against black people. I never say black I always say nigga; that word by itself carries so much more force and weight than if I say people of color or minority. It is solely more effective when you scream out "so you don't like niggas, you white muthafuckas hate us poor niggas don't you? If you don't give me what I want I'm gonna have five hundred really bad mannered niggas boycott your front door. I know you don't want that, so let's talk and I will tell you what you are going to do for me." Never for a moment let them think you are anything but serious. Always threaten and always be certain you are loud enough for everyone to hear. Never give in, always demand and always let them know that if they don't cave, you are taking it to the next step, an ofay petrifying violent protest and boycott."

The advice Tayanta had given her served her very well throughout the years of demanding things for free that other people had to earn. Another thing that Tayanta had taught her was that protests and boycotts were so easy to organize. Pay some of the professional boycotters enough and they could fill a stadium in fifteen minutes with the "herd". The majority of the people that would march in a protest had, other than the most general of ideas, no real idea of anything or even remotely of the core of the issue, they just wanted to be part of any cool sounding movement; they are the true victims of the herd mentality disease. The educated ones were superficial and shallow and as long as there were no personal consequences or commitments, were ready to scream, hold banners, and put on the show. And that is what it all really was, a show. So many black dudes got white pussy just because a white daddy's little girl thought it was so "in and super cool" to be fucking a phony nigga activist stud.

As the officer approached her window, she leaned to the left to hit the power window switch knowing that by leaning like this, her blouse would

open up fully and the officer would be able to see all the way down to her navel. "Did I do anything wrong, officer?" Noticing the open blouse come on, Sonny decided to ignore the flesh buffet and get right to business. Looking down into the car window, immediately upon seeing her face Sonny knew that he had mistaken this bitch for a young girl; from the looks of her face she appeared to be, while still attractive, a woman of at least forty. "Stick with the plan, she's as good as it's gonna get tonight, and anyway I'm committed, hurry but don't rush it and arouse her suspicions" Sonny rationalized. "Well ma'am, I just observed you leaving a bar and your driving is very impaired and I suspect that you are driving under the influence. How many drinks did you have?" "Only one or two, officer and they were very small drinks." "Please turn the motor off and step out, ma'am". Using the vehicle door as climbing wall for hand holds, Lupie pulled herself out of the auto and slightly staggering walked towards the young cop. Realizing that he hadn't kept his flashlight beam lighting up the inside of her blouse, Lupie knew that she needed to step up the game. Twice before she had been nailed driving drunk and both times, once with a very young cop and once with a long in the face veteran, with both she was able to trade a quick juicy blowjob for a no-point traffic warning. "Officer, can we work this out. I'm sure that I can convince you that a warning will do and I will promise that I will never do this again. How does a quickie blowjob sound? Let me go with a warning and I will suck your cock till your asshole collapses. Wadda you say?" she slurred.

"Lady you are drunk. So please put your hands behind your back, you are under arrest for drunken driving." "Officer I can give you the best blowjob you ever had, your car or mine. I will suck your dick until your socks go up and down. I won't make a mess, 'cause I'll swallow all your cum. Just give me a break this once, please." "Hands behind your back, now." Sonny loudly commanded. Sonny's thoughts were already envisioning this drunken bitch on the compound. By the sounds of her invitation, she just might have a lot of talent to make his tamale happy. Sonny had only twice

before had any sexual contact with Mexican girls and both times it was phenomenal. One was an anal queen and the other could suck a brick through a soda straw. His tamale sure had fun with both.

Opening the van side door, Sonny helped Lupie up to the bench. "Sit on the bench and for your own safety I am going to chain you to the bench." Lupie realizing that she was not going to walk from this one started a barrage of insults and threats; "Fuck you, you pig. When we get to the station, I am going to tell them how you reached through the window and starting fondling my tits and when I started screaming, you dragged me from the car and handcuffed and arrested me. I am a very busy activist in the Mexican rights movement and when our lawyers get done with you, you won't be able to get a job as a night watchman at a junk yard. So, asshole, if you let me go, I will forget all about your rudeness and not make buckets of trouble for you. And you can forget the blowjob too fuck face. Wadda say?"

After she had finished venting and the bench chains were in place, Sonny grabbed her by the hair, lifted her body slightly and punched her in the stomach as hard as he could. By the way she gasped and folded Sonny knew it was a home run punch. "Damn that Vinnie was so right about the punching to quiet them." Thank goodness she didn't vomit. But lying on her side still suffering from the impact of the punch, she could but whisper and wheezed out "are you crazy, I'll have your job, just wait until I tell your sergeant." "Cunt, you're never gonna see anyone, much less tell anyone anything." With that Sonny began applying the duct tape to her mouth. With her mouth sealed, Sonny slipped a pillowcase over her head and for good measure using his fingers as claws grabbed her small tits right behind the nipples and squeezed them as tightly as possible intending to deliver as much pain as possible. Her body responded by bucking and twisting hoping to wretch free from the painful pressure of his fingers. Releasing his finger grips, "This is the game plan, we are going for a little ride and when we get to my palace, we are going to have fun; well you not so much,

but for me lots. If you make any trouble while I am driving, I am going to pull over and go to work on your tits. The pinches I gave you were very minor compared to what I can do. Small titties like yours don't have much meat and are so easy to crush. If you make me pull over I am going to take a pair of pliers to your tits. You cannot begin to imagine how much that is going to hurt. Now, it's up to you; be quiet and enjoy the ride or make trouble and wish you were never born. I want to know now if you are going to be a good girl, shake your head yes or no." Naturally Lupie shook her head "yes".

The thoughts raced through Lupie's head; "who is he? What is he going to do with me or to me? Does he just want some pussy because he can't find a girl to give him some? Is he a pervert? Can I swap some kind of sex for freedom; what have I gotten myself into? if only I had walked home tonight, I would have been showered and lying in bed watching TV and drinking another one of those ready-to-drink freezer Margaritas. Fuck me." Quietly she lay on that bench for what seemed like hours. Suddenly the van started bouncing like it was on a rough bumpy road. The van stopped and Lupie heard the driver door open and footsteps on crunchy gravel and then the driver return to the van, drive the van twenty feet, exit the van and close what sounded like a gate; he did this once more before pulling to a stop and turning off the engine.

Sonny hopped from the driver's seat, opened the side door and said "We are here and we are going to have fun. From this point forward you will call me Master and only talk when I ask you questions, shake your head yes if you understand." Lupie shook her head in a yes motion and suddenly realized the extreme danger she was in. Unlocking the anchor chain, he dragged her stumbling from the van. With the pillowcase hood still in place to avoid falling, she tried to take small steps. Impatient with her, Sonny just grabbed an arm and dragged her body to the doorway. Allowing her to fall to the ground, Sonny removed his set of keys from his pocket and opened the abattoir door. Pulling her through the doorway, he stood her

up and walked her to the OBGYM table. Lupie was of course helpless to struggle. Pushing her down on the table, he spread her legs and secured them in the stirrups. Once her legs were strapped in he removed one handcuff and locked her wrist to the table frame. Pulling her other arm across her body, he opened that cuff and secured that wrist to the table frame. Sonny then cautioned her; "I am going to remove the hood and then the gag. If you do anything to anger me I promise you, you will really regret it." As the hood was removed Lupie and as her eyes adjusted to the bright lighting in the room, for the first time in her life really, really understood fear. She was in a monster's den. Everywhere and everything surrounding her spoke torture chamber, especially the tools that he had so carefully placed around the room and on the walls. This wasn't a horny kidnapper wanting a little pussy and a suck, this was a hardcore motherfucker that was into control and pain. As he painfully pulled the duct tape free, Lupie began begging, "Please mister, let me go, you can do anything you want to me, but please let me go. I have a very sick mother dying from pancreas cancer and she needs me by her side. There is no one else to take care of her. You can fuck me, I'll suck your dick, you can fuck me in the ass, anything, but please let me go." Lupie began crying.

"What is your name bitch?" "Lupie, please mister, anything, I don't have any money but you can use my body anyway you want to get off; just let me go free." "Lupie, I seem to recall that shortly ago, I gave you instructions that you were always to call me Master and you were to never talk unless I asked you a question. Do you remember me telling you that?" "Yes, Master, I am sorry, it won't happen again." "Lupie, I know it won't cause now I am going to punish you for disobeying my commands. We are going to start by removing your clothing." Taking the medical shearers, Sonny then cut up from her blue jean cuffs to her waist. Roughly tearing the strips of jeans from her body, he bunched up her yellow panties and tried to rip them free only to discover that the nylon would not tear. With the shearers he cut the panties free. "For an older chick you got a cleanly

shaved pussy. Why?" "Master I have been shaving down there since I was in college, boys always like to kiss and lick it and don't like it so much if it has a mustache." "Lupie I like bald pussies, always have. By the way that is one pretty impressive clitoris. The head is the size of a big button. We're gonna have some fun with that, I guarantee you." Sonny laughed.

Next came her blouse. When she was completely nude, Sonny said, "So let's talk a little. You pretty much fooled me, I always try for the young girls and when you walked from the bar to your car I thought that you were in your twenties, boy was I off. How old are you?" "I am fifty six years old Master." "Well Lupie, you have an extraordinary body for an old cunt, no scars, no flab, no ugly veins, good legs; if I were to dress you in a bikini and put a bag over your head, I doubt if anyone could pick you out of a lineup of twenty year olds." "Thank you, Master." "I did not give you permission to talk." Sonny then took his thumb and jabbed it in the hollow of her throat immediately causing her to choke and cough. "Listen again whore, you do not talk unless I ask you a question or give you permission to talk. Understand?" Lupie choked out a "yes, Master".

"I have always been fascinated by older women. In fact my first true love was a woman three times my age. She taught me everything about sex and the female body. She taught me the "anteater" and the "straw". Do you know what they are Lupie?" "No, Master I don't." "I am not so sure I want to take the time to teach you those, but both of them are ways to eat a vagina and bring that girl to a height of ecstasy that she has never before reached. We are talking multiple climaxes, and I mean multiple. Right now I want to do a little exploring, is that all right with you Lupie?" Not knowing what the hell he was talking about and afraid that her answer would be the wrong one, Lupie said "It is OK with me Master." "But the first thing is to cleanse your body thoroughly. There is nothing as nasty as a tuna fish smelly vagina or an ass that smells like an outhouse, don't you agree slave?" "Yes Master, I am so sorry I didn't have a chance to shower this morning and I'm not as fresh as I like to be." "Lupie, again you speak

beyond the question, all that I asked you for was a simple yes or no." With that Sonny reached over to the prep table and picked up a pair of large every day nickel plated pliers. Grabbing her breast he carefully fixed the jaws over the nipple and pushing the open jaws forward until the tips of the jaws extended beyond the perimeter of her areola, with a smile he pressured the grips closed. The pain was immediate and Lupie screamed arching her back against the relentless bolts of pain registering in her brain. He continued the tremendous pinching pressure for another ten seconds and just as he was satisfied that he had administered enough impressionable pain, he suddenly released the pressure on the grips. In response to the relief, her body collapsed. She had never, ever imagined pain as bad as this. Sobbing Lupie begged, "Please Master, no more, please." "Fuck bitch are you ever going to learn?" Pinching the pliers on the other breast Sonny put it through the same torture. Lupie, screamed and banged her head against the table, but Lupie made no more words fearful of more consequence. Seeing that she was almost on the verge of fainting Sonny released his pressure on the grips. "Good girl, I think we can say you know the rules now. Right?" Sobbing, Lupie gasped out "Yes, Master."

Sliding a chair between the leg stirrups, Sonny closely examined her vagina. "Gee, it sure looks like it's been through a lot of cock gobbling campaigns. Bet you were the number one entertainment at gang bangs. In prison, the wetback gangs used to laugh how their Mexican whores liked to fuck muy guys at parties. I can just imagine rivers of cum seeping from your twat as the next fat tamale is plunging into you. How many gang bang parties have you been to?" "Master once in college I let four guys fuck me and several times I got drunk at the bar and the guys would walk me out to car, push me in the backseat, undress me, and then take turns fucking me. I never knew how many, but when I woke up naked in the back seat the next morning there were puddles of cum on the seat upholstery and my pussy was dripping. So, I really don't know Master." "Fair answer slave. We're

gonna have to give your snatch a thorough scrubbing inside and out, you sure don't want me to foul my cock with someone else's left over semen." Reaching over to the prep table, Sonny grabbed a vaginal spreader. Separating her labias aside and opening the vaginal canal, Sonny pushed the cold metal up her canal as deeply as it could penetrate. Fixing the metal adjustment tongues as wide open as possible, he screwed the wing nuts in a locking position. "Girl that is a pretty big hole you have here. I want to be certain that we get it disinfected and smelling sweet. The water is going to be slightly hot, but once your cunt is soaped, rinsed and flushed clean and the tingling of the hot water dissipates, you will feel a lot better."

Lighting a filter cigarette, Sonny moved his lips closer to her vagina and began blowing tiny smoke rings around her violated clitoris. With another degenerate idea popping to mind, he pursed his lips and pushed them tightly between the draperies of her labias and began forcing streams of cigarette smoke from his lungs into her birth canal. Laughing he told her "bet you never in a million years ever thought you would have a smoked pussy. Placing the palm of his hand on the flatness of her stomach, Sonny pressed sharply downward. A wisp of the tobacco smoke puffed out of her vagina and formed into a small white cloud. Sonny laughed, "real interesting; never thought of that before, a smoking cunt." Later I'll tell you how smoked pussy tastes, bet it tastes a lot like smoked salmon".

Sonny began the body washing routine; first the enema, then a general body jet wetting, then scrubbing with the soap, followed by a jet rinse. Lupie, thinking it was over and with the pain from the hot water rapidly diminishing, she was hoping for a rest. Not to be! Taking his position at the chair Sonny told her "Slave, it is time for me to clean your cunt. I like to call this special cleansing, "cleaning the canon". In a moment you'll see why. But first I want to gag you, I really don't want another headache." With that Sonny forced the dental jaw spreader into her mouth and locked it down. He could never decide which tool he liked the best the jaw spreader or the cunt spreader. Both were really neat pieces of hardware. Removing

a bottle brush from the prep table Sonny was certain to pass it in front of her eyes. He saw the fear and horror reflected as she knew what he was going to do with that bottle brush. He rolled the hard bristle brush across her nose, lips, over each breast, down her stomach and rested it against her clitoris. With a sawing motion, he rubbed the stiff bottle brush bristles back and forth over her clitoris. The pain of the abrasive needle points of the bristles was immense and instant. Lupie bucked and screamed. After a dozen strokes of the hard bristles over her clitoris he again passed the brush in front of her eyes. He again slowly rolled it down her body. When the brush head was no longer in her sight, Lupie could feel it being aligned within the throat of the vaginal spreader. With a hard thrust Sonny plunged the brush head past the metal tongues and into the soft tissues of her birthing canal. The pain of those sharp bristles tearing at her insides was colossal. He pushed the brush in as deeply as he could and for more pain she could feel him slightly turning the handle causing the bristles to tear clockwise at even more soft tender vaginal wall tissue. Her screams were piercing. She could hear him laughing. With a sudden yank, she felt the brush being pulled outward causing the resistant bristles to reverse. The pain was even more severe. When the brush head was almost free of the metal tongues, he rammed it back inside her. In her mind she pleaded "Please let me die. This monster is tearing me apart. I can't take much more. Please let me die." "Wasn't that wonderful, Lupie? I so enjoyed seeing you fight the brush."

"Now that your pussy is cleaner than it has ever been, it's time for me to treat you to some fun and pleasure." Rolling his chair to the vee between her trapped legs, Sonny began the "Anteater" and "Straw". As with all of his lady guests, her body, despite the previous pain, betrayed her and mutinied to a method of going down that she never imagined any mortal man could know and practice. The "anteater" set the table for the overwhelming passion of the "straw". As she there, in a fog of spent

ecstasy, Sonny laughed and said to her "You know it actually did taste a lot like smoked salmon. If only I could bottle it, I'd be a millionaire overnight".

"You look totally exhausted, but I have been working on a tiny idea that will recharge you. I am kinda excited to try it out, wadda say?" Sonny then reached over to the prep table and came up with a small glass bottle. Placing it closely to her eyes she could now see movement, tiny specs of movement within the bottle. "I know your question, what are those little black specs? Remember that story I told you about escaping when you first got here? I tied those two bitches to a tree and put a trail of honey up into their cunts. Guess what little nasty biting and stinging house guests moved into those pussies? Fire ants, of course. It gave me an idea and I have never gotten around to trying it, you dear Lupie will be honored as my first experiment. Will they recharge you or will they just eat and sting away? Can't wait to see." With that, Sonny carefully spread her vagina lips apart and even more carefully removing the lid from the glass vial, slipped the glass tube as deeply in her vagina as it would go. The effect was immediate; as the fire ants began stinging and biting, Lupie began struggling against her bindings. Sonny smiled, "it works" he thought, "Need to catch a few more to add to my pleasure toys."

"Those ants sure are mean, aren't they? Just when you thought you had nothing left, those mean little bastards revitalized you, didn't they? Time to move on, sorry I have no idea how to remove them, so poor little Lupie, you will have to just deal with them eating away at your pussy. But first I need another cigarette break. Damn nasty habit, but just like fucking with you, I love the feeling it gives me." Once Sonny had finished his cigarette he gleefully said "Now Lupie its time so let's move on to more fun things; and afterwards the fish will be waiting. Do you like fish?"

Stacey……. A thin, blonde woman who clerked at a shoe store and just barely made enough money to pay her bills on time, Stacey had a cute face, very straight and dead blonde hair, was 23 years old, 5 foot 6 inches, 103

pounds, had been through two disastrous relationships, and was for the last 6 months avoiding male companionship. She had long legs, large breasts, a small crooked nose and thin lips. The stress of living at home and listening to the daily and nightly drunken arguments between her mother and father kept Stacey after her two disastrous love affairs, a freelancer and living in a very cheap apartment.

Stacey grew up in a lower class environment. Her father was a forever faithful factory worker, laboring every day on an assembly production line. His one repetitious job was to place a plastic cowling cover on a lawn mower motor. After fifteen years of loyal service, and never missing a day, the factory shut down and he was one of the first to be laid off. With no possible future for a fifty year old, unskilled laborer, father turned to welfare and the bottle. Rare was the day when at 5pm, Stacey returned home from school that father was not gibberish drunk or passed out sleeping in his recliner chair. Stacey remember what joy it had been for she and mom to gift father that recliner chair so he could relax after a long day at the factory bending and lifting those lawn mower covers. Now that chair represented a safe space, a space to sit, drink and curse the world for his unfortunate misfortune.

Mother had kept her figure through two pregnancies and fifteen years of a hard marriage. With large magic breasts, a pixie face, a bright smile, dimples, a page cut hairdo, and a narrow waist and hips, she still had that thing that all men desired. Mom was employed as a bar hostess; a job that paid very well in tips and kept the family's bills paid, kept food in the refrigerator, and since father's layoff, paid for and kept him in alcohol. Father always resented her job, especially after losing his and with that, she then becoming the sole wage earner in the house. Father, having spent years in the pubs, knew she nightly faced the sexual temptations of the solicitations of countless drunken men and the wandering and groping hands and fingers of aggressive drunks trying to climb up her short waitress skirt and dip their finger into her honey pot. Too many closing times he

had left the bar to see one of the bar maids climbing into the car of one of the customers. And there was good reason that he feared the temptations his wife had been exposed to, after all there were those several times when he, himself, with a promise of a little extra money, had been able to entice a young bar girl into his back seat for a quick fuck or suck. Not a single week went by that she did not receive an offer from a bar patron to make an extra fifty or one hundred dollars and not every solicitor was a drunk. A good many of the want-to-be lovers were fugitives from a boring home life. Knowing her job paid for his whiskey, he was forced to accept the the possibility of temptations overcoming his wife's pledge of forever faithfulness, but still for the sake of his self-respect, needed to degrade and insult in an argument about working as a bar girl.

Mother had secrets too. She had, to get that wonderful extra money, three suitors that she rotated early evenings with. One was a fifty dollar man; the other two were hundred dollar tricks. Knowing how suspicious father was, she knew it would be impossible to tell him she had to work late, so with a little creativity she invented the early bird. Her shift began at 6pm. Each of her lover boyfriends held 8-4pm jobs. Three times a week she would tell father that she had to go in early to set up her shift. She would leave home at 4pm, be parked on the bar parking lot by 4:30pm in an area where the lot cameras did not scan; would have that day's boyfriend pull up his car alongside hers, hop into the back seat, pop her breasts out for squeeze toys, and deep throat the man's prick until she could feel his body stiffen and feel his semen sliding down the back of her throat. After the last moan the happy camper would hand her a fifty or one hundred dollar bill and tell her how much he loved the head and could they do it again next week. For ladies of the Blue Collar poverty society, blowjobs were better than real estate investments for sure guaranteed cash flow. It was a quick two hundred and fifty dollars extra a week. Two hundred and fifty dollars for ten minutes, or less, of cock vacuuming; isn't free enterprise great! The money paid for father's whiskey and a few nice

things for the family and was especially welcome for birthdays, celebrations and at Christmas. One afternoon during a mother daughter fast food restaurant lunch, discussing futures and the dismal environment at home, mom explained how she kept her sanity. Stacey was shocked to hear that mom had three lovers, but immediately understood that was the way mom dealt with the depression of living with a negative alcoholic. Stacey walked away from this lunch with a new respect for mom. Mom had refused to allow her marriage to degrade into continuous love shattering arguments and using her body had discovered a brief pathway to escape the depression of her home life.

After dropping by to see her mother, Stacey agreed to run down to the liquor store and get a bottle for father. It was this late afternoon trip to the liquor store to spend mom's money on a pint of cheap whiskey to have ready for her father when he returned from his once a week afternoon drink-a-thon at the armpit tavern that sealed Stacey's fate. Sonny had spent less than thirty minutes down the street from where he had an excellent view and could watch both a liquor store and a convenience store when Stacey pulled onto the parking lot. Exiting her auto, dressed in a sweater and shorts, Sonny immediately homed in on Stacey's made to order body. As she exited her beat up jalopy he could see through the binoculars long thin legs, flowing blonde hair and what appeared to be sizable, keeper tits jiggling beneath a thin sweater.

Pulling away from the parking lot, Stacey had only gone less than two miles on this forsaken stretch of county back road, when she heard the blurp of a police siren and looked in her rear view mirror to see the flashing lights of a police car. "Damn, what the hell did I do wrong? Why aren't these dipshit cops chasing criminals? Where in the hell am I gonna get the money to pay for a damn ticket?" Pulling her car over to the shoulder of the road, Stacey rolled her window down and putting a big smile on her face, and as the plainclothes police officer approached, said "Good evening detective, what could I've have possibly done to get stopped?". "Ma'am please keep your

hands where I can see them, turn the motor off, and slide out of the car and with your hands over your head, walk to the back of your car." As he drove away from the scene, with the next victim bound and gagged, Sonny began envisioning the pleasures he would get from those huge breasts. He knew that they were candidates for his skin tanning taxidermy and that they would make wonderful drawstring purses or bags for the safe keeping of other of his treasures. He also wanted to try out a new idea; compressing the tits in a locked down tortilla press, then clamping pliers on the nipples and areolas. Just might be some fun in that. He could envision the smashed purple breasts overflowing from the tortilla paddles, the pliers gripping so painfully the tips of her tits and just waiting for Sonny to start twisting them. But he had to be careful if he wanted those tits for his taxidermy idea, a tear or cut from the pliers would ruin them. Goodness, he was so glad he bought that book on taxidermy; it was so helpful when he decided to clip off clitoris' to hang like a necklace of blackened mushroom trophies in his study. The rest, well the fish were always hungry and the shredder always on standby.

Lycee…….. *A daughter of first generation Vietnamese parents, Lycee was 23 years old, very pretty, with jet black hair, large breasts for an oriental, slim at 4 foot 9 inches and 85 pounds. Lycee's body was female poetry. Lycee was a college student and hated working in the family business, a Vietnamese buffet restaurant. She was funny and always comfortable and happy around her Caucasian friends. A bit of a sexual predator, but in a different way, Lycee was constantly on the hunt, seeking partners to ignite and extinguish sexual fires by exploiting a secret world that she found fascination with and much pleasure in. Girls would giggle and call her a "nympho", boys called her "slope take out".*

Life is so grand when you are young and free of life's more difficult and pressing every day grind and adult responsibilities. It was very hard and sacrificing enduring the scholarly student study work, but only because of those sacrifices, you got into an undergraduate program for electrical

engineering and with a major in computer design, you knew, without any doubt, that within three years of graduation, you will be a very successful patent holder and on the road to being the next software billionaire. You just knew that those two software programs that you have been developing, in between lovers, for the last two years cannot help but be a commercial success and make you a rich dragon lady. The file program using an ultra-secure central on demand data base should be, with a little more fine tuning, an immediate hit in both small offices and medium size offices as it eliminates at least one salary and prevents malware and virus problems. The child's mental development and intellectual growth game should be a success with both parents and teachers. The skills that children will hone using the ten simple levels of progression are guaranteed to attract big sales. You are smiling thinking about all the fun, fame, and rewards just waiting for you on the other side of the diploma. You were ready for the world and you just knew the world was waiting for you to make your IT debut.

Focusing back in the present, as you drive this lonely stretch of highway, you realize how much you dislike driving at night; it is so dismal and forsaken. Nothing but absolute darkness out there. Oh well, in another hour you will be back on campus and flopping on your dorm bed next to your boyfriend of the moment. It is so good to get away from those steam tables and especially that nasty crowded kitchen, where the illegal Mexicans your folks hire for three dollars per hour crank out tray after tray after boring tray of Vietnamese and Chinese delights. Damn, the same food and food odors over and over again, it makes your taste buds rejoice with gourmet enthusiasm to see a simple cheese burger and fries.

There is a sudden shift in the car's balance and a drag to the left side. "Shit, a flat tire." If only your cheap old man had invested in new tires, instead of these rethreads. This is the fourth flat tire this month. The same plan as always, stand to the back of the car and look helpless. Sooner or later a genuine nice guy will stop and change the tire for you. You flash

back to that black guy in the flashy pimp outfit two flat tires ago, that pulled over, rolled the power window down and said "Hey takeout, hop in my ride and I'll make you forget about that tire." A direct "fuck you, nigga" and he was off cursing gook bitches and Chinese fortune cookies. Or how about that kid in the pickup truck, "if you suck my cock, I'll fix your tire". "Suck your own dick, loser" and he was off. But mostly, it is nice people that stop to help. Such a silly statement from a young naive girl; but you can't be too over cautious; it is precisely in the dark that both four legged and two legged predators hunt their prey. As part of his detailed abduction plan which successfully kept police homicide investigators in a fog, tonight Sonny was operating six hours from his torture and murder haven and less than one mile from your destiny and in route to the very same convenience store he previously and carefully cased and sticking to that route would take him right past your flat tire breakdown.

Sonny was certainly not thinking about road assistance for stranded motorists when he noticed your car on the roadside. The few seconds it took for his mind to focus on the scene of a distressed woman with auto trouble did not allow for a safe stop so he was forced to drive by. Lycee was very disappointed as she watched the tail lights of the police van speed past her and disappears over the hill. Recovering from his daydreaming inattentiveness, Sonny had seen enough of the woman standing beside her car to know that this was a good target and a fine opportunity to make a snatch. Making a U-turn at the first wide spot in the road he smiled as he flipped the emergency lights on. Lycee thought her luck had changed and was elated thinking, finally someone to change my tire; "Damn, what great luck, here comes the police van back and with his emergency lights blazing. Bet I can get the cop to change the tire for me." As the counterfeit cop was exiting the van, Lycee, facing the man said "Officer I am so glad to see you, just my luck to have a flat tire on the loneliest stretch of road in the county." Sonny's smiled what luck, this girl was obviously Chinese or some Asian ethnicity; Sonny had never had any social dealings with an Asian

much less the luck of trapping one. "Wonder if what they say about slant eyes having slant pussies is true; cause we are about to find out." he grinned again. This was definitely going to be a very special party. Sonny smiled. "Ma'am turn and please face forward and place your hands on your head and do not make any sudden moves." "Officer I didn't do anything wrong, why do I have to do this." "Lady, there has been a shooting, now do as I tell you and there won't be any problems." "I will not, I didn't do anything wrong and you have no reason to treat me like a criminal." Drawing his weapon, Sonny said "turn around face the car and place both hands on the trunk. Do it now." "Fuck you, I didn't do anything wrong and I'm not going to let you treat me like a criminal. Those professors were right; you cops are all assholes and enjoy fucking with innocent people. I know my rights and you are violating them big time." Sonny walked up to her, holstered his gun and using a karate move, drove two knuckles into the soft spot of her throat, the incapacitating consequence immediately causing her knees to buckle, her body to stagger backwards, and her to choke, gag and gasp for air. Grabbing her by her hair he slammed her face down on the trunk lid hard enough to make her nose bleed and twisting her arms behind her painfully forced the handcuffs on her wrists. He pulled her to the van and roughly threw her up on the bench. Recovering slightly, Lycee began screaming. Sonny drove his fist into her stomach collapsing her lungs, causing her body to jackknife and she into an air deprived gasping silence. Securing her ankles to the bench chains, he wrapped duct tape around her mouth to gag her and keep her from making those irritating screams or the typical cursing, pleading, or begging victim dialogue. He then quickly slipped a pillow case over her head and secured it by wrapping duct tape around her neck. Knowing every second he lingered on the scene increased the chances of a passerby taking note of the van and parked auto and could possibly lead to a police clue, he thought to himself, "Gotta get going, this bitch is taking too much time." Slamming and locking the van door, Sonny ran to her car and careful to avoid leaving fingerprints, removed her keys and purse and then locked the

car doors. With the keys and purse missing and her auto locked the police will at first think that she caught a ride; that would buy Sonny at least four or five additional hours to distance himself and this very special catch from the scene.

As always, before he pulled away from the roadside he flicked off the police light show. Sonny then quickly removed his fake police blazer and replaced it with a dull red, pull over sweater. He knew a passing policeman would take notice; very important to shed the blazer as soon as the victim is secured and the van is on the road. As the van began to accelerate on the hard top road, he told her "I know you can hear me. I am going to explain the rules. If you obey the rules, you will get to go free; if you don't, well, there will be consequences. First you always call me Master. Second you only talk when spoken to. Third you do exactly what I tell you to do and how I tell you to do it. Fourth you always tell me how much you love whatever it is we are doing. Fifth, if you are a really good girl, I will let you go tomorrow. Now, do you understand these rules? Shake your head up and down for yes, or sideways for no." Lycee shook her head up and down. "Good. Now relax we have a long ride ahead of us."

Hours later, exhausted from the driving, Sonny was relieved to finally see the break in the trees where his private road peeked through. These long distance expeditions were exhausting but necessary. It was very unwise to keep trapping in the same zip code; sooner or later the cops would figure a pattern and patterns got you caught. The geographic part of his plan was simple enough; decide a ring of four wide zone boundaries and rotate his activities within them on a random basis. This particular one was at the extreme edge of the farthest zone, but, with two colleges close by, had proven twice before to be rich in easy and pretty young targets. This time it really paid off, he had scored a real trophy; a beautiful oriental doll.

Parking the van, Sonny opened the door, unlocked and removed her leg chains, and with her being such a light weight, just like eager sex hungry

honeymooners, he cradled her in his arms and carried her into the building. Gently setting her on the autopsy table, her removed the hood, then ripped the duct tape gag off. The pain of the tape being removed caused the girl to blurt out an "ow". Regaining her composure she began intelligently assessing her situation. As she gazed around the room, her eyes enlarged when she saw and realized what the room contained. She screamed and began crying. "What is your name?" Sobbing she replied "Lycee." "You are forgetting something are you not?" "My name is Lycee, Master." "That's better. You obviously are Asian, what kind of Asian?" "I am Vietnamese Master." "I have never been with a Vietnamese or Asian girl before. Is it true that you have a naturally hairless pussy, and your pussy goes east to west and not north to south like round eye girls and all the gook boys have very small dicks?" "Orientals do not have much body hair, Master; my pussy is the same as any girl, and it is true that oriental men are not known for large penises." "You speak perfect English, Lycee. This is so exciting, a real Vietnamese girl; Lycee we are going to have so much fun. Right now I am going to put the hood back on and place you on another cold metal table. If you fight, you will have much pain. So I suggest you co-operate." "Yes, Master." Lycee thought "what a trailer trash asshole, I speak perfect English; me a girl with a 4.0 grade average. Maybe I can work this fuck face by appealing to his prick; never had any trouble getting my way with men before. When the grades dipped a little, a little hot love from me always worked on the horny professors and one or two of the gender fence sitter lady profs. Sex is one commodity that is always in demand and always the currency of the realm, any realm".

Once Sonny had her legs and wrists secured on the OBGYN examination table, he removed the hood. Lycee thought that now was the time she should try the seduction routine and maybe with it, she could bargain her freedom. "Master, I don't know what you want. My parents are rich and will pay a ransom. I will do anything you command. I have been with many boys before and know many things about sex. I have been an ardent

student of the kama sutra. Boys have always been fascinated by my tiny size and big breasts. My breasts are very real. Nothing you could ask me to do will shame or embarrass me. I have done it all; I can drink piss or slide my long tongue up into your asshole. There is nothing I would not hesitate to do. I can make you climax many, many times. I will give you pleasures you have never imagined. Once you have used me, I only ask that you free me unharmed after my parents pay the ransom. I will not go to the police after you release me. Will you do this Master?"

"Number one, no one gave you permission to speak. Number two, I don't need or want your parent's fucking money. Number three I will make you do what I want anyway. Pain is a very strong motivator. Number four, if you think for a minute that I believe you won't go to the cops you must think that I am an idiot. Right now, I going to cut off your clothes, I really can wait to see a naturally bald pussy. I heard of them, but never personally had one." That said, Sonny removed the heavy cast shearers from prep table and begun cutting upwards from her ankles to remove her jeans. Once through the waistband, his next cut was cut up through her sweater. Contorting her hips to the side, he pulled the jeans and top free of her body. Clad only in her red bra and black panties, she looked like a beautiful doll. Sonny began to feel a stirring in his loins. There were so many things to do that flashed through his mind, but for that second her body paralyzed him, all he could do was stare at the golden skin beauty that lay bound and helpless before him.

Sonny was fascinated by first her eyes and then by the yellow tint to her complexion. The eyes were alluring and promised secrets of the Orient. The tint of the skin was luring him like a soft canvas awaiting his brush. Immediately he decided to forego the hot bath, he did not want the scalding water to ruin the yellow blush of her skin. She now being almost totally naked, Sonny could see a petite body of exciting mystery and proportions. Maybe everything he heard from men that served in the Orient was true; the women were raised and trained to be pleasure

reservoirs for men. Almost with shaking hands he cut her panties on both sides then pulled them free. He felt a weakness in his knees as before him he witnessed a perfect vagina, a vagina the likes of which he had never seen before. There was no distortion, it was beautiful and normal, no slant at all to it. Draping, no flowing from along the sides of each labia major were less than a dozen long light brown pubic hairs that so softly and delicately framed the treasure slot, the sight causing a surge of plasma to inflate and throb his dick. Her pubic hair suggested a beautiful exotic artistic and wispy Confucian beard. Suddenly he was made conscious of the wetness of his seminal lubricant leaking from his penis in anticipation of a major ejaculation. "Too soon", he thought.

Next off came the brasserie; the bright red fabric cups promising a huge bounty. Cutting through the center of the fabric he pulled the bra off her chest and when both breasts rolled side wards in freedom, he gasped in delight as he felt another jolt of plasma spurt into his cock. Her breasts were symmetrical works of art, an intriguing yellowish tinge to the skin, chestnut brown nipples the size of pencil erasers surrounded by large dark brownish pink areolas each with a grove of tiny but pronounced eruption bumps across their surfaces. Not being able to resist Sonny began sucking each nipple, sucking like he had never sucked before. Sonny was like a lamprey eel, attaching his lips to the softness of breast and trying to suck that breast as if he were indeed a vampire, drawing and enjoying a blood feast. Each time, when his lips were finally lifted from her breast and the suction vacuum broken with a loud popping noise, a seriously dark passion mark appeared. Encouraged by his hickies, he lost control and began putting love marks all over each breast while Lycee quietly endured the pain. Looking at those gorgeous globes, he was proud of his work; each square inch of her breasts now contained a circular love mark. His fires became even more ignited, "Did you like that cunt?" "Yes Master I loved it and you did it so well; you played my nipples like a violin. Can I have more Master, please?" "I heard you gook bitches are piss drinkers, love huge

dildos up your pussy and asshole, like to rim assholes, love to gargle cum, and like to suck balls, is that true?" "Yes, Master, I can do all of that." Sonny smiled at her.

Not saying anything, Sonny positioned a chair between her spread legs so he could face her pooter up close and friendly. "You know what a "6'er" is?" "No Master, I don't." "Well it's a guy that likes to "69" but doesn't necessarily need the woman to reciprocate, in other he eats her pooter and she doesn't have to suck his dick. Get it now?" "Yes, Master it sounds like something I would love." "Your oriental ethnics intrigue me so much, I am going to treat you to the pleasures of the "anteater" and once you begin panting "the straw". Do you know what these wonderful treats are, slave?" "No Master, but please do it, it sounds so exciting and sensual." Lycee was trying to use her intelligence to invest in a future moment when she could create that second where he would drop his guard long enough for her to turn the tables and escape this madman monster.

Within in minutes of Sonny putting the skills of his tongue and lips to work on her vagina, Lycee realized she was losing the fight to prevent this evil motherfucker's tongue and fingers from overwhelming the creature that lurked within the sexual sensors of her nervous system and brain. Midway through the "anteater" Lycee's body, ignoring her mind commands, began to softly rise pushing against his open lips as those lips sang the song of seduction. It only took several more sensual electrons racing through her receptors before her hips began a buckaroo rodeo, bucking against his face. Lycee began to moan loudly and scream "fuck me now, please fuck me now. I want you inside me. Please Master, give me your cock."

Smiling now but ignoring her pleads, Sonny kicked up the program into the "straw" phase. Curling his tongue into a hollow cylinder he began vacuuming the wrinkled drapery of her labia minor, first the left one then the right one. Using his fingertips he reversed them with the palm facing outward and then curled them up and deeply within her vagina. Dragging

his fingernails across the bumpy threshold of her soft tissue inner wall, her body arched and she moaned a very long moan of pleasure. If Lycee had been able to free her hands she would have tried to gasmask him and smother his face within her pussy. Her moans were closer together and louder now and reached a screaming pitch. Sweat was beading on her forehead, lips, breasts and stomach. This was a sensuous torture she had never imagined anyone capable of performing on anyone much less to her. This was fantasy sex out of a cheap boy's paperback jackoff book. Never had any boy, and she had lots of experience with boys lapping and tongue dueling her pussy, had any tongue or fingertip taken her to this level of pure ecstasy. Between screams and moans, she begged; "Cock, Master, I need your cock, my cunt is on fire, please Master fuck me and fuck me hard, please Master."

Now she could not deny the fact that this sad motherfucker was a master at eating the oyster and she was truly and wantonly experiencing pure orgasm after pure orgasm. He had taken total control of her sexual beast, tamed it and won. The "anteater" and "straw" had given her an out of body experience and mentally freed her from her present state of fear and bondage, delivering her to a level of ecstasy she had never even imagined attainable before. If only she had met him under normal circumstances, she would have loved to be his lover. Losing control, she moaned and shouted "More, Master, more, please don't stop now. Your prick, Master, stick your prick in me, please Master I need your prick so bad."

Suddenly aware that he was only seconds away from his engorged and throbbing prick jetting a hot ejaculate in his shorts, Sonny decided a short postponement was in order. "Not now China girl, time for a short break, eating pussy makes your tongue tired. I can barely talk. Let's take a fifteen minute break, I really need a smoke." Half manipulating and half out of gratification she responded; "Yes, Master that would be nice and thank you so much for this wonderful experience."

Both immediately became absorbed in their personal thoughts. Lycee silently cursing him for making her enjoy his gift while desperately trying to parlay this into a component of an escape plan, and Sonny trapped with visions of her prefect body, perfect face, perfect breasts and a masterpiece of a vagina. If only her could keep her as a sex slave, but how? There would be so much work to do to prepare a cell, he would need some type of cage, a toilet, maybe a small refrigerator, a radio or a TV. It would have to duplicate in security the cells he lived in while serving his sentence out in the penitentiary. There could be no possibility for escape. Weighing the dreams of her charms again, he decided that to create a secure place to keep her captive would be way too much work on this short a notice and besides, the prisons are filled with people that were impetuous and jumped into a situation without proper planning. The next best thing was to keep her alive for a few days and that certainly would be easy enough to do. When he got tired of her as a plaything for the day, he could place the hood back on her (hoods always worked to prevent an uprising; nobody tries to tackle something they can't see); cuff her and chain her ankles in the corner where the toilet is. If he had to, he could even feed her through a slot in the pillow case. So, smiling to himself that's what it would be, a few days of fun then a personal date with the shredder and fish pond.

Securing her back on the examination table he said "OK China girl, you almost got me to cum in my pants. That doesn't happen ever, no girl has been able to hit my high note like that. My dick has been dripping the entire time we have been sitting here on break. Now it is time for me to give some of what you begged for. Keep your mouth shut, understand?" "Yes, Master."

Now totally naked, taking a standing position between her extended elevated legs, Sonny slowly inched his penis into her. She was still oozing vaginal lubricant. Once he could feel his balls resting on that sensitive spot between the bottom vee of the vagina and the anus, Sonny pulled back to almost exiting and then with all his might plunged his dick as deeply and as

forceful as he could. She gasped, but said nothing. Ramming in and out of her he could feel the sexual electrons racing back and forth from the tip of his cock back into his balls and into the sensual control of his cortex. "Now Master, I can feel you and it is a good feeling, please let your cock explode within me and your cum squirt and warm my pussy, please, Master." "Not yet, I have several more places I want to visit." Stopping and allowing his cock to flop out he adjusted the stirrups upwards on the exam table and then grabbing both of the table's leg rest, he elevated them and locked them high enough to present a prefect shot at her asshole. "I am now going to fuck you in the ass, is that OK with you China girl?" "Yes Master I want to feel you cock as deep in my ass as you can force it. Thank you Master." With vaginal lubricant having seeped from her and coursed down through that special spot, much of it flowed over her anal passage. Sonny, centered his cock on her asshole and pushed. There was little resistance. He pushed harder and it plunged all the way in. Again she softly gasped; it hurt but the pain was not a big hurt. Thank goodness she spent that one semester with that big nosed and big thick dick college professor's prick buried in her ass at every opportunity. It served to pump her grade up from a C+ to an A+; and now here it is again that stretched asshole saving her from a most unpleasant pain.

After several thrusts and not hearing the screams and not feeling that virgin sphincter squeeze response to the cock invasion similar in most of the other girls, disappointed, Sonny pulled his cock from her bowels. "Seems you have been doing a lot of back alley work, haven't you?" "Master, many years ago a phy ed teacher with a very large penis raped me and tore my ass to shreds. He was arrested and is serving time for having sex with a minor." "You really expect me to believe that China girl. There have been more dicks in and out of your asshole then in a police station. Now tell me the truth or there will be consequences." "Yes you are right Master, many of my boy friends only wanted two things blowjobs and to fuck my ass. I enjoyed it very much Master." "Now I am going to give you

a chance to prove you are as good as you say you are." Sonny then moved from the back of the table and squared off with his cock inches from her face. "Master can you wipe your cock off first, it really smells." Sonny then reached down and grabbed a handful of her jet black hair and lifting it from the table slammed it down. Immediately Lycee recognized the danger of the situation. Fighting a moan, "I want your prick down my throat now Master. I want to feel your cum squirt on my tongue. I want to gargle your cum and swallow every drop, Master, please."

"Open your mouth." Obeying his command she almost gagged and vomited at the fresh smell of her bowels on his cock. The heightened sexual duress rocketed through Sonny and within four deep throat plunges, his cum was splashing against the back of her throat. Sliding his dick out and wiping the still oozing droplets on her lips, he made a point of saying "I didn't see anything special about your cocksucking, I did all the work, didn't I". "But Master, if you would have wiped it clean and fresh I could have given you something special, I am so sorry but I kept gagging."

"Fuck, China bitch you broke the mood now, what are the rules about talking? Now, we are going to have to punish you, you stupid fucking gook."

Reaching over to the prep table, Sonny picked up a very large dildo that was studded by hard plastic nubs. Ignoring her screaming, first he tried to ram it up her birthing canal, but even after being lubricated by the wonderful vaginal lubricants Mother Nature provided and a healthy glob of dependable shaving crème, it just wouldn't go in. Setting the dildo aside, Sonny decided on another instrument for the delivery of pain. Inserting fingers, he managed to force four in but couldn't get his hand past the thumb. That brought louder screams from Lycee. "Don't look like this is going to work, unless I slit your pussy just like they do when delivering a baby. Do you girls ever talk about the joke when the pediatrician asks the

husband after the slice, should I stitch the gap for 3 fingers or four?" Lycee in too much pain, did not answer.

"OK, Miss Lysee, here is what I am going to do to teach you about obeying my rules; picking up the electric probes from the table, Sonny switched the transformer on and holding the probes close to her eyes, he sparked the two bare probes together. The panic in her eyes was immediate. "Now Lycee the fun really begins. By the way, I always heard that you Orientals are crazy about fresh fish; how do you feel about fish; do you like fish Lycee?"

CHAPTER ELEVEN

Betty......... *A 19 year old, fun seeking, 5 foot, 4 inch, full breasted, redhead with wide hips, a narrow waist and a very outspoken personality. Betty was always the livewire at parties and never had a dull and boring weekend. From college, she had explored lesbian love and pretty much ended up AC/DC, with more of a pronounced tendency for the company of ladies and their gentle and secret places then men with their gross appendages and ejaculations.*

Through the binoculars Sonny had watched this one a little more carefully than the others; she had a butch type haircut and a man's front zipper pants and a short sleeve tee-shirt. She did not appear muscular but he was hesitant to target her as she just might be a fighter. However, focusing on those jiggling, bouncing obviously braless big tits as she got out of her car and again as she got in the car forced desire over caution and Sonny decided to pull her over; after all, he could always give her a traffic warning

and let her go if the physical threat appeared to be more than he wanted to tackle.

Three miles down the road, Betty noticed the flashing lights; "Fuck me, now what the shit did I do that this cop is going to give me hell for?

Once Sonny had her backing out of the car with her hands up he decided that he could handle the situation should she decide to struggle. Cuffing her and answering the usual questions and protests, Sonny began the pat down. When he slowing dragged his fingers across her nipples she started with the usual complaint of sexual assault and when his fingers glided down the front of her jeans and suddenly wiggled into her vagina, she exploded with indignity and even tried to break loose and launch a disabling kick at his nuts. Laughing, Sonny threw a round house that connected with her upper abdomen, driving all the air from her lungs. Now incapacitated, it was very easy for him to push her into the van and shackled her to the bench and tape a gag in place and tape a pillow case over her head. Following the practiced routine, he removed all her personal items from the car, locked the car doors, hopped in the van and began the journey to his hideaway castle.

The routine was basically the same, strap down, clothing removed, soap wash and rinse and then playtime. Sonny was delighted with this one, both of her huge tits had been tattooed by someone with talent. There were florals, skulls, snakes, lips. The right tit had one word "HOT" and the left tit had "COLD". Sonny was so impressed with the artwork that before he killed her and fed her to the ravenous fish in the lake, he skinned her tits out and then tanned them with borax and salt to keep them forever as mementoes of a girl with a sense of humor. He imagined that skinning a person alive, even if they were gagged, was something that would cause so much screaming pain and agony he could imagine and picture the unwelcome noise and struggling problems. Skinning a live breathing body was just something he wasn't ready to tackle yet. He had read in one war

story tabloid magazine that the Japs delighted in cutting a twelve inch square on a Korean woman's back, then making one inch vertical cuts from top to bottom and using pliers they would seize a corner of one of the epidermal strips and then slowly downward pull the skin free. The pain was excruciating the article said. Maybe someday, Sonny was ready to do the strip skinning torture, but right now he was more interested in the more conventional torture methods. However skinning a corpse was a different ballgame. The actual removal of breast skins wasn't very complicated and didn't take much time; you took a scalpel and made an incision completely around the breast at the chest. You then pinched the skin with a pair of pliers and began pulling it downward, everywhere it resisted, you cut it free with the scalpel. You did have to take care when you got to the inside opposite the nipple; it took many tiny cuts to free the nipple of tissue. One thing, even with a stone cold dead victim, you had to be absolutely sure that the body was strapped down tightly, the shifting and twisting, if there was any free movement to their body would cause you to make punctures or slashes in and ruin the breast skin. But once the tit was skinned out, you indeed did have a trophy that would, and by adding a simple drawstring, make a nice erotic purse to put your coins or snug your ball sack in.

Betty was a very loud screamer and Sonny was forced to clamp her mouth open with the dental jaw spreaders. Amazing even with the jaw spreaders in place, she could still force out loud screams at every stab of pain. This was a most pain sensitive victim that gave Sonny much pleasure, at even the mildest of electric jolts, she would scream like a creature from hell. Her ass was a special delight, being a ladies' lady, few things found their way into her rectum, leaving it extremely tight and a challenge to Sonny's probes, bottles, and cock. Her energy completely exhausted in three hours and her screams reduced to semi-conscious moans, Sonny reflected as he sat in his chair and watched her face turn purple as she strangled it was

such a shame to lose this one so soon, but the fish won't be disappointed; they are never disappointed with the menu fare.

Carol ...... Carol was born a generation too soon. She was a child of poverty and discovered that for her success had to be about recognition. She was a campus activist, and at 28 years old knew that to move forward she had to find the right protest and media outlets to connect with. Just like any business career, she had to locate the right theme, promote and manipulate herself within it, and use it as a means of celebrity to garner buckets full of zombie supporter dollars or fill an application with a lot of bullshit and grab a few of those grants from celebrity seeking big dollar donors. A single grant could keep her in high fashion for at least two years.

"That lazy no good for nothing asshole, sending me out in this shitty weather to get his fat ass cigarettes, chips and a six pack of beer. The fucker lays around on that sofa night and day and when he's not asleep, watches TV and then bores the living shit out me with bios of the cast characters and high lights of their celebrity life. Like dick face is some type of Hollywood critic. Well, that's all gonna change. Saturday when fuck face leaves for the bowling alley to be with his best bowling compadres, he's gonna come home and find all his shit in boxes in the driveway and all the door locks changed. I am tired of telling him to get out, this time it's the big scene. I'm gonna make sure that I'm not here to hear his whining and begging for one more chance. The fuck has played that game for the last time, not once has he ever got beyond picking up the newspaper (that I paid for and brought home) and making a single call on any work available in the Help Wanted ads. Well jobless fat ass can go home to mommy and live in that basement that I rescued him from fourteen months ago. He fooled me pretending to be an activist with stories of rock throwing, tear gas, Molotov cocktails and police violence. As an activist, a masked rioter, or really as anything, he's a big pussy and an all-around failure; the perfect 'nothing man'. I'll play the game this one last time; yes sir cigarettes, chips and beer" she thought as her car pulled up into the dimly lit parking space

of the convenience store. The rain was beating down as she exited the car and scurried to the door. The clerk looked up from his computer game and thought "nobody has been in the store since this nasty rain started pouring hours ago, she's gotta be desperate to be out in it, bet she ran out of pads, cigs, or pet food."

Another set of eyes, predatory eyes were on the outside basically thinking the same thing, why the hell would anyone be out in this wet shit unless they were victim hunting. He had gotten enough in the brief look he had of her bailing out of the car to guess that she was the right package, the rain jacket made a detailed physiological assessment impossible; however she did have the fleeting appearance of being youngish, no weight problem and with an alluring bounce in her step as he watched her hop from the car and become lost behind the steamy plate glass windows of the store front.

Her shopping was with joyous purpose; these three articles, a pack of filtered cigarettes, a large bag of cheese/taco flavored potato chips, and a twelve pack of imported lite beer represented the threshold of a new life. Tomorrow there would be no more errands in the rain and no more panoramas of a five foot eight, three hundred pound blimp lying in his crumbled underwear on her sofa, his huge hairy belly flowing from beneath a not so fresh tee shirt, shoveling her food, and burning her electric bill watching her television set. Goodbye fat fucker. Maybe he can find another desperate woman whose soul he can fool and whose whole being cherishes and melts for a man who can pretend to be devoted to anarchy, quote Shakespeare, knows the arts, and can whisper love sonnets from the golden and romantic age of the Renaissance.

Paying the clerk, she grabbed the grey plastic carry out bag and hefted the twelve pack of cans so nicely and conveniently nested in its brightly advertised cardboard case and turned for the door. Little could she realize that this was the last purchase she would ever make in this life and it was for someone whom she hated. Sprinting to the car and throwing the beer

and grocery bag in, she slid behind the wheel. Checking her side mirrors and rear view and seeing no other forms of life or transportation (who the fuck would be out on a night like this) she backed from the brightly striped parking aisle and stopping and turning the wheel she goosed the accelerator pedal and was back on the deserted highway once more. Reaching down she adjusted the defrosters and turned the music up a little higher. Thinking and smiling about she was delivering a condemned man his last meal she looked into the rear view mirror and saw flashing red lights racing to catch up with her. "Shit, what the hell did I do wrong?" Hoping that it was a police car on another call she slowed down only to find that the flashing lights were now right behind her about two car lengths. With no choice she pulled to the side, put the car in park and waited for the cop to get out and come to her window. She had been told years ago in a community awareness class, that there were several things you did not do when a policeman pulled you over; you never got out of the car unless commanded to do so and you never reached down below the car windows with your hands, you always kept your hands locked on the steering wheel and fully visible until the police officer asked you for ID.

As he pulled over to the side and slightly to the left, just like a real cop would do (protects the cops from getting clipped by a gawking or drunk driver) he knew that the next seven minutes would be the most exposed and most dangerous part of the plan. He knew or reasonably guessed that if a real cop were to drive by, the flashing dash lights would likely and immediately arouse the cop's curiosity as to who was pulling vehicles over and working in his area. If this were to happen, his choices was but one; identify himself as a police officer and as the cop was sorting that through his mind, pull his revolver and murder the cop in cold blood. There was no other escape. This was a rehearsed part of his plan, even down to the conversation; "Nasty night to be out and working ain't it? I just got hired as a junk and bunco squad detective (all big police department have squads where they train cops for promotion or hide or keep cops from the public)

in the next county and going home I observed this woman driving very erratically so I pulled her over before she either killed herself of some poor family. Have you radio'd your dispatcher yet? I haven't gotten her license or insurance card to run, so would you mind doing it? You can see that she looks like a DUI." As soon as the cop's eyes float over to the woman, draw your piece and shoot. The woman must be executed too. Be absolutely sure that you leave a dead cop and a dead woman behind, especially if he hadn't called in to the dispatcher yet; it will buy you at least an hour before someone stops, sees the dead cop and dials 911. The van's phony license plates definitely will help keeping your ass out of the back seat of a real police car.

Looking back through the rear view and side view mirrors she could see the officer was exiting a van and was dressed in a poncho type rain coat. As he approached the window, she hit the power button and dropped it full length. "What did I do wrong officer?" "Ma'am keep your hands where I can see them and slowly get out of the vehicle and with your back to me, step to the rear. Do not make any sudden moves, please." Suddenly you realize this is no ordinary traffic stop. "Officer, I haven't been drinking and just left the store on the highway. Honestly, I'm not drunk and have not been drinking." Then you remember the twelve pack sitting on the passenger front seat. "Fuck and double fuck!" you think. "Ma'am Just do as you are told and everything will be OK." "Officer the rain is coming down pretty heavy and we are getting drenched just sitting here with the window down, can I stay in my car?" "Ma'am, please do as you are instructed. Now turn the motor off, get out of the car, and back away from your car and towards my unit, start doing it now." "I don't understand." "Ma'am, I not going to tell you again, do it!" So you are now out in the rain and as commanded, you back away from the highway until you are even with the sliding side doors. "Ma'am please place your hands behind your back, I am going to handcuff you, and for my safety and yours I have to do a pat down to see if you have any dangerous weapons, then place you in

temporary custody. As there are no police women working tonight, I have to do the pat down and if you get upset, you are welcome to file a police complaint when we get to the police station" "Is this really necessary officer, I know my rights and this is bullshit." "Ma'am if you don't do what I tell you to do and do it right now I'll be forced to consider you as resisting arrest and it will be necessary for me to use force to subdue you, understand."

With that said you know you can't bluff and this cop means business, so the best option is to meekly comply. After you place both your hands behind your back, you feel a strong hand tightly squeeze your fingers, locking your hands together; one hand after the other he twists behind your back and locks them into the cold handcuffs. "Ma'am, I have to do the pat down now, sorry." He immediately and roughly reaches around from behind your body and pushes his right hand up your sweater and you can feel his hands flattening your breasts, it feels as almost a Neanderthal grope. Once satisfied there are no bazookas in your bra, his hand slides down into your slacks and glides into your panties. You feel very uncomfortable as you feel his fingers dancing over your vagina and suddenly the long one dips inside and slides the full length of it. Shocked and embarrassed you blurt out "This is degrading, is this really necessary officer?" "Yes, absolutely ma'am. You would really be surprised if you knew what we discovered hiding in that personal spot. Many years ago, a woman had a small derringer hidden in there and because there was no police woman to check, she was able to shoot the officer in the back of his head when he got behind the drivers wheel. I am sorry but it is necessary." Removing his hand from your slacks he lifts your arms enough to cause you to bend forward, he pushes his hand down the back of your slacks and again into your panties and you suddenly feel a finger probing your anus. "That is enough officer, as soon as we get to the station, I demand to see your supervisor. This is uncalled for and demeaning and I am going to file a

complaint and talk to my lawyer first thing tomorrow to see what he thinks about this degrading groping."

With the cuffs securely on your wrists he explains "Ma'am we just had a robbery and murder and a victim ID'd the shooter as a youngish female in a dark car. You fit the radio alert. If you have committed no crime then after I drive you to the station for a walk by the victim for an ID, and if the victim says you're not the one, then after you file your complaint, I will bring you back to your car. Do you understand? Now we were short patrol cars tonight and I got stuck with this damn van. You will have to sit on a very uncomfortable steel prisoner's bench, and I will have to leg cuff you; sorry it's a police procedure. It should be all over in about forty five minutes. I hope you understand." Well, other than his manhandling of her private parts and after all what did you expect, he was just a man and her big tits were always grope targets, it's not like no one has ever stolen an "accidental" feel; and he does seem like a nice cop and the inside of the van is dry and it's raining like hell, so why not just go with the flow.

One hour later, after an occasional small exchange of questions about his career and his police duties, you suddenly and panicky realize he has been driving far too long to get to a victim face view. "Officer, where are you taking me? We should have been wherever it was the crime happened or the police station at least thirty minutes ago, tell me now where you are taking me, I have my rights and I won't hesitate to report you." "Shut the fuck up bitch. One more word out of you and I coming back there to make it real unpleasant for you. Now keep still or suffer, understand?" You know now things aren't exactly right and are very frightened. "Maybe the guy is a rogue cop and is taking me somewhere to rape me. What did I read in that tabloid about abduction, do not antagonize the man, do not provoke him into violence and wait for an opportunity to alert someone or to escape. Hope the author knew what she was talking about," so for now you decide to follow that author's fantasy land game plan.

After another hour of driving, the last twenty minutes down some really bumpy roads, the van pulls to a stop. The driver gets out and opens a gate. Back in the van, he pulls through, hops out closes the gate, hops back in and the van bounces down the rough road a short distance before coming to a complete stop for another gate. Opening and closing this last one, and a minute later, he pulls into a yard type driveway and turns the van's engine off. When he opens the side door you realize two things; the rain is only a drizzle now and you are in the middle of a compound. Removing the leg chains, he drags you out of the van and pitches you down into the wet grass. "Screaming won't help; we are in the middle of nowhere. This is my party house and you are going to be my guest and we are going to have a very, very good time." He reaches down and grabs your arm hard enough to make the handcuff pressure on your wrists hurt. Half pushing, half dragging he manhandles you to the doorway of a building that from the outside looks like some kind of big stone garage. Once you are dragged inside as you look around to what looks like a medieval torture chamber you suddenly like a rifle shot, realize the dangerous situation you are in. You begin crying. He begins a series of frightening maniacal laughs.

"First thing bitch, I am your Master and you will address as such. You will do everything I tell you to do, exactly how I tell you to do it. If you expect to leave here alive you will obey and treat me as your Master. Do you understand this?" Weeping and sobbing, you mutter "yes." "Listen cunt, are you stupid? When you address me you will address me as Master; fail to say Master and I will have to give you a little pain." "Yes Master, I understand, please don't hurt me." "The first thing we are going to do is place this chain and lock around your neck." He fastens the chain tightly around your neck and you hear the padlock click shut. "Notice that the chain links have spurs on them. I can jerk the chain for a little pain or I can yank the chain hard enough to rip your throat out. Do you want to die bitch?" "No Master, please I'll do whatever you want just let me go, please." "Not yet, by the way what is your name, slave?" "Carol, Master,

my name is Carol." "OK Carol cunt, I am going remove the cuffs and then you will slowly remove all of your clothes. If you try to fight or escape, I promise you will dread that decision all the while you are here. "Now take those clothes off, slowly." As you remove your clothing piece by piece you can see the depraved want in his eyes. This is not a normal man, this is a monster, a son of Lucifer. As you remove your bra and your large breasts tumble free, you see his tongue flicker back and forth several times across his lips. You see the same serpent tongue flicking again as you roll your panties down your legs. "You got some nice tits there slave and that is so neat, a smooth and hairless shaved snatch, damn. Not a bad job of up keep, your snatch doesn't even have stubble, excellent!"

With a slight jerk of the chain and the pain it imposes on your neck he is leading you like it was a dog leash across the room to a stainless steel pelvic examination table. You have fleeting thoughts of how many times over the last decade you have kicked your legs up as your gynecologist probed the inner you for signs of infection or cancer. You hesitate at the sight of that table and it makes him mad, with a hard jerk on the chain you feel those teeth dig deeply into your neck. You scream out in pain. With another pull on the chain he pulls you to the edge of the table and pushes you down forcing you into the table's contours, the coldness of the metal is immediate. "Put both your legs up and your ankles in the stirrups, slave." With no choice you comply; "Yes, Master." He closes some type of Velcro clasping anklet securing your ankles to the stirrups. "Now, you are going to raise your hands and extend them behind your head, understand or do you want a little more of the chain." He pulls your arms up behind your head and downward where you can feel him locking some type of metal handcuff. It is uncomfortable and the strain causes your body to slightly arch upwards. "Why are you doing this to me Master?" "Damn are you going to be a talker, I can't stand talkers and noise makers. I have just thing for you miss Carol." He walks across the room and opens a drawer in a roll about tool cabinet. When he returns he has a ball gag in his hand.

"Well Carol this will keep your bullshit to a minimum and the only time it will come out is when my cock goes in." He began that maniacal laugh again as he unlocked and removes the painful neck collar.

"Now Carol I do like my girlies clean, so we are going to give you a little spritzing. She could now see him approaching the table with a white lab type water hose with a long narrow nozzle. He pointed the nozzle at her breasts and squeezed the activator lever. A jet of almost too hot water to bear fired from the tip of the nozzle and bore into the softness of her breast. It hurt and he knew he was hurting her. He adjusted the nozzle to a spray and slowing, almost with car wash precision, slowly washed down her body. He paid special attention to her nipples and areoles. When he got to her vagina he dialed the nozzle back to the jet mode and delighted in the up and down strokes pressure washing of her clitoris, the drapery of both labias and the anus. The pain was excruciating. Poor Carol had never imagined hot water could hurt so much. After the standard plan thorough body, body crevice soaping, and body purging, it finally came to an end. "Well Carol, everything is as clean as whistle and the party can start. First I'm going to eat your pussy. And guess what Miss Slave, you are actually going to enjoy it and beg me not to stop." He pushed a roller chair right between her legs pushed his face into her groin and began the "anteater" and once she started bucking and moaning, he shifted into the "straw". The "straw" really sent her into overdrive, and the passion of those electric sensations firing into her brain overwhelmed the fear and pain of minutes ago. Carol found herself arching her back to push her pussy into his face. If only her hands were free, she would pull his face as tightly as she could to get that phenomenal cosmic tongue as deeply in her as possible. No one had ever gotten her this high; not a single man had ever come close and that one special time with the waitress, was as good as she thought it could be, but no sir, this guy is really the Master, the Master of the tongue.

After fifteen minutes of pure ecstasy, he broke the spell; "Now slave, unfortunately for you it is time for me to be pleasured." She could see him

entering back into her field of vision, and in one hand he had an ugly set of clamps with trailing electric wires and in the other, he had a thick copper metal tube that looked like it was ten inches long and at least two inches thick. It also had trailing electric wires. "Well slave, I can see the questions in your eyes. The clamps are for your pussy lips, one on each side. The probe will be pushed up into your ass. It will hurt a little I'm sure, but it is necessary. The wires are connected to a voltage regulator. We will begin with a little current and gradually work up to the maximum voltage. Somewhere about half max, you gonna begin pissing and when you do the clamps will begin sparking and we will notice a smell of something burning. You are about to have what every man wants, a hot, hot pussy. We will be doing this on and off for the next day or so. Once I get bored with it, there are lots and lots of other toys that we can play with. You are one lucky girl." As he slowly forced the probe up her rectum Carol despite the pain was cursing not only this sadistic madman but that fat lazy motherfucker that sent her out and got her into this hellish predicament.

"Well Carol, I'm getting a little exhausted, bet you are too, don't you think it's time for me to take a cigarette break?" "Yes, Master if that will relax you, please take your break." Fifteen minutes later, as she heard him approach the exam table, she could see that he had a ball of some type of white cord in his hand. "Now Carol, have you ever had a case of purple tits? Probably not, but you are about to have a splendid double dose of purple tit. I really like purple tit; first I wrap the cord around each tit as close as I can get it to your chest. I tighten the cord as much as I can. Then I knot the ends. The ligatures cause your breast to swell and your nipples to jut out. Almost immediately each swollen tit begins to turn rosy, then the color transforms into a deep red, then a pastel purple, then a darker shade of purple and continues in a chameleon transformation until it almost becomes the darkest purple you can imagine. When those guns are deprived of a blood flow and the oxygen it puts in your tit cells, they protest in color. Sonny then using his left hand in a claw like compression

of her breast, began looping the cord around her left breast. Once he had that breast tightly bound he tied, he bound the right one likewise. Once he had both breasts strangled with cords, he asked her if she had any feeling in either. "Master it does hurt, could you please release the cords. Anything you wish I will do. Each second the pain increases in my breasts, please Master, have mercy." No way was Sonny going to loosen those chords. Sonny loved to watch the color phases of ligatured breasts and he loved to tease and torture purple tits.

"Now Carol, it is time for me to have fun. I am going to gag you and prop your head up so you can watch the fun." Sonny secured a ball gag in her mouth and to be certain, with the intensity of pain he anticipated, he made double sure it couldn't be shook loose by duct taping the Velcro gag bindings. Once the tape was in place, he forced her head up with a special wrap he designed and strapped her forehead to the table so she could not move it in any direction and made it impossible for her not to see everything Sonny was about to do to her breasts. Leaving the table, he returned with a large pin cushion. He slowly extracted one straight pin, careful to be certain that Carol could see its entire length. The pin was a two inch stainless steel, straight pin. Once Carol could see what it was she began behind the ball gag, making gargling noises. Staring into her eyes, Sonny delicately placed the sharp point slightly behind the areola of her right breast and ever so slowly began pushing it until it punctured the purple toned skin and then began slipping into cells of her breast. The pain, being acute, Carol tried to fight but with the Velcro strapping around her neck and abdomen, could not buck his hand away. Once Sonny had pushed the pin completely into her breast, he paused for a moment, "I bet that hurt like hell. I could see the pain in your eyes. Some of my lady guests do not have any pain and the needles don't seem to hurt them at all; others, like you unfortunately for you but fortunate for me, do have needle pain. I have twenty five needles for each tit. You are going to occasionally pass out and need reviving. I have two ways to bring lady

guests back; one is the ice water the other is this (Sonny held up the electric cattle prod). The first I guarantee you is more pleasant to wake up to then the second. I will be piercing your tits for about thirty minutes each. Because of the ligatures, there will be little or no blood, so this won't be very messy. I will need an occasional cigarette or drink break. I hope you are ready, I am, I can almost cum every time I stick a needle in a bitch's tit. So let's get the show on the road.

One hour and fifteen minutes later, after passing out six or seven times (the cattle prod was used several times and Carol had never imagined how successful at reviving a person a cattle prod in the vagina could be) Carol thought it was over and that she had survived this monster's torture. "Carol honey, I'm so sorry, but that last time you fainted, I got a little angry plus I was a little bored with your tits, so just like a Thanksgiving turkey, I skewered your pussy lips together. Now that's gonna really got to be hurting. Even though you were unconscious, you grunted like a pig each time I pushed a needle through those gray wrinkly lips; looks very good though, kinda like a pussy kabob."

She could feel the pain of the needles stuck to their pin heads with each breath and movement of her breasts and now she was aware of a second area producing pain impulses to the cortex. Allowing her thirty minutes to consider her hopelessness, Sonny walked up to her side, displayed the pin cushion and slowly pulled out an eight inch hat needle. Carol screamed a thousand gargled screams. Somewhere between the fourth and sixth hat pin being stabbed up into her vagina, Carol's heart stopped. Sonny's only comment when he realized she had died was "Selfish cunt, ruined my fun. Now I won't get to push that hose down her throat. O' well, the fish are always happy for a bloody snack."

Latoya.......... *Born in a middle class family and raised to respect the values associated with the social structure, she followed the template. Her mother was white, her father a very smart black man who rose in his corporation*

on a combination of brains and race. Her completion was a wonderfully light pastel of almond. She went to college, found a decent man, married that decent man and had and was raising two children, a boy of fourteen and a girl of sixteen. She was thirty seven years old, was very attractive, and had very big but saggy breasts but otherwise a knock out figure for a thirty seven year old matron. The ladies would always comment about how Latoya with two children managed to keep that fine trophy wife shape.

She just hated living in the upscale but remote lakeside subdivision where to get to any place major you had to drive miles and miles on these desolate county roads. She so missed the bright lights of the city, where every street was well illuminated and the malls and shops were all within a ten to fifteen minute drive. Here she was driving twenty minutes to get a gallon of milk and a carton of eggs. The small highway grocery store was reasonably stocked with items and the meat, produce and dairy products were always fresh as shopper demand ensured that all perishables were quick turnover items. The little store, before the lake development, was a family operated grocery, gasoline, and live bait store. Once the lake development lots sold out, homes were built and families began to move in, the family quickly recognized the possibilities of a smart business enterprise, took a big bank loan, modernized and expanded the square footage to accommodate the needs and convenience of the upscale trade. Worms and minnows were no larger lead items; expensive imported wines, seafood, fresh produce, and premium cut carcass meats were the mortgage payers. The residents of the development flocked to buy the overlooked items they had forgotten to buy when in town, an item that they ran out of, or something special for a last minute grill party.

As Latoya slid from the SUV seat her mind was on a grab and go mission and she had paid no attention to the possible perils of her environment and therefore did not notice nor had she, would she have given a second thought to the driver occupying the white van parked across the highway. Inside the white van, Sonny had been watching the convenience store

parking lot for only fifteen minutes. Traffic was slight at this time of the evening and customers even scarcer during the 5-7pm dinner hour. Five shoppers had come and gone since he parked the van. Three were men; two were women, both from their appearances apparently being of the retirement age and likely with wrinkled, dried out tits, undesirable targets. Sonny focused when the SUV pulled in and Latoya got out. With only seconds to watch her, he carefully and hurriedly observed her for a match to his victim profile in this very brief distance as she walked from the car to the convenience store's door. Having a fair figure, short hair, and glasses she appeared to be well within his victim profile and would be given a final look see as she walked towards her car facing him. The distance of course would prevent a positive body match, but the tiny pair of powerful binoculars would at least give Sonny a general idea of looks, age, and weight.

Paying for tomorrow's breakfast featuring scrambled eggs and cold glasses of milk, Latoya cursed again the time she was about to waste driving the long lonely highway home. Being a slave to a good breakfast makes for a better day, she also silently cursed herself for not having on hand enough of the breakfast essentials to get her through to the next time they shopped in the bigger city. Three miles down the road, Latoya looked in the rear view mirror and noticed flashing police lights. "Fuck, what could it be now." Two months ago that state game warden had pulled her over for speeding and given her a speeding ticket that cost her $375.00, court costs and points against her driver's license. Now they probably want even more money. These asshole hicks are making a fortune out of the speed traps and city slicker zones. Shit, she had heard from a long time farm resident, that after all those years of not having traffic control, two of the police precincts, seeing the potential gold mine, went and bought radar guns and a dedicated traffic control police car. "Fucking parasites, nothing but parasites. Guess it is time to get some of the home owners to run for the

local political seats and turn the tables on these vultures. Just maybe I'll be the one to step up next election" she thought.

Pulling over to shoulder of the road, Latoya reached in her purse and pushed aside her Lady Smith and Wesson .380 and pulled her wallet out. Retrieving her driver's license she leaned over, opened the glove compartment and removed her registration and insurance card. Straightening up she watched through her rear view as the man exited the police van. "A fucking detective, bet the bastard will write me a bitch of a ticket" she thought. Lowering the power window and handing him her license and papers, Latoya leaned out and asked "Good evening officer, why did you stop me; I am sure I wasn't speeding, what is wrong, I don't believe that I broke any laws." "Please step from the vehicle ma'am." "But officer, I didn't do anything wrong." "Here we go again" he thought. "Just get out and walk to the rear of the vehicle." Realizing she was aggravating him into probably writing a nasty ticket, she complied. To reduce her anticipation of a distressful situation Sonny softly commanded, "Ma'am for your safety, please step to the side of the road." He had herded her far enough behind her vehicle to be almost at the side doors of his white van. "I am sure we can talk this out officer without a ticket being necessary. Please just tell me what I did wrong and I won't do it again." With a sudden and startling change in his demeanor Sonny growled, "I am so tired of you cunts always arguing. Put your hands behind your back now." "I will not and there is no need for profanity young man. You can bet I will be having a conversation with your supervisor and I am sure........" She never finished the sentence, Sonny punched her in her midriff hard enough to collapse her lungs and drop her to her knees. Pushing her down onto her stomach, he twisted her hands backwards and upwards, he cuffed her. Opening the van door he pulled her up and then shoved her on the bench. Still incapacitated by the punch and wheezing air in and out of her lungs, she helplessly watched as he chained her legs to the bench brackets. Locking the van door, he ran to her SUV, removed the bag of groceries, removed

her purse and wallet and locked the doors. Then he remembered her glasses, if the cops found her glasses where they had fallen when he hit her, they would immediately know something bad had happened to her. Nobody goes anywhere without their prescription glasses. Going back to the side of her SUV he saw them lying on the pavement. Picking them up, he put them in his pocket. "The glasses, they might come in handy later" he thought. Sitting behind the wheel, he took a second to riffle through her purse; the first thing he discovered was her pistol. "And, what do you have this gun for lady? Didn't do you any good, did it?" Knowing that the gun was more likely than not to be registered in her name, it would be, if he were to be caught with, a very convincing and condemning piece of circumstantial evidence. Definitely he had to get rid of the gun and thought he would just throw out the window as they crossed the river bridge that they had to drive over. As a felon caught with any gun in his possession, he immediately had a ticket for the jail house; so any other gun then one with a missing person's name on it would be a minor charge compared with impersonating a police office or being a suspect in an abduction and murder.

Latoya still gasping for air trying to recover from that terrible blow, she looked about her. She saw many police things and was confused because if this was a cop why would he hit her and then manhandle her into this van and then chain her legs to this bench? Suddenly the panic of realization struck her harder than his fist. This wasn't a real cop and she was in deep trouble. Pulling onto a side road, Sonny stopped and parked the van. He climbed into the back of the van and explained first the rules and then the consequences of not obeying the rules. Latoya immediately tried begging and pleading for mercy because she was a mother and had little kids waiting for her. "I'm in a bit of a hurry tonight and we have a long drive ahead of us. I think it best that I tape your mouth shut cause I don't want to be listening to your bullshit for the next few hours." "Please mister; if its sex you want, anyway you want it you can have it. If it's money I have a

few thousand at the bank, we can get at the ATM. All I want is to go home to my babies. Please do what you want and let me go." "First bitch, you are making a habit of breaking the rules. I am your Master and you will call me that. We will talk about the consequences of that later, I am in a hurry right now. He quickly taped a gag across her mouth and then pulling a pillow case over her head he secured it tightly with duct tape. "I know you can hear every word, so we will discuss the consequences of your disobedience while we drive. Now I am going to briefly give you just a tiny taste of what happens to bad girls." Sonny reached up under her shirt and forced his hand into the cup of her bra where his thumb and forefinger began to crush her breast behind her nipple. Smiling, he could hear her muted screams. "Now one more taste." Removing a small multipurpose knife from his pocket, he opened the pliers and pushed the pliers between her legs and into her panties. Using his fingers he captured a fold of her labia minor and closed the plier jaws on that sensitive drapery causing such pain as to put her in almost a faint, again a muted scream and this time her body bucked in pain. Releasing the pliers' grip, he smiled, "Time to get on the road."

Throughout the two and one half hour drive Sonny again explained his rules and explained in great detail how the electric probe worked and a half dozen or so of the other devices that he enjoyed torturing his victims with. Latoya suspected that outside of some lucky and unlikely police intervention she would never see her children again. Here she was hooded, gagged, bound and helpless a victim of a monstrous madman. She could not help but cry and sob. "If only there was some way to bargain with him. He doesn't appear to care about sex or money and all that appears to appeal to him is hurting people." Fear causes people to lose focus and when focus is lost opportunities are lost. She heard him say "Shit, forgot to gas up this morning." Now she suspected he would have to stop for a fill-up, but how could she attract the attention of others at the gas station? Within twenty minutes she felt the van leave the highway and

pull to a stop. The sounds were the common sounds you typically heard from people at the gas pump. "But, how to attract their attention?" Opening the van door, Sonny in a barely audible voice said "You better behave; bad girls have really bad things happen to them". Hearing his footsteps leave for the cashier island, Latoya's mind was in overdrive, how could she get the attention of people at the gas islands? Drawing no plan or action, she laid there and sobbed. Once he finished refueling and they were on the road again, Sonny said "I am so glad that you didn't beat your head against the van walls or stomped your feet on the floor. That definitely would have been a situation I could have lived without. You were a good girl." "Fuck, if only I would have thought of that I might have been a free woman by now. Fuck."

Once secured and naked on the OBGYN table Sonny removed the blind fold and gag. He then asked her about her name and family. "My name is Latoya and I have two babies at home, the girl is Latessa and is two years old and the boy is Tawon and he is six months old. Please, my family needs me. I am a single parent and my babies need their mother. There is no one else to take care of them, so please mister, let me go. It has been a very long time since I had sex, but whatever way you want I am willingly to do it." Sonny smiled, and squeezing one of her baggy big tits, he said "I think you are a lying cunt. If you had a six month old baby the milk would be squirting out of your tit right now. Who are you trying to kid, these tits hadn't fed a baby in years". Releasing her breast he then positioned himself between her elevated legs and inspected her vagina. Sonny whistled; "You barely have any snatch hair and it is groomed in a nice little strip. I like that and later we will play with that. So the question is, Why would you be shaving your pussy if no there's one no to see it or eat it?"

"Now it's time to sterilize your naked ass." He began the soap and pressure washing routine. He loved to watch them squirm as the hot water jetted against every sensitive fold and body crevice.

He started laughing. She could feel that first finger forcing its way into and exploring the secrets of her vaginal canal, then a second, then a third. "Bullshit, again, someone with a horse cock has been fucking the shit out of you. Cunts tighten and dry up when no there is nobody poking them. But I got a little surprise for you. You broke the rules and refused to call me Master. You spoke out of turn. Sorry but if you break the rules you pay the penalty." Sonny made a made a point of returning her glasses to her face, "are you ready for the circus; yes or no?" Latoya shook her head in a no gesture. "No, really. I guess it hasn't quite sunk in yet. You are going to be my sex slave and you are going to do what I tell you, when I tell you and how I tell you. I want you to be a brave girl. Do not curse or complain, understand." "Yes, Master." "Now that's better, hope you remember to keep quiet, if not its' bad things again."

Walking over to the prep table, he stood there examining a number of instruments before deciding on a twelve inch bright blue, ribbed plastic dildo. He shifted his position to the head of the exam table and slowly turned the blue plastic truncheon in a clockwise motion inches from her eyes. He cradled the thick shaft as he rubbed its ribbed neck back and forth across her lips. He enjoyed seeing her eyes fluttering in fear. "Open your mouth bitch." She parted her lips; "wider cunt, say Ohio." She opened her mouth as if he was giving her a dental exam. With her mouth open, Sonny slowly pushed the dildo to the back of her mouth until she began gagging and twisting her head. I have something that I think will make this a little easier. Back to the prep table, he set the phallic device down and picked up a dental jaw spreader. Seeing what he had in his hands, Latoya began begging, "Please Master, I promise I won't gag, please don't put that on me, please". "No one gave you permission to talk; now I am going to have to punish you. Once we get done playing with the blue cock, I have something very special in mind. You might say it will run chills up and down your spine." Sonny starting laughing again, "Now back to work. I do enjoy this so much, I know it is a little unpleasant for you, but

that's what slaves are for, to be used as the Master sees fit and I see fit to fuck with you". Forcing a metal surgical spatula between her teeth he was able to force her mouth open and push the spreader between her teeth. Using the adjustment knobs, he adjusted the clamp gap as wide as her jaws would part, screwed the locks down, then pulling the straps tightly behind her head he snapped the Velcro fastening together. Latoya could now only make animal noises. Holding her throat with his left hand, with his right he pushed the phallic device as far down her throat as he could make it go. He had expected vomiting and choking, but actually Latoya had a secret, she could deep throat her husbands' fat 9 inch cock all day long; he preferred it and she thought it was so much easier then removing all her clothes for a 30 second poke. Several more times he used the phony prick as a throat swab, each time with the same results. "Hmmm, seems you are a champion cocksucker. I have never seen a bitch swallow that much plastic; are there any sword swallowers in your family; maybe your mother, a sister, a brother?" All Latoya could do was ignore the rawness of her throat, grunt, and hope this monster motherfucker has a heart attack.

"That was a little disappointing for me. I expected more gagging, but it is time to move on to the punishment. Leaving the dental spreader fastened he walked over to the prep table and donned a pair of insulated gloves. Walking over to the walk-in freezer he disappeared inside where arranged on a freezer shelf were a number of various sized and shaped bottles containing freeze proof alcohol. Contemplating the pain giving virtues of each he lifted each from its cold cradle and as if he were carefully choosing the correct golf club, he minutely examined each. Finally making his choices, when he walked out back into the room he had two bottles, one in each hand. One was a green heavy glass champagne magnum bottle the other a very long and slender neck decorative yellow liqueur bottle. She could see that Sonny had cemented a t-handle to each of their flat bottoms. Seeing the terror in her eyes, he smiled and proudly said, "Now let me explain the punishment. Years ago, I discovered that not only huge

and long cocks can be pushed up a girl's pussy or asshole, but others things would fit just as well. I had watched a porno movie with two girls making out. After the scene had heated up, one reached down and picked up a beer bottle and used that beer bottle to bottle fuck her friends' pussy and when she got tired of that flipped her over and shoved that bottle all the way up into her friends' asshole. The whole thing, can you imagine that? That was really something to see".

"With that in mind and thinking it out I invented the "glass glider". Since a bottle has no convenient handle and could become very slippery and unmanageable, I experimented with several different types of handles. After several field trials, I decided that a simple T handle would be best. It had a comfortable grip and most importantly I can twist that bottle clockwise or counter clock wise. With the handle I can also use it like a piston to plunge, push and pull the bottle in and out of your body holes. The second part of my idea was to fill the bottles with alcohol and freeze them. The alcohol of course never freezes but it stays at zero degrees. Wait till you feel that ice cock gliding up your pussy. I guarantee it's gonna take your breath away. My frozen bottle idea has proven so useful both in punishment and pleasure that I have given it a name "the glass glider", cute name huh. I am not a monster, so I am going to give you a choice, the thick green one, or the thin yellow one. Pick one."

Latoya could only wish she could die. The cocksucker was going to shove a frozen glass bottle up into her vagina and it was going to hurt, hurt a lot. With the spreader still holding her jaws apart all she could do was to grunt curses at him. "Can't make up your mind; OK so let's start with the yellow one. A little squirt of shaving crème and its gonna glide up your cunt. That shaving crème does wonders and is so much better that the fuck crème they sell at the sex store; plus it's a lot cheaper."

Only half suspecting the degree of pain she knew what he meant to create and knowing there was no escape, Latoya thought that maybe if she played

his game he might not be as cruel. She shook her head yes. Sonny smiled and after smearing the shaving crème around her vagina gateway and then fingering some in her vagina, he slowly pushed the top of the long neck yellow bottle slightly past the lips of her labia minors, resting it briefly allowing its ice cold to begin penetrating the soft and sensitive vaginal tissue. Latoya instantly felt the pain of freezing cold and began to twist and push trying to pull away from the frozen glass bottle neck. Sonny was smiling as he slowly began to rotate the bottle and millimeter by millimeter screwed it upwards. After he had forced her vagina to sheath the six inches of bottle neck, he rested it briefly and then again began forcing the bottom four inches in. With another push Latoya felt it spread her canal wide open and could feel the icy edges of the bottom as her vagina tried to close around it.

The increasing larger circumference of the bottles' tapered neck prevented a deep insertion and Sonny quickly got bored with the playground. He then re-positioned himself between her stirrup bound legs. "Shake your head bitch if you want me to treat you to more of the "glass glider." She shook her head "no". "Wrong answer again, I'm gonna jam this big boy, magnum bottle in your cunt and use it like a cannon swab, in and out, in and out. When we get done today playing, I bet your cunt will be so big, I will be able to gt my fist in there up to the elbow. Now, I know you're going to like that. Shit, we are just beginning." She moaned and bounced her head back against the hard metal table.

"Now the real test begins, how big a woman are you? Do you have an ox cunt or a two finger one?" The "glass glider" has just reached its' shoulder, from here the diameter gets larger and larger. To maximize the test I have attached this tee handle. It makes it so much easier on me; it is strong enough for me to shove on it. It's strong enough for me to use it like a corkscrew, and it's strong enough for me to use it like an in and out plunger. Feel free to scream, buck and twist. It's going in all the way. If you are a good girl I might not push it up your ass. Ooh is that gonna hurt,

not may girls can take very much of the glider in the ass. Most faint and ruin my fun." Sonny began twisting and pushing. It took almost twenty minutes to get that entire thick wide green glass bottle all the way up into her birth canal. Latoya had fainted three times from the extraordinary pain. Her screams sounded like loud gargles. Her body was drenched in sweat beads from the pain. "Hey no blood. I'll be; most girls start bleeding when the glider gets about half way in. Lady your husband must have a horse cock or you must have a glass glider hidden beneath your bed." He started laughing.

Once Sonny could see from the lessor degree of pain registering in her eyes and body that the pain from the large circumference insertion was not achieving the maximum level of results he rapidly got bored and decided to move on to another "treat". Removing the huge glass dildo from her stretched and aching vagina, Sonny informed her that he decided against jamming that ice cold oversized ramrod up into the dark passageway of her rectum. "I know you would have loved that cold buried in your ass, but I am not here to reward you, I am here to punish you. You have nice tits and they sag enough to drape to the side. That is good. The next thing we are going to do is what I call the "pincushion". I doubt very much if you are going to like this fun time very much at all, but it is something that I invented for girls that are very bad and don't follow rules". Cleaning then returning the bottles to the freezer, Sonny removed several large, tourniquet sized rubber constriction bands from his prep table. "Believe it or not, I used to use cord, but these rubbers are so much neater, you don't have to tie knots and they fit any size tit. These guys work especially well with big, flat, flabby, jelly tits, like yours. I get these big rubber bands at the novelty store. They are big and strong and are just perfect for the "pincushion". Lifting her right breast Sonny stretched the thick rubber band around her breast and looped it twice as close to her chest as possible. Her breast immediately turned purple with the whole of the breast drum tight. He did the same constriction on her left breast. Her

eyes were doing frantic scans from his hands to the prep table panicky about what was going to happen next. "See that wasn't so bad, was it?" Using his thumb and index finger he captured that part of her now very purple and swollen breast right behind the areola in that most sensitive area of the mammary gland, pinching as hard as he could, he watched her eyes. "Just wanted to test it and see if you are ready for the next phase of the "pincushion". Yep, you sure are". All Latoya could do was to gargle another scream and hoped either she died or he had a heart attack. She would welcome dying a slow death on this table if only she could see him dead lying on the floor. "What an evil motherfucker, if only I could get loose and grab one of those knives he's got lying on that table, I'd show this cocksucker what real pain is." she thought.

Once more he turned to the prep table and picked up something that she was not able to see. Switching positions back to be next to her torso he held in front of her eyes a pincushion. Removing a single pin from the cushion, he stuck it in the tip of her nose. The pain was huge. She could not imagine how such a little piece of silverish metal could hurt that much. "I wanted to give you something to focus on. I am going to fill your tits with many of these tiny pins. Once we are done, I wouldn't recommend that you try to get past the scanner at the airport anymore". Sonny laughed that strange, disconnected laugh, the laugh of a lunatic madman.

One by one, in a concentric pattern, Sonny jabbed pins in her breasts. Not satisfied with a little penetration, he pushed the pin the entire length of its shaft until its tiny round head rested against her skin. She moaned, gargling screams, rolled her head from side to side, and fought by arching her body against the pain. The "pincushion" took over one and one half hours to complete. Latoya had fainted four times and Sonny promptly revived her with a little squirt of lubricating shaving crème in her vagina and the insertion of the cattle prod. One or two bolts of electric would bring her back to consciousness. Latoya, in between bursts of pain, prayed for death. "Heck, girl, I think I am ready for a little cigarette break. You sure

have a fun body, I wish we could do this forever, I know I could. How about you? Not talking, I understand. So, let's knock off for say, thirty minutes. It will give you time to think about the next fun thing."

Four hours later, and after Latoya had succumbed to the slow death of a hogtie strangulation, the wood shredder roared to life as schools of fish raced to the feeding area. Standing there lakeside, watching the fish fight amongst their selves for the gory protein tidbits spewed from the shredder, Sonny thought about an idea he had for quite a long time; a captive slave, but how? "Going three to six months between hunts doesn't do my hunger any good. Gotta work some more on the idea. I really need to come up with something innovative to keep these bitches caged and alive for a while."

Then the thought of a plan came to him, how could I be so stupid, all those months I spent in the penitentiary cells, I know what it takes to keep someone alive and incarcerated. Sonny suddenly had an epiphany; why not build a chain link cage, say twelve by twelve, eight foot high, a three foot wide door, build it over one of the floor catch basins cleaning, in the corner with the toilet, plastic pipe a cold and hot water tap, put a sleeping carpet on the floor, and then electrify the chain link. If it was bolted to the floor with insulated rubber washers the only parts with juice would be the chain link cell walls and ceiling. I could build in a slot just like the jails to pass food through and make them push their arms through so I could handcuff whenever I wanted to play. I could keep bitches alive for as long as they were pleasure. I can see it now, there's that rest room spot in the corner where Uncle Buck used to keep all them empty cardboard meat boxes and I think it's about twenty by twenty and there is a floor catch basin for them to wash down everything to it clean. Probably build it for less than a thousand dollars. Need to see what kind of electric transformer it would take. Uncle Buck has three or four brand new in the box electric fence transformers that just might do the job. Wish I had thought of this year's ago. With a live slave, I won't have to hunt as often and it will be fun to

have someone in a cage and be there whenever I decide I need some pleasure time. Don't think the fish are gonna like the idea, they seem to really like the bonus feeds. Tomorrow, after I clean up this bitches mess, I'll draw up my list of materials and drive into the big lumber store and get want I need. This project is going to be so much fun." Two weeks later, Sonny was beaming proudly at the cage he had put together, now there was no longer the need to take the risk of hunting so often and he would have temporary companionship, reluctant and terrified companionship, but a face to look at when he decided he wanted to look at it and a body to torture with pain when he decided he wanted to pain it.

CHAPTER TWELVE

Susan.........An attractive, single 22 year old natural, blonde with huge breasts and a tiny waist who loved the attention her body's hint of sex did to men. From an early school age, Sue had always been a dominant and demanding child who enjoyed degrading and harassing classmates to tears. At twelve both parents were killed in a drunken driver vehicle accident, and she was taken in by a spinster Aunt. In her teens she discovered that she had a shameless hunger for sex and pain, the sex she learned from older men (some of them fathers of her girlfriends) who preyed on young girls, the pain she would inflict on boys twisting their cocks and squeezing their balls until they begged for mercy. Her Aunt continually lectured her on her late hours and to Sue's disgust, her loose morals as well. On high school graduation day as she left the stage with her diploma in hand, more than one boy (and several of the male staff men) with aching balls proudly smirked that those dream tits bouncing down the stage steps were certainly worth all the cash, pain and degradation necessary for the chance to explore and know them.

After dropping out of her sophomore year at the junior college and several months of working meaningless, nowhere jobs, she leaped at the opportunity to flee her aunt's boring, high horse weekly lectures and one night on a whim for freedom, she packed her cheap but very fashionable clothes, made that leap, bought a bus ticket and moved to this distant city where she knew not a single person. She immediately found another nowhere but pay the bills, job. Employed as a phone solicitor, she avoided new friendships and networking to maintain a high level of personal privacy. At 22, Sue had intimate affairs with a legion of boys and men. She adored tempting and luring married men into after hour sexual encounters in parks, alleys, motels, anywhere the opportunity presented itself. There was always that little "thing" about poaching in another woman's backyard. She had mastered the "trap'; first she would cruise a bar or restaurant looking for a mousy looking, lone male wearing a wedding ring, then it was a matter of catching his eyes, then the smile, then the tongue cruising across her lips and rolling it into a curl. When she was satisfied she had their attention, she would coyly walk to the bar or door and taking one last look and smile, hesitate for that crucial last second's eye contact which sealed the deal and she had landed her latest conquest falling over himself to pay his bill while daydreaming of a fantasy about to be reality. Almost without fail they took the bait. Once she had them in a face to face, she would smile and casually reach down and roll her fingers across their awakening penis and looking into their eyes would say; "If you want to see the guns and get these lips on your cock, it's gonna cost you $50.00. If I don't see cash by the count of five, it's good bye. Now, dig it up or back to your wife. What's it's gonna be?" She loved how they in a panicky moment afraid they were gonna lose out on this opportunity, then in a flash reached for their wallets. She was always amazed how in this modern world of credit cards, they would almost always miraculously have fifty dollars cash money hidden away in their wallets. She just assumed that it was either emergency money just in case they ran into a cock emergency and their fantasy world became a happening or spending money hidden away from

the wife. Usually with a very timid approach and stuttering words which always left her in control they timidly became submissive. Once they were semi-clothed or naked, depending on the location, she would take command as a dominix. Sue loved to mete out pain, rarely did they complain; the promise of sinning away from the beady eyes of their wives and the smell and taste of foreign pussy, huge pillowy tits, and a spurt of cum overrode any objection to a little minor discomfort. As a finale, she would always wipe what semen she either spit out or cup from her tits across Mr.Mousy's lips and face. Hundreds of dates while wiping their own cum from their faces, would without fail say "can I see you again?" She would then smile, laugh and walk from their lives.

Damn, she was out of cigarettes and it was drizzling rain; an eleven mile trip to the convenience store was absolutely necessary. The caffeine in the coffee just wasn't enough to keep her fingers from her roomies throat, the same nagging roomy that had talked her into renting this run down area, dirt cheap, but very well furnished condo, so remote from civilization and overlooking a stagnant, long dead playground lake. Of all times to run out of cigarettes, that nicotine was crucial in her crisis management and Joan, her gay roommate, with the black belt in nagging, was in high gear today; just two cigarettes and she could throw up her tolerant shields and Joan would be safe again and no longer a potential nicotine withdrawal murder victim. She hated the thought of the winding county road, but nicotine addiction was a strong motivator and each nagging syllable out of Joan's mouth this morning, reminding her of her lecturing Aunt was almost as spurring a motive to plunge into the rain for a pack of doogies.

Sonny was parked in a grove of trees across from the store parking lot and was silently listening to the radio broadcasting the weather prediction; 70% chance of light rain with storm warnings for Wednesday and Thursday, clearing Friday with sun and warm temperatures for the weekend. There had been few cars pulling in the store for last minute or forgotten or emergency things like cigarettes or milk for the kids. Three cars were

driven by men. Four cars had multiple people in them. Two had women, one was an extremely heavy set elderly woman, the second a skinny middle aged housewife looking person. Like Vinnie had underscored, the hunter had to have a lot of patience and never, never get desperate and increase the chance of a mistake. Sonny looked at his watch. He hated to sit in one spot for more than a hour, you really had to be careful not to become a suspicious entity. He was a little reluctant to give up this hunt; there were no cameras, this spot was at an extreme distance from his hideaway, it was raining, these roads did not have a lot of weekday traffic during the work hours, and the patrolling sheriff's deputies only came by on the second shift and graveyard shift, the day shift cop preferring to work the more financially rewarding state highway for pass through vacationer speeders.

A late model four door bright red sedan car pulled into the parking lot. Sonny immediately threw his binoculars up and focused the lens on the driver as she exited the car seat. He wondered to himself "Cigarettes, tampons, loaf of bread, or milk; this one looks desperate for a cigarette, so I'd say a pack of cigarettes got her out in the rain." Opening the umbrella, it gave him extra time to profile her. He could tell she was in her late teens or early twenties, looked like she had huge breasts, was definitely not over weight, and might even be pretty. The thought of warm, big, soft titties on this cold, wet, dark day sent a charge of passion into his cock, and this one won't be disposable; she could be kept caged as long as he wanted her around.

He scanned her auto carefully to be certain there were no passengers or children. Several times in the past he pulled over targets and when he got to the driver's window discovered that had a child in a child's seat or a baby in a baby seat; in those cases he just cautioned the driver about speeding and allowed them to proceed on with their lives never for a second realizing how close they had just come to torture and death. This one would most definitely do. He smiled as she walked outside, juggling

the umbrella to light a cigarette; "ah, it was a damn pack of cigarettes that put her into my spider web. If these stupid people bought their cigs in cartons they wouldn't have to make these trips and waste the gas". He waited until she backed out of the parking lot and turned on the county hardtop road. Slowly he engaged the gears on the van to "drive". He knew better then to immediately pull behind just in case someone was watching; he did not want anyone calling 911 to report a white van with suspicious behavior. Allowing a few minutes before beginning the chase, would avert any attention to him and on the plus side, as there was no one was driving these roads at this hour, so it would be a simple measure to speed up and catch up to her car.

As she looked in the side mirror she could see the flashers of a police car. "Fuck, just what I need a fucking cop to write some kind of nonsense ticket." Pulling over off the road onto the shoulder she jerked the lever into the "park" position. Smiling she just thought of something, in her hurry to keep from killing her roommate this morning she did not put on a bra. "Maybe he'll trade a little lookie see for a warning ticket." Quickly she unbuttoned her top three blouse buttons and opened her blouse to maximize the view of her large tanned boobs. Her tits have always been a super advertisement and she had commanded so many of those mousy married men to jack their rivers of semen over them (it made it easier for her to cup a handful and smear on their uncomplaining faces). If the cop is handsome, she might even bargain a blowjob to get out of a four hundred dollar speeding ticket.

As she followed the movement of the police officer from his car, she noticed he seemed a little nervous and maybe apprehensive. "Double shit, I might have a new cop and a mountain of tit scenery or no scenery, he's gonna write me a ticket." Twisting in her seat, to flare open her blouse and give a wide a view as possible, she powered the window down and carefully watching where his eyes went, asked "Did I do anything wrong

officer, I know I wasn't speeding". She disappointedly noticed that his eyes only scanned her breasts very briefly, "fuck a fag" she thought.

"Please keep your hands where I can see them, slowly use your left hand to reach over and turn off your motor and exit the vehicle. Once you are out of the vehicle, place both hands on your head and step backwards until I tell you to stop. Please begin now." "What the fuck is this?" she thought. "Yes, sir, but I didn't do anything." As she walked backwards and came abreast of the van doors, "There has been a terrible shooting and your car matches the description. If you are not involved, you will be released; but right now I have to cuff you, frisk you, and drive you to the scene for a witness to either identify you or kick you free. If the victim clears you I will drive you back to your vehicle. I apologize for the frisking but we are undermanned because of the shooting and the police woman is busy with a victim at the hospital. I hope I can count on your cooperation." "Yes, of course you can officer." With that Sonny put the handcuffs on her wrists. "Now please face the van while I frisk you." His hands began in her hair, down her shoulders, up her ribs and across the small of her back. Reaching around, he reached inside her blouse immediately confirming no bra, and traced his fingertips over under and across her nipples on each breast. Having had more finger prints on her tits then those in the FBI files at Quantico, Sue said "That feels so good, I wish that you could frisk me more. Did you like it too?" Sonny did not comment, but did crack a big smile. His hands then slide down the back of her slacks and she could feel his index finger gently plowing up the crevice of her ass, stopping briefly at her pink button hole before continuing upwards. Shifting his hand to the front he slid his hand into her panties and again she could feel that finger and combined this time with his thumb quickly rolling her clitiors then continuing up one side then down the other wrinkled drapery of her labias and finally sneaking past those lips and curling into and out of her vagina. She suddenly and expectantly started to moisten. "Oh, officer I got the chills, do you do this to all suspects?" "Ma'm I am just doing my job, if you

are offended, you make a complaint to my sergeant." "Oh no, I liked that maybe after they turn me loose, we can play around a little when you drive me back to the car. Would you like to do that, officer?" "Ma'm I'm just doing a job. Now I have to put you in the van, and secure your legs on the bench. Please continue to cooperate."

Sonny helped her into the van and chained her to the bench. Looking around, Sue saw everything she expected to see in sloppy police vehicle, a white riot helmet stenciled "POLICE" rolling around on the floor and several other pieces of trade equipment. Closing the doors, Sonny ran around to her car, opened the door and grabbed her purse and sunglasses and her pack of cigarettes. Locking the door, he returned to the van, hopped in, threw her purse and articles on the passenger seat, put the lever in "drive" and pulled onto the county road to begin the long drive to his fortress. "Relax, miss, the crime scene is on the other side of the county so enjoy the ride." A thought suddenly occurred to her, everything was labelled "police" and this was not a police jurisdiction. this was a police detective and not a sheriff's deputy or a constable, so why was he out of his jurisdiction? She remembered that cop she seduced after he pulled her over for a speeding violation and who explained who could give her tickets and who couldn't. A sheriff's deputy was county wide while most police officers were limited to the city boundaries they worked in. "Officer, I have a teeny question, which city are you a policeman in? Why are making arrests in the county, when you are supposed to only have policeman powers in the city?" "What are you some kind of lawyer lady? If you are smart you will keep quiet." "I will not, I have rights and I have the right to know who is arresting me and what for and as soon as we see your sergeant, I am going to file a sexual complaint about how you fondled my breasts and pushed your finger in my asshole and then finger fucked me. I bet when I get done, you'll never have a badge again."

Pulling the van over to a side road, Sonny slammed the lever into "park" and hopped over the console and slipped through the divider gate.

Smiling, he tore open her blouse and in a vise like grip seized her breast right behind her nipple and crushed it with as much pressure as he could mustard. Sue screamed and twisted and tried to kick for his balls but the chain kept her feet from elevating high enough. Her handcuffed hands locked to the bench could not offer any defense either. Sonny then pinched her nose and twisted it and she screamed again, this time cursing him; "You motherfucker, I'm gonna see that you go to jail. Wait till I file that complaint, your ass is fried. I was going to give you the best blowjob you ever had when we got back to my car, now their gonna take your gun and badge away and those black guys you've been arresting will be standing in line to fuck you in your ass. Just think about those big cocks ramming your ass, fuck face."

"Dear Miss Cunt are you ever in for a big surprise." Sonny grabbed a hand full of her beautifully conditioned hair, and twisting her head back, pushed a dirty sock in her mouth and grabbing a ribbon of duct tape, started taping her mouth closed. Once he had her gagged and silenced he began "This is really your unlucky day; first you run out of cigarettes and have to make a smoke run in the rain, then I snatch you, and then you make all these threats and threaten me about what you are going to do and piss me off. You shouldn't have done that. I am not a cop. I am an ex-con. I have abducted you for several reasons, the first being a little sexual the second being pleasure, you see not only do I get off with my cock, I also get off in mind doing things to you that cause you a great deal of pain. You see, I am somewhat of a student of sadism and I so enjoy testing women. I will be doing things to your tits, your cunt hole, your asshole, and even your tongue that will make you beg for death. As a very special bonus for me and curse for you, I have just finished my electric cage and will be able to keep you captive for just as long as I desire your companionship. You will truly be a slave, my slave and in a few hours you will beg for my cock and cum, you will offer to do anything and everything for freedom. The best part of this is that I am a certified hypnotist, and after I get finished using

your body, I will put you in a state of hypnosis and you will not remember me or what happened to you. (Sonny was delighted when he thought of this and added this new twist, to give the victim the hope of eventual freedom.) When I dump you in an alley all you will able to tell the real police is that you were driving and blacked out, from there you remember nothing. So, just relax while you can."

Sonny was very happy to finally end the long drive and see his lane just off the interstate. Home at last! Once in the driveway, Sonny hopped into the back and Sue immediately began to struggle against the handcuffs and leg chains. "Shit, she's gonna be a fighter. Time for the chloroform." Grabbing her hair and tilting her head back Sonny forced a chloroformed sock over her nose. After thirty seconds her body collapsed in surrender to the strong vapors. Squeezing her breast as hard as he could, and observing no reaction, he judged her safe to transfer, unchained her and carried her from the van, across the pathway, into the building and then laid her on the OBGYN examination table. Rolling her eyelids up and touching a fingertip to the eye ball, Sonny confirmed that she was still unconscious and it was safe to exchange the wrist and ankle shackles. After strapping her body to the table it was time for a cigarette and a cold beer. Sonny sat comfortably in his chair and watched as she gradually began to recover from the anesthesia. He smiled as the veil of the chloroform slowly lifted. He saw in her eyes first confusion then terror as she realized she was no longer in the van but had traded placed and was now in some sort of torture chambers. Her eyes darted around the room and noting many strange pieces of medical appearing devices sang of despair. It was great to see that panic and fear in his victims. "Fuck" she thought, "if only I had listened to Joan about these cocksucking cigarettes." For months, her roommate had begged her to give up cigarettes and if only she had listened she wouldn't be strapped to some fucking table with a madman squeezing his crotch and gawking at her.

"Well, well, look who's awake. I like a girl with a little fight and spirit in her, but not too much fight, so please remember that. I have certain rules that you must obey. The first is that you must always refer to me as Master. The second is that you only talk when spoken to. The third is you do what I command you to do, when I command you and how I command you. Pretty simple, three rules and there just might be a few more depending on a few other things. I will keep the gag on for a little while longer, but first it is time to remove all your clothes and examine the body I just caught and now belongs to me. Reaching over to the prep table he removed the shearers and within a few snips had all her clothing removed. "Goodness sweetheart, you have a beautiful and complete tan, even the underside of your tits and the valley of your pussy is tanned. Another thing, I have had many girls with good sized tits, but I have never seen tits this huge before. Poor girl, I bet you have back strain. Now let's begin the examination; first the tits to see if they are real or silicone and then your pussy to see if it's been a busy cock freeway or a lonely side street." Taking his hands and using both to grasp and wrap partly around her breast at her chest he tightened the grip and pulled them slowly downward toward the nipple to feel for any foreign implants. There were none on either. "Your tits are the real McCoy, that's a very good thing. I do find it so depressing when I encounter my guests with balloons instead of real boobies. Now let's check on the pooter." Lifting a can of shaving crème from the prep table, he placed a foam glob about the size of a fat cherry on the tips of his first two fingers. He lathered the vagina lips and opening with a smear of the white wonder lubricant. Using his left thumb and index finger he separated her labias, opening her birthing canal for the finger assault by his right hand. First one, then two, then three and folding all four fingers together with the slippery lubricant of the shaving crème, he was able to slide all four and thumb past the knuckles up to his wrist. "Very good, you are going to do fine when we get to the cold bottle fun. You might be able to set the record for the biggest, deepest and hungriest cunt ever to grace my humble domicile. Now I am going to remove your gag. I caution you about

name calling or threats. You have no power here and are at my mercy. The last bitch that persisted on calling me vile names got a knitting needle through her tongue; I don't think you want that. So be a good girl and let's find out about each other."

Sue still in the numbing state of shock of being abducted and now helplessly shackled to an examination table with her legs wide spread and elevated in stirrups, he only thoughts were how she could manipulate this situation to her advantage to be in a better position with this monster. Maybe cooperation would be a key. Immediately keying up in her memory was her special power and how many men she had commanded and degraded in the last three years after she discovered this power over those timid creatures that sought fantasy away from the bliss of matrimony; twenty, thirty, forty maybe. Once they took her bait she could command them to do anything as long as the suggestion and promise that she would allow them ejaculation existed. She was always fair, after they had tongued her ass, sucked her toes, drank a streaming fountain of piss from her, bent their dicks, pinched the tip of their dicks with her fingernails, crushed their balls, forcefully yanked their ball sacks, or any one of a hundred degrading, emasculating and humiliating things afterwards did as a good slave reward, suck their cocks or jack their dicks off. Once her passionate servant would ejaculate, almost as a brand and reward, she would collect a palm full of cum to smear across their lips and face. Rapidly thinking now in a survivor mode, if only she were able to find a weak spot in this cocksucker, she might advantage it to flip it to her advantage. Looking around the white tiled room, she noticed nothing other than items and devices of bondage or sexual depravity. An idea began to form, a plan. "It just might work" she thought to herself.

When Sonny ripped the gagging tape from her lips, she coughed the sock out and gasped with a huge and very audible intake of breathe, the noise resembled a bellows vacuum. Recovering quickly and knowing she had to adjust to and play his game if she expected any opportunity, "Master thank

you for removing the gag, please a moment to allow me to speak. I want to thank you also for the pain; I am also a student of de Sade. I understand your urges and desires. I too have urges but not to give but to receive. We are different; pain is our religion and this castle will be our altar. Destiny has brought us together. Your hands when they milked my breasts to see if I was a natural woman created an erotic feeling as they choked downward on my breasts. Those fingers that explored me were wonderful, and I felt myself moisten as they probed inside me. I am so looking forward to the pleasure games I am sure that you will be treating me to. I will scream but it will not be from the pain, it will be from the pleasure you are giving me. I have many secrets that I think we can share. I will do as you command, my Master and now I am ready for the punishment for speaking without permission." She had just successfully begun to flip the tables on Sonny. The confusion on his facial expression was obvious and she immediately noticed it. She knew if she was very careful and patiently played in his court, there was hope. Sonny now wondered what kind of woman he had in his power. Never before had he such a woman that asked for pain and understood the fires within him, even wonderful Auntie Mame who had occasionally let him play around with big dildos, titty ropes, slightly painful bites, twists, pinches, and the times they even worked up to fist penetrations, never understood the voices that beckoned to him from out of the darkness.

"We have preliminaries that must be done before we can get to the fun things." She now had an idea of his game and understood that leading sentences were part of his strategy to get her to respond to his statements and by doing so she would be breaking his rules. Wisely she said nothing. He still could not believe the size of the tits he was looking at. "Shit, bitch, those are some extreme trophy mammaries and I am going to have some fun playing with them. I have never seen tits this big, well maybe in the girlie mags." Sonny began to gently rotate his finger tip around her nipples, pushing compression pressure in a shallow in and out movement.

Within seconds, her nipples responded, popping erect like two, brown trained sentinels. "Damn girl you got blue ribbon winning knobs atop these tanned trophy jugs, I'm just gonna have to take a time out and do a little titty sucking." Sonny's lips descended first on the nipples, slurping hard enough to bring them to a pouting posture. Susan moaned; it was not a moan of pain but one of passion. Sonny immediately recognized it and smiled. Once he was satisfied that he awakened her nipples, he began to suck her breasts and left so many purple passion marks that twenty minutes later each breast looked like it had leopard spots. Twisting her head and looking downward at her tormentor's slacks, she could see the outline of a prick erection in his trousers and what looked like the beginning of a tiny wet spot. "The jackoff is getting ready to cum", she thought.

After the cleansing ritual, Sonny decided it was time to question her on her life and see if she was going to fabricate "let me go" lies. "What is your name?" My name is Susan but everyone calls me "Sue". You can call me anything, a slave has no demands, my Master." "I like Suzie better and that's what you are going to answer to. Understand, Suzie?" "Yes, Master my name is Suzie." "Tell about yourself and what you enjoy."

"My Master, I am an only child. My parents said I was a rebel. I did get good grades in school, but I was pretty wild. While other girls were babysitting I was fucking their daddies and brothers. I could never get enough sex. By time I was fourteen I had cocks in every one of my holes. When I was around eighteen and a freshman in college, I discovered how big a pussy most away from home boys were. One night, on a date, we were in the back seat burning up the passion fires when I decided to add a little extra to the make out before I let him cum. My bra was up and my shorts were down, and he was fingering me like a jack hammer. He had dropped his shorts and sticking out of his boxer shorts was a very proud eight inch cock. I was so surprised 'cause this guy was a real geek. I grabbed his cock and sank my fingernails into it while my other hand had

grabbed his ball sack above the balls and while keeping the pressure on my fingernails piercing his prick, I started yanking his ball sack as hard as I could. He stopped fingering me, and yelled. I kept at it for another second or so until his hands pulled my hands away. I smiled at him and then jacked him off. His groaned and shot his cum up my arm and over my shoulder. He had never catapulted jizz that forceful or shot that much cum before. From then on I always played rough with my dates. They never really complained and were always trying to date me again. After I dropped out of college, I hunted for married men. I could always count on them for an extra fifty or hundred bucks and most of them really did love a painful relationship. I dreamed of whipping them, subjecting them to really painful things, or smashing and cutting their cocks and balls off. I dreamed of pushing rods up their asses. I started reading books on sadism and torture. I had boundary limits that men would not allow me to violate, so much of my fantasies are unfulfilled. So, my Master, I am here as your student and slave, please teach me the black arts, please. I swear my allegiance to you. I am yours."

"Suzie you are a very interesting girl, but you did talk out of turn and you know you must be punished for being a bad girl. I think that I would like to use the shock punishment first. I am very excited for your huge soft titties and would like to watch them contract and then pulsate as the electric current bolts and charges through each titty. Understand, we are in the middle of a forest and the only things that will be hearing your screaming will be the birds and squirrels, so it is OK to scream. Damn Suzie, just thinking about those dancing titties and hard straining nipples is beginning to make my prick get hard, what do you think about that." "Please my Master, let me suck it until I get every drop of cum out of your balls. I know I am going to fall in love with your cock. Please pull it out and let me look at it while you are punishing me, please my Master, let me see it." Sonny had never imagined he would have a girl about to be tortured,

telling him, no begging that she wanted to watch his dick while he shot bolts of electric through her body.

What the fuck; what the girl had just said shifted his thoughts to another direction, just maybe she would make a good candidate for an accomplice; but how could he trust her? Like a bolt of lightning, it struck him; video, make a video of her doing something really heinous and send it to the lawyer with instructions that if he was arrested or murdered by her or anyone else, the lawyer would turn the video over to the police. Or, he could make a video then let her watch the incriminating scenes and just pretend that he was going to give it to the lawyer as insurance for her loyalty. That idea was better yet, it prevented the possibility of the lawyer's curiosity causing a premature viewing and a possible big problem with the lawyer client privilege. And if he were to just show her the packaged tape, make the run to the post office and return with a mailing receipt (for mailing something else to the law office of course) she would just assume he had actually mailed it and it was now in the attorney's safe. A great plan, but a little bit too early, there was still so much testing of her he had to do first; that had to happen.

Watching her eyes for reaction, Sonny told her "Suzie, your punishment for talking without permission will be the electric buckaroo rodeo. First I must clip your nipples to the hot leads, and then when they are in place I am going to give you jolts every few seconds. At the beginning they will be reasonably mild but as I turn this red dial, the current will increase. It starts at 0 and rotates to 24. Most girls pass out somewhere in the 10-12 range. Are you ready?" "If that that pleases you, then I am ready my Master." Sonny placed the clamps, one on each nipple. Sonny was really excited as he had never had breasts this size to play with before, they were huge, they were soft, and highlighted with a very large dark pink areola from which within the center, a knobby nipple relaxed. Turning the dial to 10 and pressing the red switch, Sonny drooled as he watched her body arch and the mammary cell mass vibrate in rhythm to the pulsating current. The

girl only squeaked out a small yelp. In the pattern that he had developed, he shocked her five more times at the 10 scale. "How did you like that Miss Suzie?" "My Master, it was so wonderful, it made my pussy wet. Thank you, my Master." "Hold the thanks for a minute, I have just decided to experiment at the high range, what do you think about that?" "Yes, my Master, the high range will be even better." As a curiosity, Sonny rotated the power dial to 20 knowing that most women would pass out somewhere between the 15 and 20 dial setting. Pressing the red button, he watched closely for her body language and vocal reactions. She began screaming as the hard bolts of electric coursed through her cells. Her breasts violently vibrated, her back arched to its extreme, urine squirted ten feet from her vagina. Her left the current surge through her for five seconds then released the red button. There was an instantaneous collapse of her body as streams of sweat on her forehead, face, stomach, and thighs poured from her pores. Piss oozed from her pussy. Her eyes had rolled back into her head. He could feel his prick throbbing screaming in a tiny voice for his hand magic or a warm body spot to plunge in and out of until that cum train came down the tracks and washed into the station. Surveying the effects of the current on her body and then looking a little closer, he noticed that she, unlike almost all of the others had not defecated (the bowel cleaning cleansed the lower bowels and rectum but the high energy electric spasms without fail to this point, would trigger a minor movement and discharge of fecal matter). Sonny took a smoke break to reflect upon the strange attitude of this girl. He was intrigued by her. Never before had any of them asked for it nor acted as if they enjoyed it. His smoke break would allow Suzie a little recovery time.

"Well, Suzie, what did you think about that. I really enjoyed it. Luckily I was standing to the side when your bladder gave, that piss really shot out of your puss. That was pretty funny. Anyway, tell me what you think about that good ole number 20." Still, at first she could not really form words, everything came out garbled. After several attempts she was finally able to

talk and speak in understandable sentences. "My Master, I have never had anything that severe. I could feel it everywhere, in my breasts, in my arms and legs, in face, and especially in my brain. I cannot describe the sweet pain it produces. I am sorry I pissed on your clean floor and will clean it up if you allow me. I am ready for more, maybe the 24. With the tingles of the electric still dancing in my body, I would love to suck you dry, my Master. I promise I will not bite or do anything treacherous."

"I can't believe this crazy cunt. She is actually asking for more" he thought to himself. "You know, Suzie that sounds really good right now. So here is how its gonna happen, reaching over to the prep table he picked up a scalpel, I will keep this scalpel resting on the table next to your throat, if you bite or do anything stupid I will slash both your eyes. The scalpel will be the last thing you ever see. A little later I will fill your pussy with a very strong caustic acid and sit in my chair with a beer and cigarette watching the caustic drain cleaner eat your cunt up. I had several girls that made me do that, I really didn't want to but you just can't let people hurt you or ignore the rules and not be punished. You wouldn't believe the caustic chemical odor and boy did they ever scream and fight the shackles. It wasn't a pleasant experience for them, that's for sure. Now that you understand the consequences, I think you sucking my cock dry is a capital idea."

Unzipping his pants, he pulled out his swollen and steely dick, while it waved in anticipation, he adjusted the head rests, allowing her head to dangle downward over the edge of the table where he could place his cock over her nose and directly in front of her lips with his balls coming to rest on the bridge of her nose. "My Master, in this position I cannot move my head enough to get your dick in and out of my throat, could you please push it in and out?" Sonny smiled and began in earnest, face fucking his captive and quickly discovered that he could hold the back of her head and hold it stationery and far enough downward draped over the edge of the table for his body to jam his cock completely down her throat. A bonus was

that his balls, with his dick completely in, would drag back and forth across her nose and eyebrows; how erotic. Another surprise, she did not gag or vomit. This was a classic deep throat maneuver he had seen in countless triple X fuck films. As an added pleasure he was able to push his knuckles and twine his fingers in the softness of her huge breasts, reminding him of the dough that he and Auntie Mame used to knead when they made bread. Then there were those other entertainment pleasures of alternating and twisting her nipples and massive breasts as hard as he could; with all these exciting and stimulating pain producers in motion, it took but a short time before he ejaculated. He ejaculated when his prick was as deep in her throat as it could go and it was a heavy load. She gargled a little but managed to swallow most with only a little dripping from the corners of her mouth. "Suzie, that was great and I really enjoyed it, but now it time for a little break, I need a cigarette and a cold beer." "Funny, she thought, I don't miss the cigarettes as much as I thought I would. Maybe that electric fright was a nicotine cure."

Thirty minutes later she could hear the screech of the chair as he stood up and began moving about tile floor room. He was out of her line of vision, but she could hear some type of door being opened and what sounded like the clink of glass. Suzie thought he was getting himself another bottle of beer. She also then realized how thirsty she was, those electric screamers had actually dehydrated her body. Maybe he was bringing her a drink. She was so thankful for this rest, her body was desperate for a break from that pain, those electric charges were overwhelming and she had never imagined pain like that. When he walked into her line of vision she could see him set down on the prep table a wire bottle holder that had at least four different colored heavy glass bottles. Strangely, they all seemed to be frosted.

"OK Suzie, I think we will do two more things and then into the cage you go. You are going to be my first guest and I am really excited about it. I think that you are I are going to get along just fine. You have been a big

surprise and I am going to treat you to something special between my little fun exercises. Now here is what is about to happen. I just love to eat pussy. You probably thought it a bit strange that I made such a big deal about soaping and washing your body when you first got here. There was a reason, of course. I make a habit of really cleaning that fun crack with the soap and hot water so that it loses that pissy taste and fishy odor and tastes sweet like a candy. It also cleans away any nasty smells from your ass and ass crack. You wouldn't believe how disgusting and unhygienic some girls are. I have standards and must have it very clean and fresh before I do my pussy pleasuring thing. Another thing, I know that every guy that had eaten your cunt badgered you to tell him that he was the best, but we both know you lied. How many guys have had their faces and tongues buried in your crack?" "My Master, there have been many and as you say, none were really able to arouse any deep passion in me." "I asked you how many?" "My Master I would say at least forty, every one after I have subjected them to a little pain, would crawl to me and beg me as their mistress to allow them to tongue me; at least forty, my Master." "That's funny, you a mistress and look at where you're at now, subjugated to a real master." Sonny laughed.

"Pay attention, not many guys know how to really eat pussy and send their woman to the top of the world. I have that talent. There are two methods I use, the first is the "anteater" and then when you think that there is nothing better, I give you the "straw" treatment. While I am working on you it will be OK for you to freely talk. But a word of caution if you go negative and start with the filthy names and threats I will stop and put you back on the electric but at the 24 level. The 24 level leaves burns on the skin wherever the contacts are clipped, and you don't want to even think about what it does to nipples. Understand?" Rolling his chair to between the stirrups, Sonny settled in between her legs. She could feel his warm breath on the lips of her vagina, a vagina that was so used to legions of men exploring it, she smiled when she thought about what that mousy

college professors' jealous nasty wife had once said after she had discovered Suzie was enhancing her grades and grade average by letting her husband do the wiener slam on her; that her pussy had more dicks going in and out of it then a police station.

Thinking this demented deviate was probably going to be no different than the scores of sloppy tongues working her groves, Suzie tried to focus on her "plan". And then it happened. At first she could sense the tip of his tongue exploring the drapery of her labias. She felt it coil around her clitoris. She felt his thumbs as they spread open the drapery that shrouded the secret spots that men overlooked as they lapped up and down or stabbed at. She could feel the hot tip of that tongue gently gliding first on left inside of her labia and then slowly wandering onto the right fleshly pinkness. She could begin to feel a warmness creeping up from her labias and as a match is struck and ignites, she pumped her thighs to greet those lips that were now whistling fire bolts driving the neurons like electric arrows up to explode like roman candles in the real " I am a selfish woman" part of her cortex. Two minutes after Sonny began, Suzie became an animal, a beast that needed prey; a creature that could only be satisfied with more. She started screaming for more as Sonny shifted into the "straw". Her body went into tremors as she felt his curled fingernails scrapping within and against the upper pad of her vagina. Forgetting that she was a kidnapped prisoner of an obviously crazy madman, Suzie had never imagined that any man could catapult her into the dimension she was rocketing to. On the verge of fainting from the pleasure, she realized she had lost or abandoned control of her body and it was bucking against his face while she screamed, creamed and schemed for more. Like a relentless infantry assault, bolt after bolt of orgasms were racking her body, realizing that she had lost control and more importantly realizing that she did not want to control this passion, she surrendered to that heated and welcomed fiery passion. If only she could free her hands, she would force his face and that wonderful

tongue so far into her cunt, that without a scuba line, he would die of oxygen deficiency.

As the hours turned into days, and the days turned into weeks, Suzie became more than a torture object. After a number of brief conversations and time spent with Sonny sitting in an easy chair outside the pen and Suzie, within the cage and sitting on her metal folding chair, Sonny began to think of her more and more as an confident and accomplice, than a captive. Sonny thought it was time to allow her a little freedom to see if he could detect any suspicious reactions or she was truly on the road to being a trust worthy accomplice. "You know Suzie, I really think that we could be a team. I am growing quite fond of you, you are an amazing woman that never complains and always seems to be on a high note. I am so pleased that you are never haunted by depression and seem to look forward to our little workouts. I am sure you have noticed that I have been limiting the workouts to things that are more sexually orientated and produce less pain than several of the methods you experienced when you first became my slave. We definitely have the same outlook and both appreciate the extremes of physical testing. I have made a decision to allow you a little more freedom when playtime comes around. You won't have to wear the handcuffs anymore when I let you out of the pen, but you will have a collar around your neck that will produce a 50,000 volt charge just in case the temptation of this freedom produces any escape ideas. I will have the collar ready by the weekend and it will have a tamper proof locking device on it. You will wear it 24/7. But once I allow you the freedom of being out of the pen no other binding will be necessary; of course for your safety, I will always strap you onto the table just so when things get hot and heavy you don't bounce off the table. To reduce any temptation of violent acts against me, I am sure you are aware that all the sharp or blunt instruments that could harm me are now locked within those medical cabinets. What do you think about this?" "My Master, I think it is a wonderful idea and I promise you that I will be a trustworthy and faithful servant. I too, have

grown a liking for you. I will never give you a reason to regret this decision. Thank you so much my Master. To celebrate, can you put the electric to my nipples again or if you prefer, may I suck your dick or tongue fuck your asshole. I adore stabbing my tongue in and out of you and I believe that you find it pleasurable as well. How would you like to celebrate, my Master, anything you wish, anything you wish."

After several sessions of the limited freedom he granted her, Suzie thought it imperative to act. "My Master I will accept your punishment without complaint for speaking out of turn, but while I do enjoy my stay here I find it so lonely that you spend so much apart in your living quarters and I have no one to speak to. Is it possible that once or twice per day, when you are not playing with my body, you could find it in your generosity to schedule perhaps thirty minutes a day so we could just speak freely to each other? I promise that I will never say anything vulgar or anything to hurt you. It would be such a reward to be able to just ask you, my Master how you are feeling or talk about some other subject that would interest you. Do you think this is possible, would you please grant me a little time each day to be human?" "Suzie, I have been thinking about this also. I am beginning to really see a partnership blossoming between us. So here is what I decided, at 10am and at 5pm when I serve you food we will have a free hour. You will be able to speak of anything you wish. You have earned a little freedom and as a bonus, I will be giving you a small TV, two sweaters (I love to see tits shake beneath a sweater) a skirt and a pair of slacks. I will also attach an intercom between your pen and my living room. You will be free to use it whenever you wish and if I have any interest in what you are saying I might respond, if not I will just shut it off. What do you think about that?" "My Master this is the most wonderful news. I can't begin to thank you for your generosity. I do have a request, I will need a trash bin, another blanket, another towel and a larger supply of sanitary napkins, next week will begin my period again. Is it possible to get these for me?" Sonny had not thought about these items and after a frown, said, "You have been

pretty good and I do have to make a food run tomorrow, I guess I can pick those things up for you."

"Oh incidentally Suzie, I have also thought about something else. How would you like to help me entertain the next girl? Of course, you will have at first with this one a minor part. You see if you agree, I will video tape you torturing the girl with the most heinous methods and make no mistake, anyone that views the video tape will definitely know it is you. Once I get you on tape, the tape will be given to my attorney and if anything should ever happen to me, say a girl like you suddenly thinks she is smart enough to stab me and escape, the attorney will turn over the video to the police department and you will be prosecuted for murder. Keeping you in a pen forever is not something I would look forward to and besides I really think you would be an asset to have as a team. You will once again be a dominix. You will have our captives screaming for mercy. You will be sitting alongside me in a chair smoking a cigarette and drinking a cold, cold beer while you watch the hogtied captives slowing choke themselves to death. Think about it and tomorrow be prepared to give me an answer. Sonny had already made up his mind that if she did not want to join the team that tomorrow after the food run, he was going to hogtie her and sitting in his recliner chair watch the life slowly leave her body. You can only fuck holes so many times before they become boring, and Suzie, despite those glorious wonderful pillowy tits, was becoming boring. As another test in the development of his ungodly partnership, Sonny had decided to remove the shock collar to better see her reaction to just a little more freedom. He was not disappointed.

That night as she sat on her bed Suzie thought for a moment about where she was in life. Abducted and knowing that not a single soul had to date or would ever miss her much less search for her, everyone would just assume that she had wandered off. Not a single soul that would ever care, not a single soul! Here she was, an accomplice to a sadistic torturer and serial killer. Trapped with video evidence displaying her torturing women and

actually slipping the strangulation cord around their necks and then sitting in a chair smoking a cigarette and sipping a bottle of beer as she watched the poor victim struggle against the ever tightening ropes until the victim's eventual death. Sonny was very shrewd when he came up with that accomplice idea. Definitely a graphic video that if a jury viewed it would see her as a monster and certainly would be compelled to send her to death row. What happens if Sonny suddenly gets bored with her, or finds someone else with colossal tits or decides that he just needs to move on? How expendable was she? How could she gain his trust to the point that he would treat her as an equal and she would rise from this slavedom? An idea began to form and as she closed her eyes she had a smile on her face.

During the next seven months, Sonny had hunted six times, aborted four times, and returned with a captive twice; a twenty seven year old black girl and a thirty year old blonde. As promised Suzie was given much freedom in the selection and execution of the tortures. Of course, Sonny made absolutely certain that each video tape was clearly focused on a step by step, almost a "how to" instructional video of the woman and the callousness and apparent joy of her personally administering the heinous torture upon her victims. Sonny would fade in and out on the faces of her victims as they desperately tried to scream out through the gag. He would also make Suzie smile and drag her tongue across her lips as she powered the electric rodeo or pierced a breast with a sharpened knitting needle. He filmed her sitting in a chair smoking a cigarette as the each of the girls slowly strangled themselves to death. As a closing, he filmed her pushing the bodies of the girls into the shredder and her watching and laughing as the fish swarmed in schools eating the shredded victim chum. He recorded enough self-incriminatory evidence to ensure that Suzie would forever be in his power as long as he had control of these videos. Sonny now looked at Suzie differently, no longer was she a captive, now because of the videos she was a criminal accomplice. While this would not allow him to

completely trust her, it would give him a feeling that she, only to protect herself, would serve him now more as a partner then as a captive.

"Suzie, I have decided that you have earned an upgrade. You will still be locked in the pen at night, but I am going to provide you better clothing, some furniture, a better TV, toilet articles, a microwave, and a small refrigerator. Once a week I will allow you an allowance so you can make a list of items you wish, both grocery and personal. I will take you to town and we will shop together. I know that the thoughts and temptation that will be racing through your mind about being one step away from freedom, but I will always have the tethering leash, the video tapes. Should you escape, within four hours my attorney will be appearing before and presenting to the local prosecuting attorney both incriminating tapes. Within six hours an arrest warrant for murder will be issued for you and if you are smart enough and lucky enough to escape the police manhunt, you can only hope to be a fugitive for the rest of your life. If you are caught, it will be the fatal injection. So as long as you are a good girl, things will improve here.

"My Master, I have an idea that may interest you. We both enjoy so much the discomfort that we produce in your victims. I had always enjoyed sexually degrading and punishing my boyfriends and the men in my life. I had no idea I would like punishing women as well. I have been very faithful in carrying out your instructions and have even made several innovative suggestions myself. I believe that I have proved my worth as your servant and without any hesitation have carried out your orders and subjugated the most extraordinary pain stimulation upon your captives. I am not asking for a reward, but offering you a suggestion; the last two captives have been females and I did enjoy exercising the tools and methods you prescribed to share our passions with them. To please you, I have become quite good at taxidermy and have preserved your clitoris trophies so they no longer have odor and no longer turn coal black.

You plan has provided us the bodies of guests to punish. I have tried to excel in performing every pain inducement to the highest degree of my ability. I only wish that we could relax and watch each torture and execution video to allow me to improve my skills with your tools. But maybe, just maybe, you would like to capture a gay male for the next subject. It will offer you a different canvas to paint and I as your devoted helper will enjoy assisting you in exercising the different applications and due to a male's peculiar physiology, offer even more pleasures for you my Master, and me your servant. Do you not think this is a good idea, my Master. On your next hunt you seek a homosexual. Also, my Master, the police will think, since no more females have been abducted, that you have retired or died, and possibly they will put the investigation file in a box set in the police station basement, only to be retrieved if girls again start disappearing. Please my Master, I hope I am not too bold for suggestion something as unusual as this?"

Sonny was about to tell her that the plan has been working, so why change and if she started nagging, she could go back to the handcuffs, no clothes, and no TV; but as she gradually explained her idea further; he began to think of Tommy. It would be a nice change to grab a cocksucker and have some different anatomy to play with. "Suzie, I think you are on to something. I need to think it through a little bit; but you are right, it will throw the cops for a loop and plus since we just fed the fishes the blonde, I can start hunting right away and we won't have to wait several months for the coast to clear. Yes, I think you are on to something. Damn, I am getting a hard on, come over here get those slacks off, and bend over I think I want to fuck your asshole till it catches fire." "Yes, my Master I love to feel your cock pushing in and out against my sphincter muscles and I know how you much love it when I tighten those muscles and strangle your cock; it really turns me on."

Sonny was loudly grunting as he rammed his prick in and out of her rectum, thinking back to those days and about how nice it was to hurt Tommy.

Sonny occasionally mourned the fact that because of that damned incarceration he lost contact with Tommy. Those escapades were a lot of fun and Tommy was always petrified and that factor gave Sonny a special feeling of superiority and made sex that much more enjoyable, for Sonny that is, certainly not for Tommy. Sonny would be shocked to know that two strange things happened: first that Tommy's mother, finally realizing that she and she alone was the reason that her sweet son Tommy turned homosexual and out of pity, monumental guilt, and the hope and chance that she could turn Tommy back to being a heterosexual, began fucking and sucking her son on a regular basis and just as hard and as earnestly as she had years ago fucked those black, white hating motherfuckers on campus; and secondly that Tommy came out of the closet and started a gay club, which in less than two years made him a millionaire. As protection against ever encountering someone like Sonny again, Tommy surrounded himself with big cock bodyguards (during the employment interview, Tommy always made them drop their pants and ordered them to allow him to massage their dicks until they reached their maximum potential; no cocks less than eight inches were ever hired). As part of his duty to momma, he always found time to once per week drop by to fuck momma. In a twisted way, Tommy did enjoy fucking her and often would get carried away a little and try to punish her for his past and all that suffering with pain. He would grab a breast and really squeeze and twist her nipple until she begged for mercy, or maybe fuck her in the ass without lube, or maybe or push her face into his ass and command her to do some of the nasties that Sonny had made Tommy do so many years ago. He especially liked to call her names, just like Sonny did to him; whore, big holed bitch, ass licker, cum sucker, useless cocksucker. Many sessions ended with her bursting into tears and sobbing and callused Tommy laughing at the tears dipping from her eyes. Oh vengeance was so sweet.

Sonny was in the hunt planning mode now. The more he thought of her idea of grabbing a gay guy the more he liked it. Bitch holes were getting

boring; it was time to move on to something else, something a bit more exotic. Grabbing a queer took a little more planning. As homosexuals or their vehicles were often the target of hate filled assholes, trailer trash, drunks, teenagers, activists, etc., and the end result generally meant a violent confrontation or property damage, every gay hangout had cameras everywhere, alley, parking lots, doorways, every single space that could be invaded by a queer stomper, Sonny knew that snatching a gay guy would take a lot of cruising and planning. One afternoon when he was in Gillette shopping for groceries in a box store, a wire newspaper display basket caught his eye. It was the local alternative life, monthly tabloid, advertising all the popular gay haunts throughout the state. On the way out, to avoid notice, he quickly grabbed a copy and pushed it into one of the shopping bags. He couldn't wait to get home to do a little shopping of his own for maybe a cocksucker or two. After he had unloaded the groceries and fed Suzie, he retreated to his bedroom and as he lay on the bed savoring a cigarette, he sorted through the gay hangouts, one by one, and area by area. He discovered very little close by, small communities generally do not welcome open gayness and gays that live in small communities usually have to travel many miles to practice his or her art with fellow believers of same sex fun club. Sonny did notice that in Ponsy a pretty big and liberal city with real suburbs and a population of several hundred thousand people, there were at least four small openly gay rendezvous, two gay social clubs, one gay bar and one lesbian after hour club. Once a year they even had a gay pride picnic. One big problem, Sonny had to weigh out the worth and reward of the travel time as Ponsy was at the extreme of Sonny's northeast boundary; it took a drive of seven and one half hours to get there. Time to sleep on it.

The next morning after weighing out the trouble and expense of the drive against the pleasure he would reap from having a new canvas to paint, Sonny decided that he would make the trip. Sonny walked over to the cage to awaken Suzie. "Honey child, I think that you have a great idea. I have

given it much thought and I have a very big surprise for you; I am going to take you out on this hunt. I don't need to warn you about the consequences of doing anything stupid, the lawyer has the videos and if I ever get caught and you're responsible, the police will be sending you to death row and we both will die holding hands together. You are going to be my female detective partner who stays in the van and when the guy sees you, he will think everything is normal and it's a routine bust. You will have the chloroform ready and once we get him handcuffed and his legs clamped down, I will headlock him and you will chloroform him. After he is out you can duct tape gag and blindfold him. It's going to be a very long trip, in fact we'll probably need a cooler for drinks and maybe a sandwich or two. I am only going to stop for gas once on the way there and twice on the way back. While he is out you can check him out. I'm getting a little excited just thinking about the fun we can have once we get him back here and on the table. Do you like the idea?"

"Oh, my Master, thank you for giving me the opportunity to earn your trust. I promise that I will be faithful and will carry out every command. I too, am very excited about having a guy captive, pussy is beginning to bore me a little, so having a penis and testicles to play with challenges us to devise new trials for this slave. If you allow it, I would like to be the first to experiment with ways to make our slave obey and appreciate our love. Is this a possibility, my Master?" "First off Suzie, he will not be "our slave", he will be "my" slave. Do not make any mistake of your place and conduct yourself in an over extended bravado. I do plan to allow you to design and decide the methods of stress that will give us both pleasure, you as you administer them, and me as I sit in my chair, enjoying a cigarette and a cold beer watching "my" slave undergoing the tests you will be giving him. I may decide to join you. Tomorrow will be a big day, the day we hunt gays. So rest and I will be here around 7am and start the journey. Back in the pen Suzie, we have a very long day ahead of us, get some rest." Into her

pen she freely went. Sonny said "good night" then locked the outside annex door and off he went to the big house for a good night's rest.

"Good night, my Master".

The very next morning, Suzie thought she saw an opportunity to begin her plan and decided that there would likely be no better time. She knew the risk she was taking, if she caught Sonny in one of his depressive moods, he could decide that he needed a new play toy and she could easily end up in the lake feeding the fish and turtles. As she heard Sonny opening the annex door and she opened the door to her pen walking to meet him, Suzie pulled all her courage together and began: "Good morning My Master, I trust that you still find my body desirable and my companionship pleasurable. I have carried out your orders and commands with the respect you have taught me to have for you as Master and for the black arts. I have shown slaves that disobedience has severe consequences. I have tortured slaves for you. I have killed slaves for you. You have filmed my actions forever linking my loyalty to you. I have long ago decided that I belong to you and belong with you. I have thought of creative ways to entertain you as I used the bodies of our captives as a canvas to paint with pain. During these last months, I have discovered that I love you, not as a slave but as a woman. My feelings for you have grown and I hesitated to demonstrate them fearing you would scorn me and the disclosure would send me to the fish tank. I know that I am taking one huge risk should you not harbor any similar, however small, feeling for me. I would like to propose marriage, you and I. We could forever enjoy the entertainment we introduce to our strange world together. If you are considering that it would involve giving me too much freedom, I would certainly accept any boundaries you think appropriate. My Master, before you say anything, please think of all the exciting things we have done together as a team. You have introduced me to your world and I have found a comfortable place in it serving you. My skills go way beyond sexuality and sadism; my Master I am both a fiend in the annex and a talented chef in the kitchen

and I always strive to maintain a clean and orderly environment. Look at my quarters, they are kept spotless. Look around this room, not a spec of blood or dirt anywhere. The freedoms you have granted me are wonderful. You no longer lock my quarters at night. I can accompany you on shopping trips. I will not leave you or betray you, my Master for I sincerely love you. Please say you have feeling for me."

Knowing that there was likely little chance of him ever again capturing a woman like Lycee, Sonny had begun to think about making a change in the arrangements with Suzie. Marriage was always an option and like his lawyer had once said, in this state, marriage was better than a court gag order as a spouse could not testify against a spouse. This sudden and unexpected declaration of love by Suzie did have merit. She was a great partner. She seemed to be into and relish being a dominix. She enthusiastically carried out all his orders and commands. Plus there was always the insurance of the video tapes clearly showing her complicity in the torture and murder of at least two victims. Maybe this is a good idea. Plus those tits were the best, soft and huge and he never got tired of sucking them, playing with them, tit fucking them, or using them as a massaging platform to launch a string of his cum up her chin across her lips and tongue and splashing on her eyes and forehead. Just thinking about them always gave him a hard on.

"Suzie I have given this a great deal more thought than you ever could imagine. From this point forward you can address me as "Sonny". You are right; you have come a long way in earning my trust and respect. We have been a good team and make good partners. I can never get enough of your luscious titties and no one gives head like you. My toenails explode when you do that tongue thing in my asshole. Over the last eighteen months, I have seen you grow from a frightened captive to a real dominix. I have enjoyed watching you evolve into a wicked bitch incapable of mercy as you dispense the devil's pain. I have grown to trust you and I have discovered feelings for you. I will think about your proposal overnight and let you

know my answer tomorrow as you serve me breakfast in bed in the big house." "My Master, if you are in bed, how will the annex door be unlocked and how will I get into the big house's kitchen." "Suzie, you are to call me Sonny now, and you will no longer be quartered in this annex building, from this point forward you will be living in the big house, cooking our meals, sleeping in our bed, and have all the freedoms a housewife would have."

"Sonny, I love you. I cannot begin to tell you how much I love you. I will be the best live-in or best wife a man could ever ask for. I will keep my fingers crossed hoping your answer tomorrow will be the one that makes me happy and then I will make you happy. Thank you my darling." For the first time ever, Suzie jumped into his arms and began French kissing him with a fervor that actually shocked Sonny. Down to the floor they went and for another first, they made out and fucked each other like first time lovers.

Suzie smiled; cooking our meals, sleeping in our bed, she was flabbergasted that he used the word "our" and would be retiring every night alongside this monster man. She loved it when a plan worked.................

CHAPTER THIRTEEN

Many, many miles away Leonard, a twenty six year old, light complexed, slim black man, looked into the full length mirror to see how his new avocado green pants matched with the lime green plunging open silky custom shirt. Satisfied that the colors smartly coordinated and it displayed his hairless chest and that the tight trousers kept his cock bulge prominent, he smiled. Today he was going to make a play for that sexy waiter. Leonard loved the way the waiter would shake his golden tresses as he teased the hopeful patrons, he himself hoping for a decent tip. To assist patrons in deciding generosity, Teddy the waiter would allow them to tuck dollars bills in his skimpy red briefs and if the owner wasn't tending bar, Teddy would allow those tipping fingers to quickly caress his eight inch cock, which by the way was always in a state of semi-hard. Today was the owner's day off, and the fill in bartender could give a fuck less who was grabbing dick and who wasn't. Leonard had a horde of five dollar bills, exactly twenty of them, plus a crisp one hundred dollar bill and several high quality condoms. Years ago when AIDS first made the gay

circuit blackboard, Leonard hurriedly read every single medical article he could find on transmission. He discovered that oral sex and ingestion of even an infected person's semen was not likely to transmit the virus. He did discover that anal virus transmission was almost a sure thing if that person plunging his cock into someone else's bowels was infected. So Leonard practiced safe sex; like the club jingle said "Rubbers are a gays' best friend". Today Leonard was going to rent one of the little cubicles and one way or another get Teddy bear's cock down his throat and later making Teddy bear don a rubber, get that wonderful wand shoved up into the darkness of Leonard's ass. That was the plan and it was a good plan, so thought Leonard.

"What a night" thought Leonard "Teddy bear cost a lot of money, almost two hundred dollars, but that enormous cock was worth every cent and boy could that guy jet out the cum. I got a sore ass and my throat still hurts a little from that choking. I never dreamed that Teddy would be a guy that liked to force his cock all the way down your throat to put that especially erotic pressure on his dick and he would then strangle you with his hands as he plunged it in and out. Don't think I could do that every night; gee a guy needs a rest when he gets a workout like that. The best part of this club besides the cute boys is how the management designed it as an entertainment center. It's just great that the management had the fore thought to lay out the club with the ultimate in privacy in mind; these little side love rooms are so convenient and so cheap to rent. No fuss no muss, everything right here in the club and convenient. What a night, but time to go home, maybe a little stop for breakfast first. Maybe I'll stop by the convenience store and get a quick café ole, and who knows maybe someone with big muscles and a hard dick will be looking for an afternoon delight."

Sonny and Suzie had been cruising by the gay bar on and off for hours and because the gays were almost always paired up when they left decided to move on to the bar with the steam room and privacy rooms. Arriving at

9am they had set on a parking lot within binocular distance of the "Boy's Club" entry. There was a steady stream of "in and outers", guys visiting the bar and steam room to get a leg up on the day by either getting or giving a quick morning blowjob. "Here Sonny check this guy out." Sonny took the binoculars and scanned the parking to observe a smiling, over weight bald man in a pink shirt and bowtie ambling towards his car after obviously scoring a throat jabber. "He's too heavy, we could get back strain lifting that fat ass on the table and remember we got to toss that body in the shredder; here take the binoc's and keep looking, someone about one hundred pounds lighter." "Look at this one Sonny, he's the right size." "Suzie, he's getting into a four door family car, and you can just barely make out the family decal in the rear window. Everybody would be looking for him fifteen minutes after he misses picking the kids up. We don't need that trouble. Keep looking." "How about him?" "Too muscular Suzie, the guy could put up a fight and beat the shit out of both of us. Find a wimpy one."

While they were sitting there, Suzie shared with Sonny some new ideas she had come up with for punishing a man. "Sonny, how much pain do you think it would cause if we were to push a glass rod up into someone's cock and then smash it again and again with a wooden or rubber mallet? Or if we were to skin his prick out or cut off his ball sack and taxidermy it just like the tits and clitoris' we have? Or maybe cut off his balls, fry them and eat them in front of him? Sonny I am always thinking of ways to make you happier. Sonny I love you so much and I could never be happier anywhere else. Thank you Sonny for saving me from the boring life I was trapped into."

It was just minutes later, when she spied Leonard getting into his little green two door imported car; "Sonny, look at this one, skinny and that's no family car." "Good job honey, an all green cocksucker, a sweet pea. This one will probably work out if we get a chance to grab him. Let's follow him and see if we can get him off the beaten path." Having no idea that he was

now hunted prey, Leonard started his jazzy little sports car and clicked on some soul tunes. The day is pretty early. Leonard loved to shop and flirt at the convenience store which was owned and operated by a tough cut, lesbian appropriately named "Butch". There were always gays hanging out and once in a while Leonard would hookup and get a "take out". The only issue was the convenience store was not very convenient; it was located in the suburbs and if one was in a hurry, he had to drive a few back roads to get there. But the double dipping lure of another hot body and the thought of relaxing naked on the bed in his air conditioned apartment messaging a white boy's balls while that white boy was gargling his cum were irresistible; the dick always wins, on to Butch's.

This was just the break that Sonny had hoped for. The little green two door vehicle suddenly turned from the highway and headed down a service road that was away from the traffic zones. When the little green car turned onto a state forest road, Sonny knew it was almost over; success was knocking at the door. Sooner or later there would be a wooded section with a pull over spot on the shoulder, and when he saw it coming, he would flick on the police lights. Bingo, he no sooner mentioned that to Suzie when he sighted in the distance a spot that would serve just that purpose. He told Suzie to flip the light switch and the show was on the road.

"Shit, now what, I can't afford another ticket. That last speeding ticket cost me two hundred dollars for a lawyer and four hundred and thirty dollars in court costs, plus those greedy insurance motherfuckers jacked my policy premium up another fifty bucks a month. Hope I can talk myself out of this." "Good afternoon, officer was I doing anything wrong; if I was going a little fast, I am really sorry and promise to watch my speed."

Sonny began the routine. "Sir we just had an assault at a gay bar and the guy said the man who slapped him was wearing a green outfit and driving a green sports car. Please turn your motor off and step from car and keep

your hands where I can see them. Please do it now." "Damn" he thought "there goes my afternoon, some fucking queer got jealous that I drained Teddy's cock before he got a chance to". "Yes, sir I have my hands up. Boy, you sure are a handsome man. I bet your partner has trouble keeping her hands off you. What is going to happen, sir." "Here's the deal, I am going to handcuff you and put in the back. I will turn off and lock up your car. Then I am going to drive you back to the police station where the complainant is and see if he can identify you. If he doesn't then my partner and I will be driving you back to your car. If he does identify you then it's a different story. Hands behind you back please." Leonard thought "what the fuck, nothing I can do so just go with the flow and when I see who lied about the assault, I promise I will really fuck him up the next time I see him at the club."

As Leonard was now cuffed and sitting on the paddy wagon bench, he was thinking "I just bet it was that black as coal, field nigga, Thomas that ratted my ass out to these police people. He's so black he's almost purple and he's always pretending he's from royalty in the Sudan. Shit, he's a third generation welfare, project nigga for sure. Niggas like him are always jealous of us refined house niggas. When I get my hands on that motherfucker, he gonna wish he never snitched on this important civilized and sophisticated career man. The nerve of that project trash; causing trouble because the handsome, tight ass waiter boy prefers a refined, articulate bottom rather than an alley tramp with a twenty word vocabulary that always starts with or ends with "ya kno". After I put the hurt to his jealous black ass, I'm gonna see to it that everyone in the club knows he's a cop snitch; I gonna make sure that if anyone holds or smokes, they know for sure that this motherfucker will be dropping their names to the local DEA man. That oughta get his ass kicked on the parking lot every time someone gets busted. Then after a couple of ass kickings, he gonna get the idea that the welcome mat don't say welcome anymore, it say, git you snitch ass outta this club and outta this town. That be the end of

jigaboo ass Thomas; damn low evolution monkey ass boogies are worse than toothless, smelly, white trash Mississippi crackers."

After Leonard had been seated and the leg manacles attached to the bench, Leonard suddenly noticed that the detective's partner did not look like a police woman and strangely there were no mounted dashboard police radio in the van. "Excuse me ma'am could I see your badge please. When we get to the police station I want to commend you and your partner to your supervisor."

"Well, looks like we got a player Suzie. Listen and listen well you ass licking, sweet pea cocksucker, you will keep your mouth closed and speak only when I or my partner speaks to you. We are going to be on the road for about eight hours and I don't want to hear a peep from you. I will be pulling over shortly and we are going to make you a little more comfortable. There is not a fucking thing you can do to change any of this; you can't beg, you can't threaten, you can't bribe, nothing. The only thing you can do is make it worse for yourself, so keep your mouth shut. Understand? Oh, one more thing, from this point forward you are to address me as "Master" and the lovely girl with the huge tits as "Mistress" but girl tits don't interest you, do they sweet pea?" Leonard just couldn't resist the racial inference of the word "master". Leonard loved the expression on whitey's faces when he played that victimization trump card and went into the aggressive disrespected mode. "Fuck you, you ofay motherfucker. Did you lose a century on your gas station wall calendar? Where the fucks do you think you're at, on a plantation in Mississippi? I don't call anyone "Master". Fuck you honkies. If you have any smarts you will take me back to my car. I am a very influential person in city government. I am director of the award winning City arts program. When they catch you and release me I am going to personally sit with the judge and tell him how this was a hate crime and that he should rule for the maximum sentence." Sonny and Suzie smiled, both knowing that unless one of the little fishes or turtles had a law degree and bench appointment,

Leonard wouldn't be discussing the finer points of law with anyone, ever. Seeing them both smiling, Leonard suddenly realized that these were no normal white milk toast motherfuckers; neither blinked an eye at his spiel, a spiel that would have had any ofay motherfucker begging for forgiveness. These mothers were hard core and bad ass.

"So you're a man of influence, sweet pea. So you're gonna call names and make threats. Hmmmm. Lookie here, Mistress, sounds like the cocksucker doesn't seem to like us very much. Guess what, asshole, I can see a lonely little dirt road up ahead. I am going to pull over and your Mistress is going to give you the first lesson. We'll see how brave you are afterwards." Sonny and Suzie began laughing. Stopping on the side road Sonny turned to Suzie and said "Forget the chloroform, for now, get him honey, teach him some respect." Suzie hopped over the console, opened the barrier gate and grabbed the duct tape. Leonard resisted by twisting his head this way and that, but eventually by clawing his nostrils, Suzie managed to get the duct tape across his mouth, silencing him. Once he was gagged, she slammed his head against the back of the metal bench and when his head floated back towards her she back handed smacked him several times across the face. Leonard was in shock now. "What was happening, how did this happen to me, who are these people, why did this happen, all I wanted to do was to entertain a white boy for the rest of the afternoon and now I was snatched and fucked up by two white crazies."

"Check his gear out, Suzie." Suzie smiled back to Sonny and pushing Leonard's body flat on the bench, first undid Leonard's sequined belt buckle; then his zipper and pulled his avocado green slacks down to his ankles. "Look he's wearing green silk underwear", they both thought it funny. Pulling his shorts down, she whistled, "Look Master, his cock is huge, not really thick, but like a pencil, long; and even soft, it's maybe five or six inches and like his face, it's kinda a yellow tone color. Wonder what it's gonna look like when it gets hard? I expected to see a coal black dick, but we got a yellow yard stick instead." Leonard thought, "yea you

motherfuckers, long like a pencil, like a yardstick, just wait until I jab it down your throat and you choke to death on your puke, just wait."

"OK, faggot, now your lesson starts." Suzie grabbed Leonard's balls and cradled them in one hand and began striking them with hammer blows with the other. With the gag now in place, Leonard could only grunt and moan. Suzie smashed those ball six times and just when Leonard thought it could not get any worse, she seized both of his nuts and began twisting the sack. Leonard began bucking against the pain. Suzie smiled and looking directly in the eyes said "You are really going to regret calling us motherfuckers. This is just a little taste of what my Master is going to allow me to do to you. You will wish you could crawl back into your mother's womb before I get done with you. Now stay still and enjoy the ride, it'll probably be your last ride, so enjoy it." Suzie started laughing and as a last salute, grabbed his finely pointed nose and twisted that too until his body arched in pain. While he was struggling to break loose his nose from her fingers, he heard Sonny tell her it was time to get up front and get on the road again.

Throughout the drive Leonard could only reflect on the pain. Whenever his moans got too noisy, Suzie would hop over the console and beat his balls again. After two treatments, suffering through the pain, Leonard was a very obedient man and became a very quiet slave for the rest of the trip.

After an all-day drive, and two short fueling stops, the van came to a halt. The mad, crazy woman got out and apparently undid and redid some kind of gate and then after one more gate opening and closing, the vehicle came to a stop and the driver cut the engine off. "Damn, I hope these crazy motherfuckers just want to fuck around a little and then let me go. I don't think they are crazy enough to really want to hurt me, I don't think they are Klu Klux Klanners maybe just fag haters. If I get any chance to fight I'm gonna show them how bad a queer can kick ass." Leonard smiled as he remembered that time on the parking lot when two husky, black

teenagers thought they could rough him up and take his money. Boy were they surprised when he fought and beat the shit out of both of them, leaving them lying on the parking lot begging for mercy. "Just give me the chance" he thought silently. "Suzie we better juice him, I think he's gonna be trouble". Grabbing a rag she saturated it with the chloroform. Leonard remembered fighting the rag, the sweet smell and then nothing.

Opening his eyes, his head a little groggy and his vision a little blurred and foggy, he immediately became aware that some device was forcing his jaws apart and he was helpless to speak. As the chloroform wore off, Leonard gradually realized he was naked and strapped to some type of cold metal table, his wrist secured to each side, a strap across his chest, another across his throat and his legs and ankles elevated and strapped in some type of stirrups. Testing the bindings it took him but a second to realize that this was the real deal, there was no way he was going to get loose. Turning his head he could see that he was in some type of horror chamber, tables full of instruments and dildos hanging from pegs on the walls. (In a vote of extreme trust, Sonny had removed all the instruments from the medical cabinets and allowed Suzie to arrange them on the prep tables). He also realized that he had been given some type of bath, he could smell the strong fragrance of bath soap and his skin still tingled from the soap and hot water they scrubbed him with. Turning to his left he could see a man and a woman sitting in chairs smoking cigarettes and both enjoying a soft drink. "Damn, this sure doesn't look good for a poor black man."

"Well, lookie, lookie if it isn't the nasty mouth man. Well trash mouth man, I think that you have exceeded the speed limit calling us all those terrible, evil names. Before you know it, you will be begging us for mercy. Unfortunately, this isn't the House of Mercy; this is the House of Pain. Your Mistress will begin with the electric rodeo. Let me explain, I love to explain to everyone exactly what going to happen. Mistress will clamp one of the electrodes to the tip of your handsome yellow cock and the other one to your yellow ball sack. Of course when she fingers that little red button on

the control board, current will bounce from one electrode to the other. At first, when the little dial is on "5" you will just a little feel displeasure, but the more she turns the dial upwards and it intensifies up to the "24" you will swear it's the worse pain you have ever had. Your back will arch, your cock will burn and even your asshole will feel like a frying donut hole. Your eyes will feel like they are exploding. You will piss yourself. To save you the embarrassment of shitting yourself, while you were unconscious, we gave you a purge and cleaned you out. All the while you are cursing me, Lady Mistress and your luck; I will be sitting here smoking my cigarette laughing my ass off. You see, you were snatched for a purpose; that purpose being to entertain us as we treat your body, mind and soul to these little kinky things we do. If you weren't such a race hater, I would have Lady Mistress remove the dental spreader gag; but since I don't really care for negative demeaning social epitaphs, you won't get the opportunity to call us names and sadly we won't be able to hear you beg and plead. Over the years we have developed some pretty sophisticated pain vehicles. Lady Mistress and myself are students of the arts of De Sade and do enjoy providing these little inconveniences to unfortunate people like you. We especially enjoy it when someone gives us a reason to be especially aggressive. All those that have preceded you on this table were women, so please excuse us if some of our devices seem a bit inappropriate or require modification; we are on a learning curve. OK, Lady Mistress, please begin."

Suzie, impressed by the fact that Sonny had actually referred to her as "Lady Mistress" and not "her" was doubly determined to prove her worth with this capture. Walking to the front of the OBGYN table, she lowered her face until eyes were directly looking into his. She could see the fear, panic and terror in them and smiled. He tried to spit at her, but the jaw separator prevented it. "Well, well, you have no idea what that just cost you." Turning she walked back the several steps to the prep table and removed a vice clamp, returning to his side, she plunged the jaws of the vice clamps past the dental jaw spreader into the open cavity of his mouth

and seized his tongue. Leonard gargled in pain, severe pain. Slowly Suzie pulled his tongue and extended as far out of his mouth as possible. Once she had reached the maximum extended length, she slowly began twisting it. Leonard desperately tried to scream out in pain, but minus the mobility of his tongue could only make drowning noises. Leonard never imagined there could be pain like this. After what seemed like an eternity, which could in real time, be measured in less than ten seconds, Suzie released his tongue. "Try spitting now, Mr. Yellow skin asshole. I think that before we get the electric rodeo going, you deserve one more little punishment." Stepping back between his elevated legs, she waved the vice clamps high enough for Leonard to see them. Leonard could feel the cold of the steel jaws slowly closing on his cock. Damn did he ever wish he could beg for mercy. As the pressure of the gripping teeth of the jaws began to crush the shaft of his cock, Leonard's damaged tongue groaned out wordless noises. Squeezing the jaws tight, Suzie jerked the pliers up and down in a masturbatory movement. The tongue pain was bad, but the dick pain was worse. Leonard hoped and prayed that death would take him; he was not sure how much more of this pain he could survive.

"Damn, Suzie you sure are a stone cold bitch. You must have been inspired by the Devil to think about the grips on his tongue and dick. Poor Leonard sure did bounce on that table. Let's move on to the electric rodeo and see how he likes that." "Yes, Sonny, I think he's ready for the juice."

Releasing Leonard's dick, she noticed something and smiled; "Look Sonny, those grips left teeth marks in his cock, it actually looks fluted". After they both inspected his dick and then laughed at the deep impressions made by the plier's teeth in the soft flesh, she moved to the control board. Grinning at Leonard, she moved the dial from the "5" to the "20" position. She held her finger up so he would be sure to see it, and then lowered it and pressed and held the red activation button down. Leonard's body instantly went into convulsion, arching as the high voltage cruised throughout each nerve ending demanding a response of every muscle, ligament and tendon.

A stream of piss four foot high jetted from his damaged cock. His head banged against the table, his arms and legs fought the restraints. A gleam of excitement flashed in her eyes. Releasing the little red button, his body collapsed in fatigue. "Did you like that my friend? I don't have much use for anyone that would stoop so low as to try spit in another person's face. I really enjoyed that and I am beginning to feel a little wet in my pussy. Should we do it again, I vote "yes" how about you Mr. Leonard? Wonder how we know your name, well it was all there in your wallet on your driver's license. OK, Leonard, just watch my little pinkie finger as it plunges down to the little red fun button."

In the next thirty minutes, Suzie without let up, had zapped Leonard every three minutes. At the end of the thirty minutes Leonard was jello. "Please unhook him, Lady Mistress." Suzie had to take a second to reflect on just what Sonny had said, never, never had Sonny ever said "please" to her in the eighteen months she was his captive, never. "Things were maybe changing" she thought, her plan was definitely working out.

"I am wondering if the electric fried his dick? Lady Mistress, I want to do a little experiment for me. Mr. Nasty Mouth, we have never had a male slave before, so a lot of this is new to us. Can you still cum? I wonder if the current dried up your cum factory. Lady Mistress I want you to jack off his prick and see if you can get any cum up. I am betting his is as dry as a box of cheap popcorn. Now Mr. Leonard, I hear that you faggots are piss sippers, so while you are enjoying Lady Mistress' attention to your cock, I am going to piss in this cup and dribble it little by little in that big, wide open mouth of yours. If you don't swallow and you begin to drown, I am going to squeeze your nose and guess what, you will swallow. Yesterday when you were probably being ass fucker by another queer, bet you didn't imagine that you would be having piss cocktails in a mysterious faraway place, did you?" Sonny stood up and walked over to where Leonard could see him. Leonard exhausted from the pain, just rested his head sideways on the exam table and stared. Leonard was vaguely conscious and aware

of the sensation that a pair of hands were pumping his cock. Unzipping his pants, Sonny rolled out his soft penis. Watching Sonny droop it over the edge of a red plastic cup, Leonard could hear the piss streaming into the cup. Sonny set the cup on the prep table and zipped up his pants. Leonard could see Sonny smiling. Making another gargling noise, Leonard tried to turn his head away from the red cup. To force his face straight up, Sonny just grabbed his nose. Picking the cup up, Sonny poured just enough of the piss into Leonard's mouth to create a drowning effect. As Leonard gagged and tried to fight, Sonny squeezed Leonard's nose shut forcing Leonard to swallow the vile tasting body waste. Again and again Sonny forced Leonard to ingest the waste. In between waves of mind exploding pain, Leonard had but one singular thought, "When I get loose these motherfuckers are going to pay and pay hard. I know some bad ass hood niggas in the drug business that use blow torches and machetes to get their points across. If it takes every penny I got, these motherfuckers are going to pay. While they are screaming as my niggas blow torch bar b que her pussy and turn his cock into cinders, I am going to be sitting in a chair smoking a tote and sipping a real cocktail enjoying every scream for mercy. Yes sir, as soon as I get loose."

"I can't get his dick hard. I did get a little of that lube to squeeze out of the spout. But his dick is really dead. I am so sorry Sonny, he just won't cooperate." "I think this afternoon has been a little overwhelming for Mr. Nasty Mouth. I getting hungry, how about you, Suzie? Let's take a break to the big house and make a little lunch. Leonard I would invite you but it would be a waste of food and I bet that you haven't much of an appetite anyway. That electric seems to be a great dietary aid; no one is hungry after a jolt or two of it. So Leonard, we are going to leave you to your thoughts, which will likely be escape and fantasizing about what you are going to do to us when you do escape. Right! Not to be a wet blanket or anything, but the bindings are extremely strong and even if you were to get loose, there is nowhere to go. You are in the middle of a huge forest

preserve and the closest town is twenty miles away. Twice I had to hunt down girls that managed to get loose of the handcuffs, and I made both of them really, really sorry that put me to that extra trouble. I don't think you would want to see that side of me. So my best advice is to rest, we have more fun in store for you. OK Suzie what are you cooking for lunch? I think I would like a couple of BLTs and an icy cold beer." "Not a problem Sonny, Leonard we'll be back in about an hour, maybe longer if Sonny gets horny and wants to fool around a little."

Of course, poor Leonard never got the chance to hire those "bad ass hood niggas" and he never got to enjoy that cocktail. Upon Sonny's urging, Suzy had removed his ball sack and skinned out his dick; the ball sack when properly preserved would make a wonderful cigarette case, and the cock tubing made a very unusual and unique souvenir. Leonard had not been a particularly great victim; he constantly had to be revived and when Suzy started cutting his cock skin loose, the shock and pain of what he was undergoing, stopped Leonard's heart. One hour later, the normal forest sounds were interrupted with the roar of the wood shredder's giant diesel engine. The sound and vibration triggered a marine migration, every little fishy in the brook keyed for a Leonard main course, feeding frenzy.

Sonny and Suzie were a team from the pits and fires of Hell. To keep police investigators puzzled, they alternately abducted a woman then a gay man. In a stroke of depraved genius, Suzie suggested that they occasionally do a late Friday night or Saturday night cruise of the highways surrounding the University campus and be on the lookout for hitchhikers with backpacks. They too, made excellent targets as no one would report them missing for weeks. Hitchhiking being illegal gave Sonny's police plan even more credibility as most, being young and inexperienced in life matters, knew they were breaking the law but were usually very naïve about police stops and civil rights and very submissive to any authoritarian figure. The plan's "we just got a radio call about a robbery and shooting and you certainly fit the description, so please place your hands behind your back" worked so

well on these college kids Sonny and Suzie regretted that it was so obvious a crime pattern that would eventually lead to their apprehension, so couldn't be used very often. Sonny and Suzie, to keep the real police off track, also found it necessary to expand their hunting boundaries, occasionally roaming ten hours or more from their retreat. Suzy even created her own horrific and cruel drills designed to produce agony of the highest order.

On their infrequent trips for groceries and supplies, it was easy for fellow shoppers to mistake them for just another harmless husband and wife couple. On a whim and with the encouragement and approval of his attorney, Sonny decided to marry Suzie. They became infused in the community with an occasional appearance at a house of worship, an occasional trip to the small town to make small purchases, an occasional dinner out at the local diner, and an occasional donation to the school or a charity event. To insure their privacy, they carefully seeded the rumor that they were both authors and needed absolute concentration with absolutely no distractions to pursue their lines of creative thought. The people in the community respected that privacy need and other than a wave or a "hi" sought no more from the solitary seeking couple.

To this day, with a lake full of well-fed fish, Sonny and Suzie still hunt victims. They decided, for safety, to only hunt four times per year. The cage accommodation made it possible to keep and entertain captives for just as long as Sonny and Suzie wished. No medieval cellar ever offered as many options of physical and mental torture as the "redo" of Uncle Buck's vacation and hunting get-away. The $550,000 life insurance policy payout guaranteed that Sonny would never have to worry about a job or money. Auntie Mame's attorney made it possible, for a price of course, to exist off the radar of the mainstream. Thank you Auntie Mame and Uncle Bob and Uncle Buck for making all this possible.

With a range of many hundreds of miles, and little connection between the missing persons, there is no police or news bulletin to warn anyone that there is a predatory team stalking back roads. In this modern age, caution and an awareness of your surrounding is still the best counter to thieves, muggers, and predators such as Sonny and Suzie.

They are real; They are out there and They are hunting Their next victim. Will you let it be you?

Made in the USA
Columbia, SC
27 November 2018